# Thistledown

A Book of Scotch Humour, Character, Folk-lore, Story & Anecdote

Robert Ford

Alpha Editions

This edition published in 2023

ISBN : 9789357941259

Design and Setting By
**Alpha Editions**
www.alphaedis.com
Email - info@alphaedis.com

As per information held with us this book is in Public Domain.
This book is a reproduction of an important historical work. Alpha Editions uses the best technology to reproduce historical work in the same manner it was first published to preserve its original nature. Any marks or number seen are left intentionally to preserve its true form.

# Contents

PREFACE ........................................................................- 1 -
CHAPTER I THE SCOTTISH TONGUE—ITS GRAPHIC FORCE AND POWERS OF PATHOS AND HUMOUR ..........- 3 -
CHAPTER II CHARACTERISTICS OF SCOTCH HUMOUR ......................................................................- 15 -
CHAPTER III HUMOUR OF OLD SCOTCH DIVINES .......- 29 -
CHAPTER IV THE PULPIT AND THE PEW .......................- 45 -
CHAPTER V THE OLD SCOTTISH BEADLE—HIS CHARACTER AND HUMOUR............................................- 68 -
CHAPTER VI HUMOUR OF SCOTCH PRECENTORS .......- 85 -
CHAPTER VII HUMOURS OF DRAM-DRINKING IN SCOTLAND .........................................................................- 97 -
CHAPTER VIII THE THISTLE AND THE ROSE ...............- 114 -
CHAPTER IX SCREEDS O' TARTAN—A CHAPTER OF HIGHLAND HUMOUR......................................................- 130 -
CHAPTER X HUMOUR OF SCOTTISH POETS .................- 145 -
CHAPTER XI 'TWEEN BENCH AND BAR—A CHAPTER OF LEGAL FACETIÆ ..............................................................- 171 -
CHAPTER XII HUMOURS OF SCOTTISH RURAL LIFE.- 187 -
CHAPTER XIII HUMOURS OF SCOTTISH SUPERSTITION..................................................................- 206 -
CHAPTER XIV HUMOUR OF SCOTCH NATURALS ......- 221 -
CHAPTER XV JAMIE FLEEMAN, THE LAIRD OF UDNY'S FOOL ..................................................................................- 233 -
CHAPTER XVI "HAWKIE"—A GLASGOW STREET CHARACTER ....................................................................- 241 -
CHAPTER XVII THE LAIRD O' MACNAB .......................- 256 -
CHAPTER XVIII KIRKYARD HUMOUR..........................- 262 -

# PREFACE

An eminently learned and genial ex-Professor of one of our Universities not long since pointed out how Scotland was remarkable for three things—Songs, Sermons, and Shillings. And whilst it may not be disputed that she has enormous and ever-increasing store of these three good things—and that, moreover, she loves them all—there is a fourth quality of her many-sided nature which is more distinctly characteristic of Auld Caledonia and her people, and that is the general possession of the faculty of original humour. Not one in ten thousand of the Scottish people may be able to produce a good song, or a good sermon; not one in twenty thousand of them may be able to "gather meikle gear and haud it weel thegither;" but every second Scotsman is a born humourist. Humour is part and parcel of his very being. He may not live without it—may not breathe. Consequently, it is found breaking out amongst us in the most unlikely as well as in the most likely places. It blossoms in the solemn assemblies of the people; at meetings of Kirk-Sessions; in the City and Town Council Chambers; in our Presbyteries; our Courts of Justice; and in the high Parliament of the Kirk itself. Famous specimens of it come down from the lonesome hillsides; from the cottage, bothy, and farm ingle-nooks. It issues from the village inn, the smiddy, the kirkyard; and functions of fasting and sorrow give it birth as well as occasions of feasting and mirth. It drops from the lips of the learned and the unlearned in the land; and is not more frequently revealed in the eloquence of the University *savant* than in the gibberish of the hobbling village and city natural.

Humorous Scottish anecdotes have been an abundant crop; and collectors of them there have been not a few. Dean Ramsay's garrulous and entertaining *Reminiscences*, and Dr. Charles Rogers' *Familiar Illustrations of Scottish Life* excepted, however, the published collections of our floating facetiæ have been "hotch-potch" affairs. Revelations each of some little industry, no doubt, but few of them affording any proof of the compiler's familiarity with the subject. And as none of them have reached farther back than Dean Ramsay, and all have been content to take the more familiar of Ramsay's and Rogers' illustrations and anecdotes, and supplement these in hap-hazard fashion with random clippings from the variety columns of the daily and weekly newspapers, the individual result has been such as Voltaire's famous criticism eloquently describes:—They have contained things both good and new; but what was good was not new, and what was new was not good.

To the present work the critical aphorism of the "brilliant Frenchman" may not in fairness be applied. In any attempt to afford an adequate representation of the humours of the Scottish people, illustrations must of necessity be drawn from widely different sources, and I have, consequently, to confess my indebtedness to various earlier gleaners in the same field, chiefly to Dean Ramsay, Dr. Rogers, and the genial trio, Carrick, Motherwell, and Henderson. But for representative illustrations of Scottish life and character I have gone further back and come down to a later period than any previous writer on the subject. And so, whilst the reader will discover here much that is old and good, he will find very much that is new, which, as illustrative of Scottish humour and character, will compare with the best of the old.

No pointless or dubiously nationalistic anecdote or illustration has been admitted. The work has been carefully and elaborately classified under eighteen distinct headings, each class, or section, being introduced by an exposition of the phase or phases of life and character to which it applies, and cemented from first to last by reflective and expository comment.

Essentially a book of humour, it is hoped that the reader will find it to be something more than a merely funny book. If he does not, the writer will have failed to realize fully his aim.

ROBERT FORD.

[1891.]

# CHAPTER I
## THE SCOTTISH TONGUE—ITS GRAPHIC FORCE AND POWERS OF PATHOS AND HUMOUR

We are frequently told—and now and again receive unwelcome scraps of evidence in confirmation of the scandal—that our dear old mother tongue is falling into desuetude in our native land. Already, it must be confessed, it has been abrogated from the drawing-rooms of the ultra-refined upper circles of Scottish society. The snobbish element amongst the great middle-class, ever prone to imitate their "betters," affect not to understand it, and blush (the sillier of them) when, in an unguarded moment, a manifest Scotticism slips into their conversation. There is a portion of the semi-educated working population, again, who, imitating the snobbish element of the middle grade, speak Scotch freely only in their working clothes. On Sundays, and extra occasions, when dressed in their very best, there is just about as much Scotch in their talk as will show one how poorly they can speak English, and just about enough English to render their Scotch ridiculous. Observing all this, and taking it in conjunction with the other denationalising tendencies of the age, there are those who predict that the time is not far distant when Burns's poems, Scott's novels, and Hogg's tales will be sealed books to the partially educated Scotsman. That there is a growing tendency in the direction indicated is quite true, but the disease, I believe, is only skin deep as yet, and the bone and sinew of the country remain quite unaffected. That there will be a sudden reaction in the patient must be the sincere desire of every patriotic Scot. If the prediction of obsoletism is ever to be realized, then, "the mair's the pity." Scotland will not stand where she did. For very much—oh, so much—of what has made her glorious among the nations of the world will have passed away, taking the sheen of her glory with it. What Scotsmen, as Scotsmen, should ever prize most is bound up inseparably with the native language. Ours is a matured country, and the stirring scenes of her history on which the mind of the individual delights to dwell, are so frequently enshrined in spirited ballad and song, couched in the pithy Scottish vernacular, that, to suppose these latter dead—they are not translatable into English—is to suppose the best part of Scottish history dead and buried beyond the hope of resurrection. For its own sake alone the Scottish tongue is eminently deserving of regard—of cultivation and preservation. Scotsmen should be—and so all well-conditioned Scotsmen surely are—as proud of their native tongue as they are of their far-famed native bens and glens. For why, the rugged grandeur of the physical features of our country are not more worthy of admiration than the language in which their glories have been most fittingly extolled. They have characteristics in common; for rugged grandeur is as truly a feature of the Scottish language as it is the dominant feature of Scottish scenery. True, its various dialects are somewhat tantalising. The

Forfar man is vividly identified by his "foo's" and his "fa's," and his "fat's" and his "fans"; and the Renfrewshire man by his "weans," his "wee weans," and his "yin pound yin and yinpence," etc. Taking a simple phrase as an example—(*Anglice*):—"The spoon is on the loom." The Aberdonian will tell you that "The speen's on the leem." The Perthshire man will say "That spun's on the luim"; and the Glasgow citizen will inform you that "The spin's on the lim." In a fuller example, a Renfrewshire person will vouchsafe the information that he "Saw a seybo synd't doon the syvor till it sank in the stank." A native of Perthshire will only about half understand what the speaker has said, and may threaten to "rax a rung frae the boggars o' the hoose and reeshil his rumple wi't," without sending terror to the soul of his West country confederate. Latterly, an Aberdonian may come on the scene and ask, "Fa' fuppit the loonie?" and neither of the forenamed parties will at once perceive the drift of his inquiry. To illustrate how difficult it may be for the East and the West to understand each other, I will tell a little story. An Aberdonian not long ago got work in Glasgow where they used a quantity of tar, and was rather annoyed to see his fellow-workmen wash the tar off their hands while he washed and rubbed at his in vain. His patience could stand it no longer, and going up to the foreman, and, stretching out his hands, he asked:—"Fat'll tak' it aff?" "Yes," replied the foreman, "fat'll tak' it aff." "Fat'll tak' it aff?" "Yes, I said fat would tak' it aff." "But *fat'll* tak' it aff?" persisted the Aberdonian. The foreman pointed to a tub, and roared: "Grease, you stupid eediot!" "Weel than," retorted the Aberdonian, "an' fat for did you no say that at first?"

There are, however, dialects and provincialisms in the language of every country and people under the sun, and the Scottish vernacular is not worse—not nearly so bad as many are. Our dialects are mainly the results of a narrowing and broadening of the vowel sounds, as exemplified in the instance of the words "spoon" and "loom." I have spoken of the rugged grandeur of the Scottish Doric, and its claims to preservation. There are single words in Scotch which cannot be adequately expressed in a whole sentence in English. Think of "fushionless," "eerie," "wersh," "gloamin'," "scunner," "glower," "cosie," "bonnie," "thoweless," "splairge," and "plowter," etc., and try to find their equivalents in the language of the school. Try and find a sentence that will fairly express some of the words. "A gowpen o' glaur" is but weakly expressed in "a handful of mud"; "stoure" is not adequately defined by calling it "dust in motion"; "flype yer stockin', lassie," is easier said than "turn your stocking inside out, girl." "Auld lang syne" is not expressible in English. "A bonnie wee lassie" is more euphonious and expressive by a long way than "a pretty little girl." "Hirsle yont," "my cuit's yeukie," "e'enin's orts mak' gude mornin' fodder," "spak' o' lowpin' ower a linn," and "pree my mou'," are also good examples of expressive Scotch. Nowhere, perhaps, is the singular beauty and rare expressiveness of the

Scottish national tongue seen to better advantage than in the proverbial sayings—those short, sharp, and shiny shafts of speech, aptly defined as "the wit of one and the wisdom of many,"—and of which the Scottish language has been so prolific. "The genius, wit, and wisdom of a nation are discovered by their proverbs," says Bacon; and, verily, while the proverbs of Scotland are singularly expressive of the pith and beauty of the vernacular in which they are couched, they also reveal in very great measure the mental and social characteristics of the people who have perpetuated them. "A gangin' fit's aye gettin', were't but a thorn;" "Burnt bairns dread the fire;" "A'e bird in the hand's worth twa in the bush;" "A fool an' his siller's sune parted;" "Hang a thief when he's young an' he'll no steal when he's auld;" "There's aye some water whaur the stirkie droons;" "Moudiwarts feedna on midges;" "When gossipin' wives meet, the deil gangs to his dinner;" "Hungry dogs are blythe o' bursten puddin's;" "He needs a lang-shankit spune that wad sup wi' the deil;" "A blate cat maks a prood mouse;" "Better a toom house than an ill tenant;" "Lippen to me, but look to yoursel';" "Jouk an' lat the jaw gang by;" "Better sma' fish than nane;" "The tulziesome tyke comes hirplin' hame;" "Ha' binks are sliddery;" "Ilka cock craws best on his ain middenhead;" "Lazy youth mak's lowsy age;" "Next to nae wife, a guid wife's best;" "Lay your wame to your winnin';" "It's nae lauchin' to girn in a widdy;" "The wife's a'e dochter an' the man's a'e coo, the tane's ne'er weel, an' the tither's ne'er fu'." These give the evidence.

Ours is a language peculiarly powerful in its use of vowels, and the following dialogue between a shopman and a customer is a convincing example. The conversation relates to a plaid hanging at a shop door:—

Customer (inquiring the material)—"Oo?" (wool?).

Shopman—"Aye, oo." (yes, wool).

Customer—"A' oo?" (all wool?).

Shopman—"Ay, a' oo" (yes, all wool).

Customer—"A' a'e oo?" (all one wool?).

Shopman—"Ou, ay, a' a'e oo" (oh, yes, all one wool).

A dialogue in vowel sounds—surely a thing unique in literature!


In his Scotch version of the Psalms—"frae Hebrew intil Scottis"—the late Rev. Dr. Hately Waddell, of Glasgow, gives many striking illustrations of the force and beauty of idiomatic Scotch. His language partakes rather much of the antique form to be readily perceptible to the present generation, but its purity is unquestionable, and its beauty and power inexpressible in other words than his own. Let us quote the familiar 23rd Psalm.

"The Lord is my herd; na want sal fa' me.

"He louts me till lie amang green howes; He airts me atowre by the lown waters.

"He waukens my wa'gaen saul; He weises me roun for His ain name's sake, intil richt roddins.

"Na! tho' I gang thro' the dead-mirk dail; *e'en thar* sal I dread nae skaithin; for Yersel' are nar-by me; Yer stok an' Yer stay haud me baith fu' cheerie.

"My buird Ye ha'e hansell'd in face o' my faes; Ye ha'e drookit my head wi' oyle; my bicker is *fu'* an' *skailin'*.

"E'en sae sal gude guidin' an' gude gree gang wi' me ilk day o' my livin'; an' ever mair syne i' the Lord's ain howff, *at lang last*, sal I mak bydan."

Hear also Dr. Waddell's translation of the last four verses of the 52nd chapter of Isaiah, they are inexpressibly beautiful:—

"Blythe and brak-out, lilt a' like ane, ye bourocks sae swak o' Jerusalem; for the Lord He has hearten'd His folk fu' kin'; He has e'en boucht back Jerusalem.

"The Lord He rax'd yont His hailie arm, in sight o' the nations mony, O; an' ilk neuk o' the yirth sal tak tent an' learn the health o' our God sae bonie, O!

"Awa, awa, clean but frae the toun: mak nor meddle wi' nought that's roun'; awa frae her bosom; haud ye soun', wi' the gear o' the Lord forenent ye!

"For it's no wi' sic pingle ye'se gang the gate; nor it's no wi' sic speed ye maun spang the spate; for the Lord, He's afore ye, *ear' an' late*; an' Israel's God, He's ahint ye!"

These suggest "The Lord's Prayer intill Auld Scottis," as printed by Pinkerton, and which is cast in more antique form still:—"Uor fader quhilk beest i' Hevin, Hallowit weird thyne nam. Cum thyne kinrik. Be dune thyne wull as is i' Hevin, sva po yerd. Uor dailie breid gif us thilk day. And forleit us our skaths, as we forfeit tham quha skath us. And leed us na intill temtation. Butan fre us fra evil. Amen."

No writer of any time—Burns alone excepted—has handled the native tongue to better purpose for the expression of every feeling of the human heart than has Sir Walter Scott; and in Jeanie Deans' plea to the Queen for her sister's life there is the finest example of simple pathos, dashed with the passion of hope struggling with despair, that is to be met with anywhere in literature. It shows the extent in this way of which the native speech is capable.

"My sister—my puir sister Effie, still lives, though her days and hours are numbered! She still lives, and a word o' the King's mouth might restore her to a heart-broken auld man, that never, in his daily and nightly exercise, forgot to pray that His Majesty might be blessed with a lang an' a prosperous reign, and that his throne, and the throne o' his posterity, might be established in righteousness. O, madam, if ever ye kend what it was to sorrow for and with a sinning and a suffering creature, whase mind is sae tossed that she can be neither ca'd fit to live or dee, hae some compassion on our misery! Save an honest house from dishonour, and an unhappy girl, not eighteen years of age, from an early and dreadful death! Alas! it is not when we sleep saft and wake merrily oursel's that we think on other people's sufferings. Our hearts are waxed light within us then, and we are for righting our ain wrangs and fighting our ain battles. But when the hour of trouble comes to the mind or to the body—and seldom may it visit your leddyship—and when the hour of death comes, that comes to high and low—lang and late may it be yours!—oh, my leddy, then it isna what we hae dune for oursel's, but what we hae done for others, that we think on maist pleasantly. And the thought that ye hae intervened to spare the puir thing's life will be sweeter in that hour, come when it may, than if a word o' your mouth could hang the haill Porteous mob at the tail o' a'e tow."

Then the vigour and variety of the Scottish idiom as a vehicle of description has perhaps never received better illustration than in Andrew Fairservice's account of Glasgow Cathedral:—"Ay! it's a brave Kirk," said Andrew. "Nane o' yere whigmaleeries and curliwurlies and open steek hems aboot it—a' solid, weel-jointed mason wark, that will stand as lang as the warld, keep hands and gunpowther aff it. It had amaist a douncome lang syne at the Reformation, when they pu'd doon the Kirks of St. Andrews and Perth, and thereawa', to cleanse them o' Papery, and idolatry, and image-worship, and surplices, and sic like rags o' the muckle hure that sitteth on the seven hills, as if ane wasna braid enough for her auld hinder end. Sae the commons o' Renfrew, and o' the Barony, and the Gorbals, and a' aboot, they behoved to come into Glasgow a'e fair morning, to try their hand on purging the High Kirk o' Popish nick-nackets. But the townsmen o' Glasgow, they were feared their auld edifice might slip the girths in gaun through siccan rough physic, sae they rang the common bell, and assembled the train-bands wi' took o' drum. By gude luck, the worthy James Rabat was Dean o' Guild that year (and a gude mason he was himsell, made him keener to keep up the auld bigging). And the trades assembled, and offered downright battle to the commons, rather than their Kirk should coup the crans, as others had done elsewhere. It wasna for love o' Papery—na, na!—nane could ever say that o' the trades o' Glasgow. Sae they sune came to an agreement to tak a' the idolatrous statues o' sants (sorrow be on them) out o' their neuks—and sae the bits o' stone idols were broken in pieces by Scripture warrant, and flung into the Molendiner burn, and the Auld Kirk stood as crouse as a cat when the flaes are kaimed aff her, and a' body was alike pleased. And I hae heard wise folk say that if the same had been dune in ilka Kirk in Scotland, the Reform wad just hae been as pure as it is e'en now, and we wad hae mair Christianlike Kirks; for I hae been sae lang in England, that naething will drive out o' my head, that the dog-kennel at Osbaldistone-Hall is better than mony a house o' God in Scotland."

No man, it is well known, had ever more command of the native vernacular than Robert Burns. In a letter written at Carlisle, in June 1787, to his friend William Nicol, Master of the High School, Edinburgh, he has left a curious testimony at once to the capabilities of the language and his own skill in it. "Kind, honest-hearted Willie," he writes, "I'm sitten doon here, after seven-and-forty miles' ridin', e'en as forjeskit and forniaw'd as a forfoughten cock, to gie you some notion o' my land-lowper-like stravaigin' sin' the sorrowfu' hour that I sheuk hands and parted wi' Auld Reekie.

"My auld ga'd gleyde o' a meere has huchyall'd up hill and doun brae in Scotland and England, as teuch and birnie as a vera deevil wi' me. It's true, she's as puir's a sang-maker, an' as hard's a kirk, and tipper taipers when she tak's the gate, jist like a lady's gentlewoman in a minuwae, or a hen on a het girdle; but she's a yauld, pouthrie girran for a' that, and has a stamach like Willie Stalker's meere, that wad hae digeested tumbler-wheels, for she'll whip me aff her five stimparts o' the best aits at a down-sitten', and ne'er fash her thoom. Whan ance her ring-banes and spavies, her crucks and cramps, are fairly soupl'd, she beets to, beets to, and aye the hindmost hour the tightest. I could wager her price to a thretty pennies, that for twa or three wooks, ridin' at fifty miles a day, the deil-stickit a five gallopers acqueesh Clyde and Whithorn could cast saut on her tail.

"I hae dander'd owre a' the country frae Dunbar to Selcraig, and ha'e forgather'd wi' mony a gude fallow, and mony a weel-faur'd hizzie. I met wi' twa dink queynes in particular. Ane o' them a sonsie, fine, fodgel lass, baith braw and bonnie; the ither was a clean-shankit, straught, tight, weel-faur'd wench, as blythe's a lintwhite on a flowerie thorn, and as sweet and modest's a new blawn plum-rose in a hazel shaw. They were baith bred to mainers by the beuk, and ony ane o' them had as muckle smeddum and rumblegumption as the half o' some Presbytries that you and I baith ken. They played me sic a deil o' a shavie, that I daur say if my harigals were turn'd out ye wad see twa nicks i' the heart o' me like the mark o' a kail-whittle in a castock.

"I was gaun to write you a lang pystle, but, Gude forgi'e me, I gat mysel' sae noutourously bitchify'd the day, after kail-time, than I can hardly stoiter but and ben.

"My best respecks to the guidwife and a' our common friens, especiall Mr. and Mrs. Cruikshank, and the honest guidman o' Jock's Lodge.

"I'll be in Dumfries the morn gif the beast be to the fore, and the branks bide hale.

"Gude be wi' you, Willie! Amen!"

That letter might fairly be made the "Shibboleth" in any case of doubt regarding one's ability to read Scotch. It would shiver the front teeth of some of your counterlouper gentry. Yet it is not an overdone example of the Scotch Doric as it was spoken in Edinburgh drawing-rooms a hundred years ago—*vide*, Henry Cockburn's *Memorials*. Between it and the "braid Scotch" of half a century earlier there is a marked difference.

In the *Scots Magazine* for November, 1743, the following proclamation is printed:—

"All brethren and sisters, I let you to witt that there is a twa-year-auld lad littleane tint, that ist' ere'en.

"It's a' scabbit i' the how hole o' the neck o'd, and a cauler kail-blade and brunt butter at it, that ist'er. It has a muckle maun blue pooch hingin' at the carr side o'd, fou o' mullers and chucky-stanes, and a spindle and a whorle, and it's daddy's ain jockteleg in't. It's a' black aneath the nails wi' howkin' o' yird, that is't. It has its daddy's gravat tied about the craig o'd, and hingin' down the back o'd. The back o' the hand o'd's a' brunt; it got it i' the smiddy ae day.

"Whae'er can find this said twa-year-auld lad littleane may repair to M—o J—n's, town-smith in C—n, and he sall hae for reward twall bear scones, and a ride o' our ain auld beast to bear him hame, and nae mair words about it, that wilt'r no."

Hogg, in his "Shepherd's Calendar," referring to the religious character of the shepherds of Scotland in his day, tells that "the antiquated but delightful exercise of family worship was never neglected," and, "formality being a thing despised, there are no compositions I ever heard," he continues, "so truly original as those prayers occasionally were; sometimes for rude eloquence and pathos, at other times for an indescribable sort of pomp, and, not infrequently, for a plain and somewhat unbecoming familiarity." He gives several illustrations, quite justifying this description, from some with whom he had himself served and herded. One of the most notable men for this sort of family eloquence, he thought, was a certain Adam Scott, in Upper Dalgleish. Thus Scott prayed for a son who seemed thoughtless—

"For Thy mercy's sake—for the sake o' Thy puir, sinfu' servants that are now addressing Thee in their ain shilly-shally way, and for the sake o' mair than we daur weel name to Thee, hae mercy on Rab. Ye ken fu' weel he's a wild, mischievous callant, and thinks nae mair o' committin' sin than a dog does o' lickin' a dish; but put Thy hook in his nose, and Thy bridle in his gab, and gar him come back to Thee wi' a jerk that he'll no forget the langest day that he has to live." For another son he prayed:—"Dinna forget puir Jamie, wha's far awa' frae us this nicht. Keep Thy arm o' power about him; and, oh, I wish Ye wad endow him wi' a little spunk and smeddum to act for himsel'; for, if Ye dinna, he'll be but a bauchle i' this warld, and a back-sitter i' the neist." Again:—"We're a' like hawks, we're a' like snails, we're a' like slogie riddles; like hawks to do evil, like snails to do good, and like slogie riddles to let through a' the gude and keep a' the bad." When Napoleon I. was filling Europe with alarm, he prayed—"Bring doon the tyrant and his lang neb, for he has done muckle ill this year, and gie him a cup o' Thy wrath, and gin he winna tak' that, gie him kelty" [*i.e.*, double, or two cups].

Very graphic, is it not! It reminds us of the prayer of one Jamie Hamilton, a celebrated poacher in the West country. As Jamie was reconnoitring a lonely situation one morning, his mind more set on hares than on prayers, a woman approached him from the only house in the immediate district and requested that he should "come owre and pray for auld Eppie, for she's just deein'."

"Ye ken weel enough that I can pray nane," replied Jamie.

"But we haena time to rin for ony ither Jamie," urged the woman, "Eppie's just slippin' awa'; and oh! it wad be an awfu' like thing to lat the puir bodie dee without bein' prayed for."

"Weel, then," said Jamie, "an I maun come, I maun come; but I'm sure I kenna right what to say."

The occasion has ever so much to do with the making of the man. Approaching the bed, Jamie doffed his cap and proceeded:—"O Lord, Thou kens best Thy nainsel' how the case stands atween Thee and auld Eppie; and sin' Ye hae baith the heft and the blade in Yer nain hand, just guide the gully as best suits her guid and Yer nain glory. Amen."

It was a poacher's prayer in very truth, but a bishop could not have said more in as few words.

But it is easy to be expressive in Scotch, for it is peculiar to the native idiom that the simpler the language employed the effect is the greater. Think how this is manifested in the song and ballad literature of the country. In popular ballads like "Gil Morrice," "Sir James the Rose," "Barbara Allan," and "The Dowie Dens o' Yarrow"; in Jane Elliot's song of "The Flowers of the Forest"; in Grizzel Baillie's "Werena my heart licht I wad dee"; in Lady Lindsay's "Auld Robin Gray"; in Lady Nairne's "Land o' the Leal"; in Burns's "Auld Lang Syne"; in Tannahill's "Gloomy Winter"; in Thom's "Mitherless Bairn"; and in Smibert's "Widow's Lament." I do not mean to say that the making of these songs and ballads was a simple matter; but the verbal material is in each case of the simplest character, and the effect such that the pieces are established in the common heart of Scotland. Burns did not go out of his way for either language or figures of speech to describe Willie Wastle's wife, yet see the graphic picture we have presented to us by a few strokes of the pen:—

"She has an e'e—she has but ane,

The cat has twa the very colour;

Five rusty teeth, forbye a stump,

A clapper-tongue wad deave a miller;

A whiskin' beard about her mou',

Her nose and chin they threaten ither—

Sic a wife as Willie has,

I wadna gie a button for her.

"She's bow-houghed, she's hein-shinn'd,

Ae limpin' leg, a hand-breed shorter;

She's twisted right, she's twisted left

To balance fair in ilka quarter:

She has a hump upon her breast

The twin o' that upon her shouther—

Sic a wife as Willie has,

I wadna gie a button for her."

No idea there is strained. Every word is common. The same may be said of Hew Ainshe's lyric poem in a different vein, "Dowie in the hint o' Hairst," which I make no apology for quoting in full:—

"It's dowie in the hint o' hairst.
At the wa'-gang o' the swallow,
When the wind grows cauld, and the burns grow bauld,
An' the wuds are hingin' yellow;

But oh, it's dowier far to see
The wa'-gang o' her the heart gangs wi',
The dead-set o' a shinin' e'e.
That darkens the weary warld on thee.

"There was meikle love atween us twa—
Oh, twa could ne'er be fonder;
And the thing on yird was never made,
That could ha'e gart us sunder.
But the way o' Heaven's aboon a' ken,
And we maun bear what it likes to sen'—
It's comfort, though, to weary men,
That the warst o' this warld's waes maun en'.

"There's mony things that come and gae,
Just kent, and just forgotten;
And the flowers that busk a bonnie brae,
Gin anither year lie rotten,
But the last look o' yon lovely e'e,
And the deein' grip she ga'e to me,
They're settled like eternitie—
Oh, Mary; gin I were wi' thee."

By these illustrations I have endeavoured to shew forth, to all whom it may concern, the verbal beauty, the graphic force, and the powers for the expression of pathos and humour there is in the vernacular speech of Scotland. Like our national emblem—the thistle—it is, of course, nothing in the mouth of an ass. But well spoken, it is charming alike to the ear and the intellect; and, for the reasons already urged in this paper, is worthy of more general esteem and more general cultivation than the current generation of Scotch folk seem disposed to award it. Lord Cockburn pronounced it "the sweetest and most expressive of living languages;" and no unprejudiced reader of his *Memorials* will dispute the value of his opinion on the subject. He wrote excellent Doric himself, and made it the vehicle of his conversation in his family, and casually throughout the day, as long as he lived. Ho! for more such good old Scottish gentlemen! Ho! for another Jean, Duchess of Gordon, to teach our Scottish gentry how to speak naturally! That we had more men in our midst, with equal influence and education, and charged with the fine spirit of patriotism which animates Scotland's ain "grand auld man"—Professor Blackie! It has been the fashion for English journalists with pretensions to wit, to animadvert by pen and pencil on what they regard as the idiosyncracies of Scottish speech and behaviour. *Punch* is a frequent offender in this way. I say *offender* advisedly, for no *Punch* artist, so far as I have seen—and I have scanned that journal from the first number to the last—ever drew a Scotsman in "his manner as he lived." The originals of the pictures may have appeared in London Christmas pantomimes, but certainly nowhere else. Then the language which in their guileless innocence they expect will pass muster as Scotch, is a hash-up alike revolting to the ears of gods and men. We don't expect very much from some folks, but surely even a London journalist should know that a Scotsman does not say "mon" when he means to say "man." Charles Macklin put it that way, and the London journalist apparently can never get beyond Macklin. Don't go to London for your Scotch, my reader! Listen to it as it may still be spoken at your granny's ingleside. Familiarise yourself with it as it is to be found in its full vigour and purity in the Waverley Novels; in Burns's Poems and Songs; in the "Noctes Ambrosianæ" of Professor Wilson; in Galt's Tales; in the writings of the Ettrick Shepherd; in the stories of George MacDonald, J. M. Barrie, and S. R. Crockett; in the pages of "Mansie Wauch," "Tammas Bodkin," and "Johnny Gibb." Don't learn English less; but again, I say, read, write, and speak Scotch more frequently. And, when doing so, remember you are not indulging in a mere vulgar corruption of good English, comparable with the barbarous dialects of Yorkshire and Devon, but in a true and distinct, a powerful and beautiful language of your own, "differing not merely from modern English in pronunciation, but in the possession of many beautiful words, which have ceased to be English, and in the use of inflexions unknown to literary and spoken English since the days of Piers Ploughman and Chaucer." "The Scotch," as the late Lord Jeffrey said, "is not to be considered as a provincial dialect—the vehicle only of rustic vulgarity and rude local humour. It is the language of a whole country, long an independent kingdom, and still separate in laws, character, and manners. It is by no means peculiar to the vulgar, but is the common speech of the whole nation in early life, and with many of its most exalted and accomplished individuals throughout their whole existence; and though it be true that, in later times, it has been in some measure laid aside by the more ambitious and aspiring of the present generation, it is still recollected even by them as the familiar language of their childhood, and of those who were the earliest objects of their love and veneration. It is connected in their imagination not only with that olden time which is uniformly conceived as more pure, lofty, and simple than the present, but also with all the soft and bright colours of remembered childhood and domestic affection. All its phrases conjure up images of school-day innocence and sports, and friendships which have no pattern in succeeding years."

---

# CHAPTER II
## CHARACTERISTICS OF SCOTCH HUMOUR

Various writers have attempted to define Scotch humour, but it is a difficult task, and in all my reading of the subject I do not remember to have ever seen a very satisfactory analysis of the subtle quantity. The famous Sydney Smith did not admit that such an element obtained in our "puir cauld country." "Their only idea of wit which prevails occasionally in the North," said he, "and which, under the name of 'wut,' is so infinitely distressing to people of good taste, is laughing immoderately at stated intervals." Further to this, the same sublime authority declared that it would require a surgical operation to get a joke well into a Scotch understanding. It has been presumed that the witty Canon was not serious in his remark; that it was a laboured effort of his to make a joke. This may be true; and the idea of a surgical operation was possibly suggested by feeling its necessity on himself in order to get his joke *out*. Be that as it may, but for the fact that the genial Charles Lamb, curiously, entertained a somewhat similar notion on the subject, the rude apothegm of the Rev. Sydney Smith would never have misguided even the most hopelessly opaque of his own countrymen. No humour in Scotch folk! No humour in Scotland! There is no country in the world that has produced so much of it. Of no other country under the sun can it be so truly said that humour is the common inheritance of the people. Much of the kind of humour that drives an Englishman into an ecstacy of delight, would, of course, only tend to make a Scotsman sad; but that is no evidence that the Scotch are lacking in their perceptions of the humorous. It only shows that "some folks are no ill to please." "The Cockney must have his puns and small jokes," says Max O'Rell. "On the stage he delights in jigs, and to really please him the best of actors have to become rivals of the mountebanks at a fair. A hornpipe delights his heart. An actor who, for an hour together, pretends not to be able to keep on his hat, sends him into the seventh heaven of delight. Such performances make the Scotch smile—but with pity. The Scotsman has no wit of this sort. In the matter of wit he is an epicure, and only appreciates dainty food." In so far as the above quotation applies to the denizens of the "North," it is perfectly true. In such circumstances the Scotch will "laugh immoderately at stated intervals," but the laughs will be like angels' visits, "few and far between."

Superficially regarded, Scotland is a hard-featured land; yet Scotch folk are essentially humorous. Do not go to the places of public amusement—to the theatres and music halls—particularly in the larger towns, where the populations are so mixed; do not go there to learn the Scottish taste and humour. This practice has led to the proverbial saying that "a Scotchman takes his amusement seriously." In such places you may learn something of the English character and humour, but nothing of the Scotch. For an Englishman's wit (he has little or no humour) being an acquired taste, comes out "on parade"—it is a gay thing—while Scotch folks' humour being the common gift of Nature to all and sundry in the land, differing only in degree, slips out most frequently when and where least expected. Famous specimens of it come down from our lonely hillsides—from the cottage and farm inglenooks. It blossoms in the solemn assemblies of the people—at meetings of Kirk Sessions, in the City and Town Council Chambers, in our Presbyteries, our Courts of Justice, and occasionally in the high Parliament of the Kirk itself. In testimony of this read the *Reminiscences* of Dean Ramsay, Dr. Rodgers' *Century of Scottish Life*, *The Laird of Logan*, and other similar collections of the national humour; or study the humours of our Scottish life and character as they are abundantly reflected in the immortal writings of Burns, and Scott, and Galt, and Wilson.

One of the chief characteristics of Scotch humour, as I have already indicated, is its spontaneity, or utter want of effort to effect its production. Much of it comes out just as a matter of course, and without the slightest indication on the part of the creator that he is aware of the splendid part he is playing. Then it has nearly always a strong practical basis. The Scotch are characteristically practical people, and very much of what is most enjoyable in humorous Scotch stories and anecdotes, as Dean Ramsay truly says, arises "from the simple and matter-of-fact references made to circumstances which are unusual."

There are others, of course, but these are the main characteristics of Scotch humour. Our best anecdotes illustrate this. Here is a good instance of the native wit and humour:—

"Jock," cried a farmer's wife to her cowherd, "come awa' in to your parritch, or the flees 'ill be droonin' themsel's in your milk bowl."

"Nae fear o' that," was Jock's roguish reply. "They'll wade through."

"Ye scoondrel," cried the mistress, indignantly, "d'ye mean to say that ye dinna get eneuch milk?"

"Ou, ay," said Jock, "I get plenty o' milk for a' the parritch."

"Jock," cried a farmer's wife to her cowherd, "come awa' in to your parritch, or the flees 'ill be droonin' themsel's in your milk bowl." "Nae fear o' that," was Jock's roguish reply. "They'll wade through." "Ye scoundrel," cried the mistress, indignantly, "d'ye mean to say that ye dinna get eneuch milk?" "Ou, ay," said Jock, "I get plenty o' milk for a' the parritch."

The colloquy was richly humorous, and at the same time sublimely practical. The same may be said of the following:—

During the time of the great Russian War a countryman accepted the "Queen's shilling," and very soon thereafter was sent to the front. But he had scarcely time to have received his "baptism of fire" when he turned his back on the scenes of carnage, and immediately struck of in a bee line for a distant haven of safety. A mounted officer, intercepting his retreat, demanded to know where he was going.

"Whaur am I gaun?" said he. "Hame, of course; man, this is awfu' walk; they're just killin' ane anither ower there."

A brother countryman took a different view of the same, or a similar situation. Just before his regiment entered into an engagement with the enemy, he was heard to pray in these terms:—"O, Lord! dinna be on oor side, and dinna be on the tither side, but just stand ajee frae baith o' us for an oor or twa, an' ye'll see the toosiest fecht that ever was fochen." What a fine, rough hero was there!

Speaking of praying prior to entering into engagements, recalls another good and equally representative anecdote. It is told of two old Scottish matrons. They were discussing current events.

"Eh, woman!" said one, "I see by the papers that oor sodgers have been victorious again."

"Ah, nae fear o' oor sodgers," replied the other. "They'll aye be victorious, for they aye pray afore they engage wi' the enemy."

"But do you no think the French 'ill pray too?" questioned the first speaker.

"The French pray!" sneered her friend. "Yatterin' craturs! Wha wad ken what they said?"

What a charmingly innocent auld wife! Surely it was this same matron who once upon a time entered the village grocery and asked for a pound of candles, at the same time laying down the price at which the article in question had stood fixed for some time.

"Anither bawbee, mistress," said the grocer. "Cawnils are up, on account o' the war."

"Eh, megstie me!" was the response. "An' can it be the case that they really fecht wi' cawnil licht?"

A Scotch blacksmith, being asked the meaning of metaphysics, explained as follows:—"Weel, Geordie, ye see, it's just like this. When the pairty that listens disna ken what the pairty that speaks means, an' when the pairty that speaks disna ken what he means himsel', *that's metapheesics.*" Many a lecture of an hour's length, I am thinking, has had no better results.

No anecdote can better illustrate the practical basis of the Scotch mind than the following:—"John," said a minister to one of his congregation, "I hope you hold family worship regularly."

"Aye," said John, "in the time o' year o't."

"In the time o' year o't! What do you mean, John?"

"Ye ken, sir, we canna see in the winter nichts."

"But, John, can't you buy candles?"

"Weel, I could," replied John, "but in that case I'm dootin' the cost would owergang the profit."

And practical in the management of their devotional exercises, there is a practical side to the grief of Scotch folk. "Dinna greet amang your parritch, Geordie," said one to another, "they're thin eneuch already." And the story is told of an Aberdeenshire woman who, when on the occasion of the death of her husband the minister's wife came to condole with her, and said—"It is a great loss you have sustained, Janet."

She replied, "Deed is't, my lady. An' I've just been sittin' here greetin' a' day, an' as sune as I get this bowliefu' o' kail suppit I'm gaun to begin an' greet again."

"You have had a sore affliction, Margaret," said a minister once to a Scotch matron in circumstances similar to the heroine of the above story. "A sore affliction indeed; but I hope you are not altogether without consolation."

"Na," said Margaret, "an' I'm no that, sir; for gin He has ta'en awa' the saul, it's a great consolation for me to think that He's ta'en awa' the stammick as weel."

Ah, poor body! No doubt she gave expression to a thought that had for some time been having a prominent place in her mind. As Tom Moore reminds us, in the midst of a serious poem, "We must all dine," and if the bread-winner has been laid aside for a time, the means of subsistence are sometimes difficult to obtain, and when "supply" is wholly cut off, a decrease in "demand" is sometimes not unwelcome.

A splendid instance of the matter-of-fact view of things celestial frequently taken by the Scotch mind is in that story which Dean Ramsay tells of the old woman who was dying at Hawick. In this Border seat of tweed manufacture the people wear wooden-soled boots—clogs—which make a clanking noise on the pavement. Several friends stood by the bedside of the dying person, and one of them said to her—

"Weel, Jenny, ye're deein'; but ye've done the richt gaet here, an' ye'll gang to heaven; an' when ye gang there, should you see ony o' oor fouk, ye micht tell them that we're a' weel."

"Ou," said Jenny half-heartedly, "gin I see them I'se tell them; but ye maunna expect that I'm to be gaun clank, clankin' about through heaven lookin' for your fouk."

Of all the stories of this class, however, the following death-bed conversation between a husband and wife affords perhaps the very best specimen of the dry humour peculiar to Scotch folk:—An old shoemaker in Glasgow was sitting by the bedside of his wife, who was dying. Taking her husband by the hand, the old woman said, "Weel, John, we're to pairt. I hae been a gude wife to you, John."

"Oh, middlin', middlin', Jenny," said John, not disposed to commit himself wholly.

"Ay, I've been a gude wife to you, John," says she, "an' ye maun promise to bury me in the auld kirkyard at Stra'von, beside my ain kith and kin, for I couldna rest in peace among unoo fouk, in the dirt an' smoke o' Gleska'."

"Weel, weel, Jenny, my woman," said John, soothingly, "I'll humour ye thus far. We'll pit ye in the Gorbals first, an' gin ye dinna lie quiet there, we'll tak' ye to Stra'von syne."

And yet there is on record a retort of a Scotch beadle, which is almost equally moving. Saunders was a victim to chronic asthma, and one day, whilst in the act of opening a grave, was seized with a violent fit of coughing. The minister, towards whom Saunders bore little affection, at the same time entering the kirkyard, came up to the old man as he was leaning over his spade wiping the tears from his eyes, and said, "That's a very bad cough you've got, Saunders."

"Ay, it's no very gude," was the dry response, "but there's a hantle fouk lyin' round aboot ye that wud be gey glad o't."

Speaking of beadles reminds me of another good illustration of the "practicality," if I may dare to coin a word, of the Scottish mind. A country beadle had had repeated cause to complain to his minister of interference with his duties on the part of his superannuated predecessor. Coming up to the minister one day, "John's been interfeerin' again," said he, "an' I've come to see what's to be dune?"

"Well, I'm sorry to hear it," said the minister, "but as I have told you before, David, John's a silly body, and you should try, I think, some other means of getting rid of his annoyance than by openly resisting him. Why not follow the Scriptural injunction given for our guidance in such cases, and heap coals of fire on your enemy's head."

"Dod, sir, that's the very thing," cried David, taking the minister literally, and grinning and rubbing his hands with glee at the prospect of an early and effectual settlement of the long-standing feud. "Capital, minister; that'll sort him; dod, ay—heap lowin' coals on his head, and burn the wratch!"

We are proverbially a cautious people. "The canny Scot" is a world-wide term; but the Paisley man who described Niagara Falls as "naething but a perfect waste o' water," was canny to a fault. And yet the Moffat man—his more inspiring native surroundings notwithstanding—was scarcely more visibly impressed by the same scene. "Did you ever see anything so grand?" demanded his friend who had taken him to see the mighty cataract.

"Weel," said the Moffat man, "as for grand, I maybe never saw onything better; but for queer, man, d'ye ken, I ance saw a peacock wi' a wooden leg."

How naturally the one thing would suggest the other will not readily appear to most folks.

He was more of a true Scot who, when the schoolmaster in passing along one day said to him, "I see you are to have a poor crop of potatoes this year, Thomas," replied—

"Ay, but there's some consolation, sir; John Tamson's are no a bit better."

"Hame's aye hamely,"—some homes are more so than others. The "Paisley bodies" have some reason for being proud of their native burgh, as they are. I have heard of one who was on a visit to Edinburgh many years ago, and during his brief stay there was discovered by one of the city guides lying on his face on the Calton Hill, apparently asleep. The summer sun was scorching the back of his uncovered head, and the guide thought it his duty to rouse him up.

"I'm no sleepin'," responded the Paisley man, to the touch of the guide's staff, "I'm just lyin' here thinkin';" then turning himself round and looking up, "Ay, freend," continued he, "I was just lyin' thinkin' aboot Paisley."

"Well," responded the guide, "I don't see why any thought of Paisley should enter your head while you can feast your eyes on fair 'Edina, Scotia's darling Seat,' as the Poet Burns has called our city here."

"Maybe ay, an' maybe no, freend; but it's no easy gettin' the thocht o' Paisley oot o' a Paisley man's head, even although he is in the middle o' Edinburgh. Up in yer braw college there, the maist distinguished professor in it is John Wilson, a Paisley man. In St. George's kirk, ower there, yer precentor, R. A. Smith—an' there's no his marrow again in a' Scotland—is a Paisley man. In the jail ower by fornent us there's mair than a'e Paisley callan' the noo. Syne, ye see the Register House doon there, weel, the woman that sweeps out the passages—an' my ain kissen to boot—is a Paisley woman. An' so ye see, freend, although ane's in Edinburgh it's no sae easy gettin' thochts o' Paisley kept oot o' his head."

The next illustration is also truly Scotch. Two Lowland crofters lived within a few hundred yards of each other. One of them, Duncan by name, being the possessor of "Willison's Works," a rarity in the district, his neighbour, Donald, sent his boy one day to ask Duncan to favour him with a reading of the book. "Tell your father," said Duncan, "that I canna lend oot my book, but he may come to my hoose and read it there as lang as he likes." Country folk deal all more or less in "giff-gaff," and in a few days after, Duncan, having to go to the market, and being minus a saddle, sent his boy to ask Donald to give him the loan of his saddle for the occasion. "Tell your father," said Donald, "that I canna lend oot my saddle; but it's in the barn, an' he can come there an' ride on it a' day if he likes."

The cannyness characteristic of our countrymen, sometimes as a matter of course, is found manifesting itself in ways which, to say the least of them, are peculiar, as witness: A Forfar cobbler, described briefly as "a notorious offender," was not very long ago brought up before the local magistrate, and being found guilty as libelled, was sentenced to pay a fine of half-a-crown, or endure twenty-four hours' imprisonment. If he chose the latter, he would, in accordance with the police arrangements of the district, be taken to the jail at Perth. Having his option, the cobbler communed with himself. "I'll go to Perth," said he; "I've business in the toon at ony rate." An official forthwith conveyed him by train to the "Fair City"; but when the prisoner reached the jail he said he would now pay the fine. The Governor looked surprised, but found he would have to take it. "And now," said the canny cobbler, "I want my fare hame." The Governor demurred, made inquiries, and discovered that there was no alternative; the prisoner must be sent at the public expense to the place where he had been brought from. So the crafty son of St. Crispin got the 2s. 8½d., which represented his railway fare, transacted his business, and went home triumphant, 2½d. and a railway journey the better for his offence.

Our next specimen is cousin-german to the above. It is of two elderly Scotch ladies—"twa auld maids," to use a more homely phrase—who, on a certain Sunday not very long ago, set out to attend divine service in the Auld Kirk, and discovered on the way thither that they had left home without the usual small subscription for the "plate." They resolved not to return for the money, but to ask a loan of the necessary amount from a friend whose door they would pass on the way. The friend was delighted to be able to oblige them, and, producing her purse, spread out on the table a number of coins of various values—halfpennies, pennies, threepenny, and sixpenny pieces. The ladies immediately selected a halfpenny each and went away. Later in the course of the same day they appeared to their friend again, and said they had come to repay the loan.

"Toots, havers," exclaimed old Janet, "ye needna hae been in sic a hurry wi' the bits o' coppers; I could hae gotten them frae you at ony time."

"Ou, but," said the thrifty pair, in subdued and confidential tones, "it was nae trouble ava', for there was naebody stannin' at the plate, so we just slippit in an' saved the bawbees."

Now that is just the sort of anecdote which an Englishman delights to commit to memory and retail in mixed companies of his Scotch and English friends; and, lest he may have heard that one already—may have worn it threadbare, indeed—I will tell another which, if not quite so good, has the advantage of being not so well known. A Scotchman was once advised to take shower baths. A friend explained to him how to fit up one by the use of a cistern and colander, and Sandy accordingly set to work and had the thing done at once. Subsequently he was met by the friend who had given him the advice, and, being asked how he enjoyed the bath—

"Man," said he, "it was fine. I liked it rale weel, and kept mysel' quite dry, too."

Being asked how he managed to take the shower and yet remain quite dry, he replied—

"Dod, ye dinna surely think I was sae daft as stand ablow the water without an umbrella."

That's truly Scotch. So is the next specimen, as you will presently perceive. Two or three nights before the advent of a recent Christmas, a Scotch laddie of ten years old, or so, was sitting examining very gravely a somewhat ugly hole in the heel of one of his stockings. At length he looked towards his mother and said—

"Mither, ye micht gie me a pair o' new stockin's?"

"So I will, laddie, by and by; but ye're no sair needin' new anes yet," said his mother.

"Will I get them this week?"

"What mak's ye sae anxious to hae them this week?"

"Because, if Santa Claus pits onything into thir anes it'll fa' oot."

How naturally a Scotsman drops into poetry, too, will be seen from the following:—

Mr. Dewar, a shopkeeper in Edinburgh, being in want of silver for a bank note, went into the shop of a neighbour of the name of Scott, whom he thus addressed—

"I say, Master Scott,

Can you change me a note?"

Mr. Scott's reply was—

"I'm no very sure, but I'll see."

Then going into the back-room, he immediately returned and added—

"Indeed, Mr. Dewar,

It's out o' my power,

For my wife's awa' wi' the key."

It is by furnishing him with choice and representative examples that one can best convey to a stranger a knowledge of the characteristics of our national humour. So much of it depends often on the quaintness of the Scottish idiom, that it defies explanation, and must be seen, or better still, be heard, to be understood. This course I have pursued in the present paper; and the examples deduced, I think, fairly demonstrate the strong substratum of practical common-sense which underlies, and yet manifests itself in, the lighter elements of the Scottish character, frequently making humour where pathos was meant to be. Take a few more:—

The wife of a small farmer in Perthshire some time ago went to a chemist's in the "Fair City" with two prescriptions—one for her husband, the other for her cow. Finding she had not enough of money to pay for both, the chemist asked her which she would take.

"Gie me the stuff for the coo," said she; "the morn will do weel eneuch for *him*, puir body. Gin *he* were to dee I could sune get another man, but I'm no sure that I could sae sune get anither coo."

The late Rev. Dr. Begg, was wont to tell of a Scotch woman to whom a neighbour said, "Effie, I wonder hoo ye can sleep wi' sae muckle debt on your heid;" to which Effie quietly answered, "I can sleep fu' weel; but I wonder hoo they can sleep that trust me."

"Are you a native of this parish?" asked a sheriff of a witness who was summoned to testify in a case of distilling.

"Maistly, yer honour," was the reply.

"I mean, were you born in this parish?"

"No, yer honour, I wisna born in this parish; but I'm maistly a native for a' that."

"You came here when you were a child I suppose, you mean?" said the sheriff.

"No, sir; I'm here just aboot sax year noo."

"Then how do you come to be mostly a native of the parish?"

"Weel, ye see, when I cam here, sax year syne, I just weighed eight stane, an' I'm fully seventeen stane noo; so, ye see, that aboot nine stane o' me belangs to this parish, an' I maun be maistly a native o't."

Not very long ago a countryman got married, and soon after invited a friend to his house and introduced him to his new wife, who, by the by, was a person of remarkably plain appearance. "What do you think o' her John?" he asked his friend, when the good lady had retired from the room for a little. "She's no' very bonnie!" was the candid and discomforting reply. "That's true," said the husband; "she's no muckle to look at, but she's a rale gude-hearted woman. Positeevly ugly *outside*, but a' that's lovely *inside*." "Lord, man, Tam," said the friend gravely, "it's a peety ye couldna *flype* her!"

At a feeing market in Perth a boy was waiting to be hired, when a farmer, who wanted such a servant, accosted him, and after some conversation, enquired if he had a written character. The lad replied that he had, but it was at home. "Bring it with you next Friday," said the farmer, "and meet me here at two o'clock." When the parties met again, "Weel, my man," said the farmer, "ha'e ye got your character?" "Na," was the reply, "but I've gotten *yours*, an' I'm no comin'!"

"There's anither row up at the Soutars'," said Willie Wilson, as he shook the rain from his plaid and took his accustomed seat by the inn parlour fire. "I heard them at it as I cam' by just noo."

"Ay, ay; there's aye some fun gaun' on at the Soutars'," said another of the company, with a laugh.

"Fun? I shouldn't think there's much *fun* in those disgraceful family disturbances," said the schoolmaster.

"Aweel, it's no' so vera bad, after a'," said the other, who had *his* share of matrimonial strife. "Ye see, when the wife gets in her tantrums she aye throws a plate or brush, or maybe twa or three, at Sandy's head. Gin she hits him *she's* gled, and gin she misses him *he's* gled; so, ye see, there's aye some pleasure to a'e side or the ither."

The Laird of Balnamoon, riding past a high, steep bank, stopped opposite a hole in it, and said, "John, I saw a brock gang in there."

"Did ye?" said John; "will ye haud my horse, sir?"

"Certainly," said the Laird, and away rushed John for a spade.

After digging for half an hour, he came back nigh speechless to the Laird, who had regarded him musingly.

"I canna find him, sir," said John.

"Deed," said the Laird, very coolly, "I wad hae wondered if ye had, for it's ten years an' mair sin' I saw him gang in."

On one occasion, when the gallant Highlanders were stationed at Gibraltar, Sandy Macnab was sergeant of the guard, and in due course of duty had sent his corporal to make the last relief before four o'clock in the morning. Whilst proceeding to one of the outlying posts the corporal missed his footing, fell over the cliff, and was killed. Meantime Sergeant Macnab had been filling up the usual guard report, preparatory to dismounting. Now, at the foot of the form on which such reports are made out there is a printed inquiry—"Anything extraordinary occurred since mounting guard?"

Macnab, unaware of the accident to his corporal, filled the query space up with the word "*Nil*," and, having no spare copy of the form, sent this in to the orderly-room to take its chance. When the Colonel and Adjutant attended in the orderly-room at ten o'clock, learned of the mishap, and read Macnab's report, the latter was peremptorily ordered to appear before them.

"Macnab," cried the Colonel, in a rage, "what the devil do you mean by filling up your guard report in this way? You say 'Nothing extraordinary occurred since mounting guard,' and yet your poor comrade fell over the cliff and was killed."

Sandy, finding himself in a fix, pulled himself together, and after a moment or two of deliberation answered, coolly, "Weel, sir, I dinna see onything very extraordinar' in that. It would hae been something very extraordinar' if he hadna been killed; he fell fowr hunder feet!"

In Mr. Barrie's *Little Minister*, a discussion takes place in the village Parliament as to whether it is possible for a woman to refuse to marry a minister. "I once," said Snecky Hobart, "knew a widow who did. His name was Samson, and if it had been Tamson she would hae ta'en him. Ay, you may look, but it's true. Her name was Turnbull, and she had another gent after her, named Tibbets. She couldna make up her mind atween them, and for a while she just keeped them dangling on. Ay, but in the end she took Tibbets. And what, think you, was her reason? As you ken, thae grand folk hae their initials on their spoons and nichtgowns. Ay, weel, she thocht it would be mair handy to take Tibbets, because if she had ta'en the minister, the *T's* would have to be changed to *S's*. *It was thochtfu' o' her.*"

Our next two specimens show how waggish the Scotch can be.

A farmer, returning from a Northern tryst, accompanied by his servant Pate, not many years ago, halted for refreshment at the Inn of Glamis, where, meeting with a number of friends, a jolly party was soon formed. Under the cheering hospitality of the gude wife of the inn they cracked their jokes and told their tales, till at length the farmer proposed that his attendant, Pate, should enliven the meeting with a song. One of the party, who professed to have an estimate of the shepherd's vocal abilities, sneeringly replied, "Whaur can Pate sing?"

"What d'ye say?" answered the farmer. "Can Pate no sing? I'm thinkin' he's sung to as good fouk, an' better than you, in his time. I'll tell ye o' a'e place whaur he has been kent to sing wi' mair honour to himsel' than ye can brag o', and that's before the Queen. Ay, an' if it will heighten him ony in your estimation, I'll prove to you, for the wager o' a bottle o' brandy, that he even sleepit, an' that no' sae lang syne, in the same hoose she was in."

Thinking this latter assertion outstretched the limits of all probability, the wager was immediately taken by the party, when, to the satisfaction of all the others present, the worthy farmer proved the truth of his allegations by telling how, accompanied by Pate, he had been to the Kirk of Crathie on the Sunday previous, and that during the service, and in presence of Her Royal Majesty, Pate had both sung and slept. The farmer won the wager, and the bottle circulated, amid continued outbursts of stentorian laughter.

A worthy laird in a Perthshire village made the, for him, wonderful journey to see the great Exhibition of 1851. On his return, his banker, a man who was well known to have the idea that he was by far the most influential and potent power in the shire, invited the laird, with some cronies, to a glass of punch. The banker meant to amuse the company at the old laird's expense, to trot him out, and get him to describe the sights of London. "An' what, laird, most of all impressed you at the great glass house?" asked the banker, with a sly wink at the company. "Ah, weel, sir," replied the laird, as he emptied his glass, "I was muckle impressed wi' a' I saw—muckle impressed! But the thing abune a' that impressed me maist was my ain insignificance. Losh, banker, I wad strongly advise you to gang; it would do *you* a vast amount o' guid, sir!"

The next example affords the promise of an abundant harvest of humour off the rising generation of Scotsmen.

A little boy, whom we shall call Johnnie, just because that is his name, was not very long since employed as message-boy to a grocer in a small country town in the west, said grocer being an ardent advocate and supporter of the Conservative party in the State. One morning Johnnie was an hour or so late in turning out for duty, and on entering was promptly interrogated by his master as to the cause.

"The cat's had kittlins this mornin'," asseverated the lad, assuming a look of great earnestness; "four o' them, an' they're a' Conservatives."[1]

[1] By the simple transposition of the words "Conservatives" and "Leeberals" the politics of this story may be adapted to suit any select company or association of individuals in these realms, as by the same practice I have seen it made to serve the interests of various Liberal and Conservative newspapers since I first printed it in the *People's Journal* some years ago.

"Get in bye and tidy up that back shop," said the shopkeeper gruffly, not at the moment in a mood to enquire fully into the extraordinary feline phenomenon. One day, nearly a fortnight afterwards, the following sequel added itself, however, and there was a perfect understanding established. A commercial traveller, who is also a true-blue Tory, called at the shop, and was discussing with the grocer the chances of victory or failure to their party in an approaching bye-election. Said the grocer, "Our party is gaining strength in the country, of that I am convinced, and with reason; why, my message-boy was telling me recently that his mother's cat has had kittens—four of them—and they are all Conservatives." The traveller laughed, as only travellers who are anticipating an order can laugh. When Johnnie entered the premises with his basket on his arm and a tune in his mouth.

"Hillo, Johnnie!" exclaimed the commercial, "and so your cat has had kittens, has she? Eh?"

"Ay," replied Johnnie, "four o' them."

"And all Conservatives, too, I believe?" remarked the traveller.

"Na," said Johnnie: "they're Leeberals."

"Liberals! you told me a fortnight ago they were Conservatives," interposed the master.

"Ou, ay; of course," returned Johnnie, with the utmost gravity. "They were Conservatives yon time, *but they're seein' noo*!"

Just one more here. There is a cobbler in a little town in the North—a worthy old soul, as it would appear, whose custom has been for many years to hammer and whistle from morn to night in his little shop, and to discharge both functions so lustily as to be easily heard by the passers-by in the street. One day not long since the minister, happening to pass, missed the whistling accompaniment to the measured click on the lapstone, and looked in to ascertain the cause. "Is all well with you, Saunders?" he asked. "Na, na, sir; it's far frae bein' a' weel wi' me. The sweep's gane an' ta'en the shop ower my head." "Oh, that's bad news, indeed," responded the minister, "but I think you might see your way out of the difficulty soon if, as I always urge in cases of emergency, you would make the matter a subject of earnest prayer." Saunders promised to do this, and the preacher departed. In less than a week he returned, and found the old cobbler hammering and whistling away in his old familiar "might and main" fashion. "Well, Saunders, how is it now?" "Oh, it's a' richt, minister," was the reply. "I did as ye tell'd me, an'—*the sweep's deid.*"

# CHAPTER III
## HUMOUR OF OLD SCOTCH DIVINES

The late Lord Neaves, himself a man of a genial, humorous nature, was wont to complain pleasantly of his friend Dean Ramsay for having drawn so many specimens of Scottish humour from the sayings and doings of the native clergy. But the worthy Dean, to employ a figure of his own recording, simply "biggit's dyke wi' the feal at fit o't;" in other words, he gathered most grain from the field which had produced the most abundant crop—the field of clerical life and work. Your typical pastor, it is true, has not to any extent been remarkable as a humourist—the reverse may with more truth be said of him. At the same time the Scottish pulpit has contained many earnest, good men, who were also genuine humourists. Yea, than the good old Scotch divines, certainly no other class or section of the community has laid up to its credit so many witty and humorous sayings that are destined to live with the language in which they are uttered. Every parish in the land has stories to tell of such pastors. It is only necessary to mention such prominent names as the Revs. Robert Shirra, of Kirkcaldy; Walter Dunlop, of Dumfries; John Skinner, of Longside, the author of "Tullochgorum"; Mr. Thom, of Govan; and the late Drs. Norman Macleod and William Anderson, of Glasgow, to suggest many other bright and shining lights. There have been many ministers of the Gospel, of course, who, not at all witty themselves, yet, by reason of certain idiosyncrasies of nature and eccentricities of character, have been the cause of wit in others. These, however, do not come within the scope of the present paper. Here we shall deal not with *negative* but with *positive* clerical humorists only.

Much of the old clerical humour of Scotland came direct from the pulpit, and was part and parcel of the pastoral matter and method of the time. The preaching of to-day gives but the faintest idea of the preaching of a hundred years ago. The sermon of the old divine was very much in the style of an easy conversation, interspersed with occasional parentheses applicable to individual characters or to the circumstances which arose before his eyes in church.

Dean Ramsay, in his faithful *Reminiscences*, tells of a clergyman who, observing one of his flock asleep during his sermon, paused, and called him to order, thus—"Jeems Robson, ye are sleepin'. I insist on your wauking when God's word is preached to ye."

"Look at your ain seat and ye'll see a sleeper forby me," answered Jeems, pointing to the clergyman's lady in the minister's pew.

"Then, Jeems," said the minister, "when ye see my wife asleep again haud up your hand."

By and by the arm was stretched out, and sure enough the fair lady was caught in the act. Her husband solemnly called upon her to stand up and receive the censure due to her offence, and thus addressed her—"Mrs. B., a'body kens that when I got ye for my wife I got nae beauty; yer freens ken I got nae siller; and, if I didna get God's grace, I hae gotten a puir bargain indeed."

It is fortunate for some folks, both you and I know, my reader, that Church discipline is not so rigorously enforced nowadays.

Mr. Shirra, of Kirkcaldy, distinguished for his homely and remarkable sayings, both in the pulpit and abroad, was greatly given to personal reproof in the course of divine service, and had a happy knack of sometimes killing two birds with one stone. One day, observing a young girl with a large and rather gaudy new bonnet, with which she herself seemed immoderately pleased, and also noticing or suspecting that his wife was indulging in a quiet nap, he paused in the middle of his sermon and said—"Look ony o' ye there if my wife be sleepin', for I canna see her for thae fine falderals on Jenny Bain's new bonnet." One day a weaver entered Shirra's kirk dressed in the new uniform then procured for the volunteers, just raised. He kept walking about for a time as if looking for a seat, but really to show off his finery, which he perceived was attracting the attention of some of the less grave members of the congregation. He came to his place, however, rather quickly on Shirra quietly remarking, "Just sit down there, my man, and we'll a' see your new breeks when the kirk skails."

This same Shirra was addicted to parenthetical remarks when reading the Scriptures, and one day, when reading from the 116th Psalm, "I said in my haste, all men are liars," he quietly remarked—"Indeed, Dauvid, gin ye had lived in this parish ye might hae said it at your leisure."

This, good as it is, was almost equalled by the remarks of an Edinburgh minister. The Rev. Mr. Scott, of the Cowgate, was a man of some popularity, but was seldom on good terms with his flock. One day, as he was preaching on Job, he said—"My brethren, Job, in the first place, was a sairly tried man; Job, in the second place, was an uncommonly patient man; Job, in the third place, never preached in the Cowgate; fourthly, and lastly, if Job *had* preached here, gude help his patience."

The Rev. James Oliphant, of Dumbarton, was especially quaint in the pulpit. In reading the Scriptures, his habit was to make parenthetical comments in undertones. On this account the seats in nearest proximity to the pulpit were always best filled. Reading, one day, the passage which describes the possessed swine running into the deep and being there choked, he was heard to mutter, "Oh, that the deevil had been chockit too." Again, in the passage as to Peter exclaiming, "We have left all and followed Thee," the remark was, "Aye boasting, Peter, aye bragging; what had ye to leave but an auld, crazy boat, and maybe twa or three rotten nets?" There was considerable ingenuity in the mode by which Mr. Oliphant sought to establish the absolute wickedness of the devil. "From the word *devil*," said Mr. Oliphant, "which means an *enemy*, take the d and you have *evil*; remove the e and you have *vil* (vile); take away the v and it is *ill*; and so you see, my brethren, he's just an *ill, vile, evil devil*."

A late minister of Crossmichael, in Galloway, did not disdain to illustrate his subjects with such images and allusions as were within the comprehension of his homely hearers. Accordingly, one Sabbath morning, he read a verse from the book of Exodus, as follows—"And the Lord said unto Moses—shut that door; I'm thinkin' if ye had to sit beside the door yersel' ye wadna be sae ready leavin' it open; it was just beside that door that Yedam Tamson, the bellman, gat his death o' cauld, an' I'm sure, honest man, he didna let it stey muckle open.—And the Lord said unto Moses—put oot that dog; wha is't that brings dogs to the kirk, yaff-yaffin'? Lat me never see ye bring yer dogs here ony mair, or I'll put you an' them baith oot.—And the Lord said unto Moses—I see a man aneath that wast laft wi' his hat on; I'm sure ye're clean oot o' the souch o' the door; keep aff yer bonnet, Tammas, an' if yer bare pow be cauld, ye maun jist get a grey worset wig like mysel'; they're no sae dear; plenty o' them at Bob Gillespie's for tenpence." This said, he again began the verse, and at last made out the instructions to Moses in a manner more strictly in accordance with the text and with decency.

Another, remarkable for the simplicity and force of his style, was discoursing from the text, "Except ye repent ye shall all likewise perish," and in order to impress upon his hearers the importance of attending to the solemn truth conveyed in the passage—"Yes, my freens," he emphatically exclaimed, "unless ye repent ye shall all perish, just as surely as I'm gaun to ding the guts oot o' that muckle blue flee that's lichtit on my Bible." Before the blow was struck the fly got away, upon which he struck the book with all his might and exclaimed at the top of his voice, "My freens, there's a chance for ye yet!"

Dr. Paul, in his *Past and Present of Aberdeenshire*, tells of a minister who, while preaching on the subject of the wiles and crafts of Satan, suddenly paused, and then exclaimed—"See him sittin' there in the crap o' the wa'. What shall we do wi' him, my brethren? He winna hang, for he's licht as a feather; neither will he droon, my brethren, for he can soom like a cork; but we'll shoot him wi' the gun o' the Gospel." Then putting himself in the position of one aiming at an object, and imitating the noise of a shot, the minister called out exultingly, "He's doon like a dead craw!"

This incident would have greatly delighted the man who thus described the kind of minister he was in search of—"Nane o' your guid-warks men, or preachers o' cauld morality for me! Gie me a speerit-rousin' preacher that'll haud the deil under the noses of the congregation and mak' their flesh creep!"

It is related of a certain divine, whose matrimonial relations are supposed not to have been of the most agreeable kind, that one Sabbath morning, while reading to his congregation the parable of the Supper, in which occurs the passage—"And another said, I have bought five yoke of oxen, and I go to prove them; I pray thee have me excused. And another said, I have married a wife, and therefore cannot come," he suddenly paused at the end of this verse, drew off his spectacles, and, looking on his hearers, said with emphasis—"The fact is, my brethren, one woman can draw a man farther away from the kingdom of heaven than fifty yoke of oxen."

They were hard nuts to crack, many of these old preachers.

A late Earl of Airlie, when Lord High Commissioner, had the retiring Moderator to dinner with him on the evening previous to the opening of the General Assembly. In a spirit of mischief, the Earl tried to unfit him for his duties on the following day. As often as the reverend gentleman would endeavour to retire, the Earl met him with the exclamation, "Another glass, and then!" In spite of his late potations, the minister was in his place on the following day, and preached from the words, "The wicked shall be punished, and that right early." Notwithstanding the manifest impatience of the Commissioner, the sermon was spun out to an inordinate length, the minister repeating with meaning emphasis each time that the sand glass which showed the half-hours was turned, "Another glass, and then! The wicked shall be punished, and that right *early*."

A certain divine—or perhaps we should say an *un*-certain divine—preaching a sermon from the parable of the prodigal son, took as his text the words, "And when he came to himself," and gave a reading of the passage at once unique and original. "We have here, brethren," said he, "an instance of the wonderful depth of meaning there is in Scripture. We see how low this unprincipled young man had fallen. 'When he came to himself'—what does it mean? Well, look at home. What do we do when our money's gone and we've no credit? What do we turn to? The pawnshop. So did he. First, his coat would go; he might live a week on that. Then his waistcoat; that wouldn't serve him long. Lastly, his shirt would follow; and then—ah, then, my friends, he came to *himself*! He couldn't pawn himself, and so he went home to his father."

The older style of preaching was often wonderfully graphic as well as amusing. Preaching from that text in Ecclesiastes—"Dead flies cause the ointment of the apothecary to send forth a stinking savour; so doth a little folly him that is in reputation for wisdom and honour," a north country divine illustrated his subject by this example:—"See John at the kirk, an' he looks amon' folk like a man o' mense; but follow him to the peat-moss, an' ye'll hear him tellin' coorse stories to the loons an' queans, haudin' them lauchin' at sin. There's a dead flee in John's sowl." Sometimes, in his endeavour to give a vivid description, this same preacher became delightfully grotesque. Referring to Jonah—"The whawl," he said, "shoutherin' awa' the waves, got at last geyan near the shore, and cried *Byock-up*. But Jonah didna come. Then the whawl cried [speaking it louder, and imitating the whale retching], BYOCK-UP! But na! Jonah aye stack. Then the whawl cried [speaking it very loud and slow], BYOCK-UP! Noo, sirs, divna ye see Jonah rinnin', dreepin', up the beach." Once he described the progress of a sinner in a course of vice to the last stage of his hopelessness, when there is nothing left for him but a cry of pain—"Sirs, oot owre yon knowe there's a sheepie tether't, an' in o' reach o' its tether there's a breem buss [broom bush], an' it gangs roond the buss, an' roond the buss, till it's hankit at the head, an' then, what does it dee? It cries, *Bae*! That's just the sinner cryin' oot in its meesery." In the same sermon, looking down upon the old women who sat near the pulpit and on the pulpit stair for the purpose of better hearing, in their clean white mutches, he said—"Here ye're a' sittin', wi' yer auld wither't faces, that's bonnier to me than a lass in her teens, for I ken ye hae seen sixty or seventy years, ilka ane o' ye, an' yer auld faces just say to me, 'We hae served our Maister threescore years thegither, an' we're no tired servin' Him yet.'" It does not surprise one to be told that this reference to the old women put them in a state of visible emotion.

The quaint homeliness thus manifested in the lesson and in the sermon found a place now and again in the prayers; and a west country divine, in the course of a wet harvest, in praying for more suitable weather, expressed himself thus:—"O Lord, gie us nae mair watter for a season, but wind—plenty o' wind, an' yet, O Lord, nane o' yer rantin', tantin', tearin' winds, but an oughin', soughin', winnin' wind."

Another, similarly circumstanced, prayed "that the floodgates of heaven might be shut for a season." This was towards the close of a protracted period of rain and storm, and the weather had never been worse than on this particular Sabbath. And, just as the good man persisted in his petition, a fierce gust of wind bore the roof-window of the church down with a crash, which was succeeded by a terrific clatter of broken glass. "Oh," he exclaimed, assuming an attitude of despair, "O Lord, this is perfectly ridiculous!"

He was more of a philosopher who, when his good lady told him that he did not *insist* enough when praying for a change of weather, replied, "Nae use o' insistin', Marget, until the change o' the mune."

The pastor of a small congregation of Dissenters in the West of Scotland, who, in prayer, often employed terms of familiarity towards the Great Being whom he invoked, was praying one day that such weather would be granted as was necessary for the ripening and gathering in of the fruits of the earth, when, pausing suddenly, he added in a lower tone of voice—"But what needs I talk! When I was up at the Shotts the other day, everything was as green as leeks!"

The Rev. Dr. Young, of Perth, used to be annoyed by a couple coming to church, sitting away in the gallery, "ssh-ssh" as they talked in lovers' language all through the service. He could stand it no longer, so one Sunday he stopped in the middle of his sermon, looked up to the gallery, and said, "If that couple in the right hand gallery there will come to me on Monday I will marry them for nothing, if they will stop that 'ssh-ssh'!"

The Rev. John Ross, of Blairgowrie, indulged a propensity for versifying in his pulpit announcements, and one day, at the close of the service, intimated that

"The Milton, the Hilton, Rochabie, and Tammamoon,

Will a' be examined on Thursday afternoon."

And now we are induced to follow our subject out of the pulpit and into the wider sphere of pastoral life. It was here more particularly that the pungent and ready wit of the famous Watty Dunlop got full reign and enjoyed free play. The best known anecdote of this worthy relates to an occasion when he happened to be accompanying a funeral through a straggling village in the parish of Caerlaverock. Entering at one end of the hamlet he met a man driving a flock of geese. The wayward disposition of the feathered bipeds at the moment was too much for the driver's temper, and he indignantly cried out, "Deevil choke ye!" Mr. Dunlop walked a little further on, and passed a farm-stead where a servant was driving a number of swine, and banning them with "Deevil tak' ye!" Upon which Mr. Dunlop stepped up to him, and said, "Ay, ay, my man, yer gentleman'll be wi' ye i' the noo; he's just back the road there a bit chokin' some geese till a man."

Than Mr. Dunlop few ministers were more esteemed by their congregations as faithful and affectionate pastors, and so much respected by all denominations. And no doubt his freedom of speech and frankness of manner were important factors in bringing about this happy result. Here we have a capital example of his free and easy manner. While pursuing his pastoral visitations among some of the country members of his flock, he came one evening to a farmhouse where he was expected; and the mistress, thinking that he would be in need of refreshment, proposed that he should take his tea before engaging in *exercise*, and said she would soon have it ready. Mr. Dunlop's reply was, "I aye tak' my tea better when my wark's dune. I'll just be gaun on. Ye can hing the pan on, an' lea the door ajee, an' I'll draw to a close when I hear the ham fizzlin'." With the frankness so characteristic of him, this divine did not hesitate occasionally to intimate how agreeable certain presents would be to himself and his better-half. Accordingly, on a further "visitation" occasion, and while at a "denner-tea," as he called it, at the close of a hard day's labour, he kept incessantly praising the ham, and stated that Mrs. Dunlop at home was as fond of ham as he was. His hostess took the hint, and kindly offered to send Mrs. Dunlop the present of a ham. "It's unco kind o' ye—unco kind o' ye," replied the divine; "but I'll no put ye to sae muckle trouble. I'll just tak' it hame on the horse afore me." On leaving, he mounted, and the ham was put into a sack, but some difficulty was experienced in getting it to lie properly. His inventive genius, however, soon cut the Gordion knot. "I think, mistress," said he, "a cheese in the ither end o' the poke would mak' a grand balance." The gudewife could not resist an appeal so neatly put, and, like another John Gilpin, the crafty and facetious divine moved away with his "balance true." Mr. Dunlop's *penchant* for "presents" was, of course, well known, and on one occasion at least brought him into rather an awkward predicament. While engaged in offering up prayer in a house at which he was visiting, a peculiar sound was heard to issue from his greatcoat pocket. This was afterwards discovered to have proceeded from a half-choked duck which he had "gotten in a present," and whose neck he had been squeezing all the time to prevent its crying.

On one occasion two irreverent young fellows determined, as they put it, "to taigle (confound) the minister." Therefore, coming up to him in the High Street of Dumfries, they accosted him with much apparent solemnity, saying—

"Mr. Dunlop, hae ye heard the news?"

"What news?"

"Oh, the deil's dead."

"Is he?" quoth Mr. Dunlop; "then I maun pray for twa faitherless bairns."

On another occasion, Mr. Dunlop met, with characteristic humour, an attempt to play off a trick on him. It was known that he was to dine with a minister whose house was situated close to the church, so that his return walk must be through the churchyard. Accordingly, some idle and mischievous fellows waited for him in the middle of the kirkyard, dressed in the popularly accredited habiliments of a ghost, hoping to put him in a terrible fright. "Is't a general risin'?" inquired Watty, as he leisurely passed by the unco figure, "or are ye just takin' a daunder yer lane?"

The celebrated Edward Irving had been lecturing at Dumfries, and a man who passed as a wag in the locality had been to hear him. He met Watty Dunlop the following day, who said—

"Weel, Willie, man, an' what do you think o' Mr. Irving?"

"Oh," said Willie, contemptuously, "the man's crackit."

"Ah, Willie," rejoined Dunlop, patting the man quietly on the shoulder, "but ye'll aften see a bright light shinin' through a crack." No rejoinder was ever more pat.

Of similar grit with the facetious Watty Dunlop was another Watty: to wit, the Rev. Walter Morrison, a well-known north country divine. It is told of this worthy that when he was entreating the commanding officer of a regiment at Fort-George to pardon a poor fellow who had been sent to the halberts, the officer declared he would grant the culprit a free pardon on the condition that Mr. Morrison should accord with the first favour he (the officer) asked. The preacher at once agreed. The favour was to perform the ceremony of baptism for his young puppy. A merry party was invited to the christening, and much fun was expected at the minister's expense. But they had been reckoning without their host. On his arrival, Mr. Morrison desired the officer to hold up the pup. "As I am a minister of the Kirk of Scotland," said he, "I must proceed accordingly." The Major said he asked no more. "Well then, Major, I begin with the usual question—You acknowledge yourself the father of this puppy?" The Major saw he had been over-reached, and threw away the animal amid the loud laughter of his brother officers.

The humour of John Skinner, for sixty-four years the Episcopal minister of Longside, who was the friend and correspondent of Robert Burns, and the author of "Tullochgorum," "The Ewie wi' the Crookit Horn," "John o' Badenyon," and many other capital songs, was of the finest quality, standing in that respect in striking contrast to the humour of the U.P. minister of Dumfries. One specimen will suffice here, and I give it exactly as recorded by Dean Ramsay. Being present at a party (I think, says the Dean, at Lord Forbes's), where were also several ministers of the Establishment, the conversation over their wine turned, among other things, on the Prayer Book. Skinner took no part in it till one minister remarked to him—

"The great fault I hae to your Prayer Book is that ye use the Lord's Prayer sae aften. Ye just mak' a dishclout o't."

Skinner's rejoinder was, "Verra true; ay, man, we mak' a dishclout o't, an' we wring't, an' we wring't, an' the bree o't washes a' the lave o' our prayers." The reply was witty and clever, and without gall.

Here you have another admirable example of the retort courteous. An old Edinburgh Doctor of Divinity, whose nose and chin were both very long, lost his teeth, and the nose and chin were thus brought, like the nose and chin of Willie Wastle's wife, to "threaten ither." A friend of his, accordingly, looking him broad in the face, jokingly observed—

"I am afraid, Doctor, your nose and chin will fight before long; they approach each other very menacingly."

"I am afraid of it myself," was the ready and good-humoured reply, "for a great many words have passed between them already."

The Rev. Dr. Lawson, of Selkirk, a pious, able, and esteemed man, was reputed for indulging in those sallies of humour which not unfrequently avail in conveying salutary council when a graver method would prove ineffectual. His medical advisor, says Dr. Charles Rogers, had contracted the unworthy habit of using profane oaths. The Doctor had sent for him to consult him upon the state of his health, when, after hearing a narrative of his complaints, the physician rather angrily said, "Damn it, sir, you are the slave of a vile habit, and you will not soon recover unless you at once give it up."

"And what is the habit you refer to?" inquired the patient.

"It is your practice of smoking—the use of tobacco is injuring your constitution."

"I find it is an expensive habit," said Dr. Lawson, "and if it is injuring me I shall abandon it; but will you permit me to give you a hint, too, as to a vile habit of your own; and which, were you to give it up, would be a great benefit to yourself and comfort to your friends?"

"What is that?" inquired the M.D.

"I refer to your habit of profane swearing," replied the divine.

"True," said Dr. —, "but that is not an expensive habit, like yours."

"Doctor!" rejoined Lawson, "I warn you that you will discover it to be a very expensive habit indeed when the account is handed to you."

Another anecdote of a similar nature is recorded of this divine. He was dining at a friend's house. A gentleman of the party was, in conversation, frequently employing the words, "The devil take me." Dr. Lawson at length arose, and ordered his horse. The host was surprised, and insisted upon his remaining, as dinner had scarcely begun. But nothing could prevail on him to do so; and when pressed to give a reason for his abrupt departure, he replied, "That gentleman there" (pointing to him) "has been praying that the devil would take him; and as I have no wish to be present at the scene, I beg to be allowed to depart."

At a subsequent period of his ministry, Dr. Lawson was appointed Professor in the Divinity Hall of the Associate Church. One morning he appeared in the Hall with his wig somewhat *tousie* and all on one side. A student whispered to his neighbour, "See, his wig is no redd the day." The Doctor heard, but took no notice of it at the time; but when it came to the turn of this student to deliver a discourse, he was invited to the pulpit with these words from the professor—"Come awa, Mr. —, and we'll see wha's got the best redd wig."

Dr. Macfarlane, in his biography of Dr. Lawson, gives a story of another Selkirk minister—Mr. Law, afterwards of Kirkcaldy—who was equally remarkable with Dr. Lawson for wit and satire, piety and talent. There was a sort of scoffing character in the town in which Mr. Law lived, commonly called Jock Hammon. Jock had a nickname for Mr. Law, which, though profane, had reference to the well-known evangelical character of his ministry. "There's the grace of God," he would say, as he saw the good man passing by; and he actually talked of him under that designation. It so happened that Mr. Law had on one occasion consented to take the chair at some public meeting. The hour of meeting was past, the place of meeting was filled, but no minister appeared. Symptoms of impatience were manifested, when a voice was heard from one corner of the hall—"My freends, there will be nae 'Grace of God' here this nicht!" Just at this moment the door opened and Mr. Law appeared, casting, as he entered, a rather knowing look upon Jock Hammon, as Jock ejaculated these words. On taking the chair Mr. Law apologised for being so late. "I had," he said, "to go into the country to preside at the examination of a village school, and really the young folks conducted themselves so well that I could scarce get away from them. If you please, I will give you a specimen of the examination. I called up an intelligent-looking girl, and asked her if she had ever heard of any one who had erected a gallows for another and who had been hanged on it himself? 'Yes,' replied the girl, 'it was Haman.' With that up started another little girl, and she said, 'Eh, minister, that's no true; Hammon's no hanged yet, for I saw him at the public-hoose door this forenoon, and he was swearing like a trooper!'" (Upon this there was a considerable tittering among the audience, and eyes were directed to the corner where Jock was sitting.) "You are both quite right, my dears," said Mr. Law. "Your *Haman* was really hanged, as he deserved to be; and" (turning towards the other) "your *Hammon*, my lammie, is no hanged yet—by 'the grace of God,'" he added, with a solemnity of tone which removed every thought of irreverence from the allusion.

Very sharp and stinging was the wit and satire of the well-known Thom of Govan. One day when he was preaching before the magistrates, he is reported to have suddenly halted and said, "Dinna snore sae loud, Bailie Broon, ye'll wauken the Provost." On another occasion, the circumstances of which were very similar, he suddenly stopped in his discourse, took out his snuff-box, tapped it on the lid, and took a pinch of snuff with the greatest of deliberation. By this time the whole congregation was agog with eager curiosity to know what was wrong. Mr. Thom, after a little, gravely proceeded to say, "My friends, I've had a snuff, and the Provost has had a sleep, and, if ye like, we'll just begin again."

A country laird, near Govan, who had lately been elevated to the position of a county magistrate, meeting Mr. Thom one day on horseback, attempted jocularity by remarking that he was more ambitious than his Master, who was content to ride upon an ass. "They canna be gotten noo," replied Thom; "they're a' made Justices o' the Peace."

Of the Rev. James Robertson, of Kilmarnock, who was possessed of high attainments as a theologian and scholar, there are many good stories. Like many another divine, Mr. Robertson was often annoyed by those busybodies who take charge of everyone's business but their own. One day, when preaching upon the besetting sins of different men, he remarked, using a well-known Scottish saying—"Every ane, my friends, has his ain draff-pock. Some hae their draff-pock hingin' afore them; ithers, again, hae their draff-pock hingin' ahent them; but I ken a man that sits in my ain kirk that has draff-pocks hingin' a' around him. An' wha dae ye think that is? A'body kens wha I mean—nae ither than Andro' Oliphant."

Mr. Robertson's precentor displeased him very much by his loud singing, and accordingly was not only often reproved, but even stopped by him after commencing the psalm. One morning a tune was started upon a key a little higher even than usual, when Mr. Robertson rose up in the pulpit, and, tapping the musical worthy on the head, thus addressed him—"Andro', Andro', man, do you no ken that a toom barrel aye soonds loudest?"

Preaching before the Associate Synod at Glasgow, he introduced the probability of a French invasion as a punishment for national sin; and while admitting the immoral character of the infliction, he assured his hearers that "Providence wasna always nice in the choice of instruments for punishing the wickedness of men." "Tak'," he continued, "an example frae amang yersel's. Your magistrates dinna ask certificates o' character for their public executioners. They generally select sic clanjamphrie as hae rubbit shouthers wi' the gallows themsel's. And as for this Bonyparte," continued the preacher, "I've tell'd ye, my friends, what was the beginning o' that man, and I'll tell ye what will be the end o' him. He'll come doon like a pockfu' o' goats' horns at the Broomielaw!"

The Rev. Dr. M'Cubbin, of Douglas, had a humorous faculty peculiarly his own, and once at least was able to turn the tables on such an incorrigible joker as the Hon. Henry Erskine. They met at the dinner-table of a mutual friend. There was a dish of cresses on the table, and the doctor took such a hearty supply, and devoured them with such relish, using his fingers, that Erskine was tempted to remark that his procedure reminded him of Nebuchadnezzar. "Ay," retorted Dr. M'Cubbin, "that'll be because I'm eatin' amang the brutes, I suppose."

But the wit of the old fathers and brethren was generally keenest when turned against the wearers of their own cloth.

On one occasion, when coming to church, Dr. Macknight, who was a much better commentator than preacher, having been caught in a shower of rain, entered the vestry soaked through. Every means were employed to relieve him from his discomfort, but as the time drew on for divine service he became very querulous, and ejaculated over and over again, "Oh, I wish that I was dry! Do you think that I am dry? Do you think I am dry enough now?"

Tired by these endless complaints, his jocose colleague, Dr. Henry, the historian, at last replied, "Bide a wee, Doctor, an' ye'll be dry enough, I'se warrant, when ye get into the poopit."

It was a very *dry* joke indeed.

The Rev. Dr. Dow, of Errol, and the Rev. Dr. Duff, of Kilspindie, long maintained a warm and uninterrupted intimacy. Once, on a New Year's Day, Dr. Dow sent to his friend, who was a great snuffer, a snuff-box filled with snuff, and inscribed thus—

"Dr. Dow to Dr. Duff,

Snuff! Snuff! Snuff!"

The minister of Kilspindie resolved not to be outdone either in generosity or pungent humour. The pastor of Errol, though withal a sober and exemplary man, was known to enjoy a glass of toddy with his friends. So his clerical brother retaliated on him with the present of a hot-water jug, bearing on the lid this couplet—

"Dr. Duff to Dr. Dow,

Fou! Fou! Fou!"

Shortly after the disruption of the Church of Scotland, two clergymen—father and son—were discussing the comparative merits of the Churches to which they belonged. The father, an upholder of Erastianism, had remained faithful to the Church in which he had been ordained; the son had joined the Non-intrusion party, and attached himself to the Free Church. The son expatiated at great length on the superiority of his Church over that of his father; of the advantages of its freedom from State control; of the privilege of its members to elect their own ministers; of its activity and zeal for the diffusion of religion, etc.; and while he did so, did not hesitate to pick holes large and many in the discipline and government of the Church with which his father had been so long connected, and from which he himself had so recently seceded. In *his* estimation the Auld Kirk had faults innumerable, the Free Church none. After hearing him for a while, the father closed the conversation by saying—

"When *your* Kirk's lum, Andrew, has been as lang reekin' as mine, I'm thinkin' ye'll find, lad, it will then need sweepin' too."

The Rev. Dr. Gillan, of Inchinnan, was a ready wit, of whom a number of capital stories are told, among them being the following:—One day a young elder, making his first appearance in the Glasgow Presbytery, modestly sat down on the very edge of a bench near the door. By and by the minister who had been sitting at the other end rose, and the young elder was just falling off when the door opened and Dr. Gillan entered, who, catching him in his arms, with his usual readiness exclaimed, "Sir, when you come to this place you must try and stick to the *forms* of the Church."

Among the preachers who occupied the pulpits in Scotland in the days of other years, these fitful glances tend to reveal, were men not less famous for their eloquence and earnest preaching than for their wit and humour and popular eccentricities of character; and they were certainly not the less effective as pastors and preachers that they now and again gave reign to their fancies, and were moved to laughter like ordinary men. How much have the keen humorous sensibilities of Spurgeon, and Moody, and M'Neill, and others that might be named, contributed to the effectiveness of their pulpit ministrations? Indeed, there have been few great preachers, in any time or place, who have not had a lively sense of humour; although the converse, of course, does not obtain. The great Dr. Guthrie; the grand Dr. Norman Macleod; the erudite Dr. Anderson, of Glasgow; and the eloquent Gilfillan, of Dundee, were all humourists of the first water.

Referring to the fact that each successive generation considers itself a vast improvement on its predecessor, Dr. Guthrie once said, "I thocht that my father really didna ken very muckle, but my laddies seem to think I'm a born idiot."

Dr. Norman Macleod's faculty of humour was well known everywhere, for it manifested itself in various ways—most effectively, perhaps, in lyrical measures such as "The Waggin' o' oor Dog's Tail," "Captain Frazer's Nose," etc., but always to the order of uproarious fun. It is told of Norman that when walking down Buchanan Street, Glasgow, arm-in-arm with a merchant friend of the West, one day, the two were passed, first by the Most Rev. Bishop Irvine, of Argyll, then by the Bishop's valet, following a few steps behind him; the one short and slim and the other long and thin, but both dressed clerically and seeming much alike. They each saluted the popular minister of the Barony as they passed, whereupon his merchant friend turned to him and enquired, "Who was the man with the choker on, walking behind the Bishop, who saluted you just now, Doctor?"

"Oh," said Norman, "that's the *valet* of the shadow of death."

When Norman, not yet great, began his ministry in the Ayrshire parish of Loudoun, among his parishioners were some rather notable freethinkers, whose views the young divine, with the energy and earnestness characteristic of him, thought it proper to assail and denounce. Naturally this caused a good deal of commotion and excitement in what had hitherto been rather a sleepy parish. One of his elders, who thought his minister's zeal outran his discretion, one day thus addressed him—"Mr. Macleod, hoo is it we ne'er heard o' unbelievers hereaboot till ye cam' among us?" "John," said the ready minister, "saw ye ever a wasp's bike?" "Hoot aye, aften." "Weel, lat them be, and they'll lat you be; but put your stick through the heart of it, and it'll be anither story."

No minister was ever more beloved by his people than was Dr. Macleod by the inhabitants of the Barony parish. There is a story which reveals this with rare effect, and which the great Norman himself told with much gusto. A dissenting minister in the district had been asked to come to a house in the High Street, and pray with a man who was thought to be at the point of death. He knew by the name and address given that the people were not connected with his congregation. Still, he went off at once as desired. When he had read and prayed—having previously noted how tidy everything looked about the room, and being puzzled by the thought of a family of such respectable appearance having no church connection—he turned to the wife and mother of the household, and asked if they were not connected with any Christian body in the city?

"Ou, ay," she replied, "we're members o' the Barony."

"You are members of the Barony! Then why didn't you call in Dr. Macleod to pray with your husband, instead of sending for me?"

"Ca' in the great Dr. Norman Macleod?" skirled the matron, with uplifted hands. "The man's surely daft. Dinna ye ken it's a dangerous case o' *typhus*?"

Norman Macleod, Anthony Trollope, the novelist, and John Burns of Castle Wemyss, were great friends, and went together once on a tour in the Highlands. On arriving at an inn late at night they had supper, and then told stories, and laughed without stint half the night through. In the morning an old gentleman, who slept in a bedroom above them, complained to the landlord that he had not been able to sleep on account of the noise from the party below; and added that he regretted that such men should "take more than was good for them."

"Well," replied the landlord, "I am bound to say there was a good deal of loud talking and laughing; but they had nothing stronger than *tea and herrings*."

"Bless me," rejoined the old gentleman, "if that is so, what would Dr. Macleod and Mr. Burns be *after dinner*!"

"Willie" Anderson's well-known "three-a-penny" story is perhaps the very best one which rumour persistently attaches to his name. The Doctor had been walking towards John Street Church one Sunday evening, when it suddenly commenced to rain, very much to the discomfiture of three well-dressed young men, who had come out to air their clothes and to see and be seen, who occupied the pavement immediately in front of the popular preacher. "What's to be done?" exclaimed one; "we canna walk the streets in a nicht like this." "We're just comin' on to John Street Kirk," remarked another, "we'll go an' hear Willie Anderson preachin'." The mention of his name caused the minister to play the part of eavesdropper for a moment, during which the young gentlemen made the discovery that two halfpennies formed the sum total of their united small cash. This fact, however, was not to be allowed to bar their entrance to the place of worship, "for," said one, addressing the other two, "I'll drap in a bawbee, an' *he'll* drap in a bawbee, an' *ye'll* mairch past the plate atween the twa o's, an' the thing'll never be noticed." Immediately this was agreed to, the erratic divine shot past the objects of his temporary attention. When they reached the church door he was standing beside the elder at the plate, and as they marched past a second later, and the "twa bawbees" were noisily dropped in, "There they go," exclaimed the Doctor, "three-a-penny—three-a-penny!"

Dr. Anderson was a man of very fine musical taste, and one Sabbath, in John Street, after the first psalm had been sung, and sung badly, he addressed the congregation thus—"Are ye not ashamed of yourselves for offering up to God such abominable sounds? If you had to offer up a service of praise before Queen Victoria in her presence, then you would have met every night, if necessary, for weeks on end, but as God is unseen you evidently think anything is good enough for Him. I am ashamed of you." Then, taking a pinch of snuff out of his waistcoat pocket, he said solemnly, "Let us pray."

Gilfillan of Dundee was distinguished for his largeness of heart and generosity as well as for his erudition and oratorical powers. No deserving—seldom an undeserving—beggar went from his door unaided. To the poor of his own flock he was a true friend and faithful pastor. On a melancholy occasion, a member of School Wynd Church called at the manse in Paradise Road to invite the Rev. George to come and officiate in his clerical capacity at the funeral. After the usual condolence, the preacher remarked to the bereaved, "By the by, I have missed you from the church for some time. What is wrong?"

"Well, to be plain with you, Mr. Gilfillan," said the man, "my coat is so bare, I'm ashamed to come."

The big man immediately disrobed himself of his coat, and handing it to the distressed member of his congregation, said, "There, my man, let me see that coat every Sabbath until it becomes bare, and then call back."

After so delivering himself, the divine returned to his study in his shirt-sleeves, and being observed by his worthy spouse, she approached and asked what he had done with his coat. His answer was, "I have just given it to God, my dear."

To correct the popular but erroneous idea that the child receives its name at baptism from the minister, Gilfillan's practice on occasions of the kind was not to mention the child's name at all. Once, however, when the sacrament was asked to be administered, the parents insisted beforehand that the child's name should be announced. "Very well," was the reply. Accordingly, when the little one had been with all due solemnity received into the Church visible, the minister, looking abroad over the congregation, raised his voice and exclaimed, "The parents of this child wish the congregation to know that its name is John."

George was never again asked to announce the name in a case of baptism.

Kindly and generous in the main, that Gilfillan could be severe too when he liked, is well known. Speaking of the county town of Forfarshire, which has no very high character for morality, he said, "When Satan was showing our Lord all the kingdoms of the earth, we may be sure he *kept his thumb on Forfar.*"

# CHAPTER IV
## THE PULPIT AND THE PEW

When discoursing on the humours of old Scotch divines, I designedly recounted only such anecdotes as revealed the minister holding the "heft end" of the argument. In the present paper, which is wider in its scope, the honours will be found more equally divided, and the illustrations of the national character and humour laid under contribution will, on that account, prove not less entertaining and amusing.

To "get the better" of the minister has always meant fame of a kind—largely because of the rarity of such an achievement—and one can imagine how the parish would ring during the proverbial "nine days" with the fame of the old dame who, when her spiritual adviser called at her house to enquire of her the reason why recently she had suddenly turned "Seceder," retorted, "Weel, ye just took a hale fortnicht to put Jonah into the whawl's belly, and anither hale fortnicht to tak' him oot; and what sort o' fool's preachin' d'ye ca' that?"

A Fifeshire laird, in a somewhat similar way, scored heavily against the minister of his parish. The latter had called on the laird to solicit a subscription from him to aid in putting a stove in the church, which, he said, the congregation found very cold. "Cauld, sir, cauld?" snorted the chief heritor; "then warm them up wi' your doctrine, sir. John Knox never askit for a stove in his kirk."

Equally pungent was the retort which issued from a country pew on the north of the Tay. "Ye're sleepin', John," said the minister, pausing in the middle of a humdrum discourse, and looking hard in the direction of the drowsy member thus addressed—"Tak' a snuff, John." "Put the snuff in the sermon," grunted John; and the broad grin that scampered over the upturned faces of the congregation showed how much the suggestion was deemed *fit*. But it is seldom the sleeper is found so *wide-awake*, if the expression will be allowed. His mental condition for the time being acts against the ready exercise of wit, and he is generally caught napping in a double sense. And, indeed, many who are popularly termed "*pillars* of the kirk," might with equal appropriateness be termed *sleepers*. In a certain church in Forfarshire, there was no worse offender in this way than the minister's own wife. One Sabbath she was actually asleep before the text was given out, a fact which her husband was not slow to observe. The minister had a quiet humour of his own; and the passage chosen for treatment that day had more than its original meaning to many present, when, "fixing his glassy eye" on the family pew he said, "The words, my brethren, to which I wish to direct your particular attention at the present time, are these—'*He giveth His beloved sleep.*'"

Some folks apparently make a mistake in not taking their nightcaps to church with them. It has been told of a Dumbartonshire cattle-dealer that, going to hear (?) a young minister of repute who was preaching for a day in the parish kirk at Bonhill, immediately after the opening devotional services and the reading of chapter, he spread his hands on the book-board, forming them into a temporary pillow, on which he laid his drowsy head and prepared to enjoy a comfortable "snooze." The preacher's voice was powerful, and the style of his declamation such as to admit of considerable grandiloquence. Accordingly, after some minutes, minister and people were attracted by Bauldy raising his head just a little, and saying, quite audibly, "Ye're just fully lood for me—ay, fully lood." He laid down his head again, and the preacher, proceeding, waxed more eloquent and more vociferous as he warmed with his theme. At length, after a grand burst which closed some great passage, Bauldy sat right bolt up, and looking up at the minister, said, "Hang it! ye're far ower lood. There's nae mortal man could sleep wi' a noise like that."

It is frequently only one step from the sleeping to the wide-awake members, and, the latter being preferable company, we will now see how some of those have conducted themselves. Perhaps the prejudice against read sermons lingered longer in Scotland than anywhere else; and, of course, it was among the class that distinguished clearly between the legitimate uses of a pew and a bed that the individuals who concerned themselves in these matters were found.

"Eh, he's a grand preacher!" whispered an old spinster to her sister, as they listened for the first time to a young minister.

"Wheesht! Bell," was the reply, "he's *readin*!"

"Readin', is he?" said the eulogist, changing her tone. "The paltry fellow! We'll gang hame, Jenny, and read our Book."

In 1772, when Dr. Thomas Blacklock, the well-known poet, who was blind, was preaching one of his trial discourses on the occasion of his being presented, by the Earl of Selkirk, to the living of Kirkcudbright, an old woman who sat on the pulpit stairs inquired of a neighbour if she thought he was a reader.

"He canna be a reader," was the reply, "for he's blind."

"I'm glad to hear it," said the ancient dame; "I wish they were a' blind!"

The ladies have always exercised a lively surveillance of the pulpit, and vended many an apt criticism.

"How did you like that young man we had to-day?" was once asked of a discerning village matron.

"Weel, I had just three fauts to his sermon," was the reply.

"And what were these, if I may ask?"

"Weel," said she, "firstly, it was read; and, secondly, it wasna weel read; and, thirdly, it wasna worth readin'!"

"Weel, I had just three fauts to his sermon: firstly, it was read; and, secondly, it wasna weel read; and, thirdly, it wasna worth readin'!"

A sweeping criticism, and no mistake.

Dr. Norman Macleod was once preaching in a district in Ayrshire, where the reading of a sermon was regarded as the greatest fault a minister could be guilty of. When the congregation dispersed, an old woman, overflowing with enthusiasm, addressed her neighbour with, "Did ye ever hear onything sae grand? Wasna that a sermon?"

"Oh, ay," replied her friend sulkily, "but he read it."

"*Read* it," reiterated the other with indignant emphasis, "I wudna hae cared gin he had *whustled* it."

How the great Norman would enjoy this we can easily imagine! And yet it was not always plain sailing with the preacher who was a victim to "the paper."

A certain minister had a custom of merely writing the heads of his discourses on small bits of paper, which he arranged and placed on the Bible before him, to be used in succession. One day, while he was expounding the second head, he became so excited in his manner that by a wave of his arm the ensuing slip was, unperceived by himself, swept over the edge of the pulpit, and, being caught in an air current in falling, was carried right out through the window, which for ventilation sake had been left partly open. On reaching the end of the second, he looked down for the third slip, but, alas! it was not to be found. "Thirdly," he cried, looking round him with great anxiety. After a little pause, "Thirdly," he again exclaimed, but still no thirdly appeared. "Thirdly, I say, my brethren," pursued the bewildered clergyman, but not another word could he utter. At this point, while the congregation were partly sympathising in his distress, and partly rejoicing in such a decisive instance of the evil of using notes in preaching, an old woman came to the minister's rescue with the remark—"Deed, sir, ye needna fash yersel', for *thirdly* gaed oot at the window a quarter o' an hour syne."

That clergyman had not the inventive ingenuity of a Perth minister I have heard about. The latter had one really good sermon, which he styled the "White Horse," and on occasions when he was called out to preach, which were few and far between, he invariably trotted out his "White Horse." On one occasion he arranged to conduct the forenoon service in a church at some considerable distance, the regular minister of which being from home expected to return in time to preach himself in the afternoon. In the forenoon, the "White Horse" did the usual gallant service, but in the interval of public worship, the intelligence arrived that some untoward circumstance had prevented the native clergyman's return, and that he (the Perth divine) would require to conduct the afternoon service also. Here was a demand which our Boanerges from the Fair City had not calculated on. He had brought no other sermon with him, and, even although he had, it would not have sustained the impression made by the "White Horse." What was to be done? A moment's reflection, and the difficulty was removed. "My dear brethren," said he, when he stood up in the place of execution in the afternoon, "it was told to me in the interval that some of you when leaving the church were saying that the sermon which I preached from this place in the forenoon was not sound doctrine. I maintain that it was perfectly sound;

and as I wish to convince everyone of you that it was so, I now ask you to give me your attentive hearing and I will preach the sermon over again." And he did.

The hero of the next story was like unto the author of the "White Horse":—

A Scotch gentleman, previous to a Continental tour, engaged as a travelling companion, a rather dissolute and ignorant Highland student, named Alexander Macpherson. Before they had been long abroad, the gentleman, to his regret, found himself compelled to part with his *compagnon de voyage* owing to his intemperate habits, and heard no more about him for several years. Happening, however, to drop into a secluded little Dissenting chapel in Wales, presided over by the Rev. Jonas Jones, as the board at the little gate revealed, he was astonished to find his dismissed servitor officiating in the pulpit, and astounded to hear him several times during the reading of the preliminary chapter turn the English into Highland Gaelic, prefacing his translation always in a sententious manner by the words, "or, as it is in the original," and he was further astonished to hear from several of the congregation that Mr. Jones passed among them as a man of deep learning. After the conclusion of the service, he accosted the minister as he was leaving the church without any signs of recognition on that worthy's part. "Do you not know me?" cried the gentleman, grasping his hand.

"Really, I beg your pardon, but there must be some mistake," said the minister, endeavouring to move on.

"Oh, no mistake whatever, I assure you," returned the gentleman. "Are you not Mr. —?"

"I am Mr. Jonas Jones," put in the pastor, hastily.

"Aye," replied the gentleman, sarcastically, observing that he was determined to ignore all recollection of him, "or, *as it is in the original*, Sandy Macpherson o' Inveraray!"

To be "sound" was the main essential in those days. A certain clergyman had been suspected of leanings towards Arminianism, or of being a Rationalist, and much anxiety in consequence was felt by the flock he was called on to superintend. He put their fears suddenly to flight, however, for he turned out to be a sound divine as well as a good man. On the Monday after his sermon had been delivered, he was accosted in his walk by a decent old man, who after thanking him for his able discourse, went on—"Od, sir, the story gaed that you was a rational preacher; but glad am I, and a' the parish wi' me, to find that you are *no' a rational preacher* after a'." The minister thought it a dubious compliment, no doubt.

An old farmer, wishing to pay his minister a compliment on the occasion of his being made a D.D., said, "I kent ye wad come to something, sir, for, as I have aye said, ye neither fear God nor regard man."

Speaking of the old-fashioned "rousing sermons" with which some ministers used to delight and terrify their hearers, Mr. Inglis, in his recent work *Our Ain Folk*, relates a conversation that took place between two severe old Covenanters after hearing a sermon of this type. "What do you think o' that sermon, Jamie?" said Willie, as they wended their way down the street. "Think o't," said Jamie. "Man, it was jist a gran' sermon. I havena heard ane I likit better for mony a day. What do you think o't yersel'?" "Ae, man," said Willie, "it was an awfu' sermon, a fearfu' sermon. It fair gar'd my flesh a' grue. I'm shiverin' yet, an I'm sure I canna tak' my denner." "What?" said Jamie, wi' a snort o' indignation; "what do you want? What wad ye ha'e, man? Do you want the man to slide ye down to hell on a buttered plate!"

A little band of old women on their way home from the kirk on the evening of a special day's preaching, shortened the road by discussing the merits of the various divines who had addressed them, when one worthy dame thus honestly expressed herself, "Oh, leeze me abune them a'," exclaimed she, "for yon auld, beld, clear-headed man that spoke sae bonnie on the angels. When he said, 'Raphael sings, and Gabriel tunes his goolden herp, and a' the angels clap their wings wi' joy,' oh, but it was grand! It just put me in mind o' oor geese, at Dunjarg, as they turn their nebs to the south an' clap their wings when they see rain comin' after a lang drouth."

The Rev. Mr. Yule, a Perthshire divine, was in the habit of going through the village on the Sabbath afternoons in summer, and inviting the people to open-air service on the green in the evening. Entering one afternoon where there were a number of the inhabitants congregated for no special purpose further than the discussion of current local events, the good man had not time to declare his mission when a douce village matron folded her hands complacently on her lap, and, looking towards the minister, said, "Eh! yon was a grand sermon ye ga'ed us this forenoon, Mr. Yule."

"I am glad you were pleased with it, I am sure," the minister modestly replied.

"Pleased!" echoed the matron. "I was just so perfectly *feasted* wi' it that I cam' hame an' ga'rd Tammas turn up 'Matthew Hendry,' and read it a' ower again to me."

In Perth, about twenty years ago, there lived one, Kirsty Robertson, who earned her living by washing. The poor body had to work from morning till night to keep herself in food and clothing. She managed, however, to make a respectable appearance on Sundays, and was a regular attender of the kirk.

The minister observed her decent and obvious poverty, and thought he ought to call on her, and see if he could assist her. He accordingly did so, and going in one night he saw Kirsty sitting by the fire, wearied out with her day's labour. On hearing the minister come in Kirsty started up with an exclamation of surprise. He bade her be seated, and kindly enquired into her welfare, both spiritual and temporal. Before leaving, he inquired: "And I hope, Mrs. Robertson, you receive much good from your regular attendance at the ordinances?" "Ou ay, sir," replied Kirsty, "it's no' every day I get sic a nice seat to sit on, an' sae little to think aboot."

Two men were talking about sermons. "Hoo did your minister get on last Sabbath?" asked the one. "Get on!" said the other; "he got on—just like a taed amang tar."

A well-known Edinburgh lecturer—the late "Sandy" Russel of the *Scotsman*—was some years ago, it is said, enjoying a brief holiday in a quiet Highland retreat, which afforded excellent scope for the plying of the "gentle art," and the Sabbath coming round in due course, he resolved, in order to dispel the tedium of the day, to attend the village church. The worthy parson noted the intellectual-looking stranger among his sparse congregation, and, on making enquiries, was informed of his personal identity. On the Monday following, the parson took a walk along the river side and very soon encountered the popular editor busy with rod and line.

"You are a keen fisher, I believe, Mr. Russel," was the preacher's introductory remark.

"Yes, I am, pastor," was the instant and decided reply.

"I am a fisher too," remarked the minister dreamily, "*but a fisher of men*;" the latter words were delivered with great unction.

"Oh, indeed," dryly responded the editor, "I had a keek into your creel yesterday; ye didna seem to ha'e catch'd mony."

"I'm a fisher too," remarked the minister dreamily, "*but a fisher of men*;" the latter words were delivered with great unction. "Oh, indeed," dryly responded the angler, "I had a keek into your creel yesterday; ye didna seem to ha'e catch'd mony."

Taking a walk through his parish one day a minister came upon a woman seated at her door reading a book, which he at once concluded was the New Testament, but which was really Blind Harry's *Wallace*. Expressing his gratification at finding her so well employed, he said it was a book which no one would ever grew weary reading.

"Atweel, sir," said she, "I never weary o't; I've read it through an' through I dinna ken hoo aften, an' I'm just as fond o't yet as ever."

"Ah, Janet," exclaimed the enraptured divine, "I am glad to hear you say so; and how happy I would be if all my parishioners were of the same mind, and what benefit it would be to themselves, too! For oh, to think, Janet, what He did and suffered for us!"

"Deed, ay, sir, an' that's true," answered Janet, "an' to think how he soom'd through the Carron water on a cauld frosty mornin', wi' his braidsword in his teeth. It was awfu'!"

The Rev. Mr. M'Dougall was one of those preachers who keep their hearers awake by sheer strength of lung. Preaching one day in a strange church, he espied an old woman applying her handkerchief very frequently to her eyes. Attributing her distress to a change for the better, he kept his eye on her, and at the close of the service, found an opportunity to speak to her, and said, "You seemed to be deeply affected, my good woman, while I was preaching to-day?"

"Ay, sir, I was rale muckle affected," she replied.

"I am truly glad of that," quoth the minister; "and I hope the impression may be a lasting one."

"I doot, sir," said she, "ye're takin' me up wrang. I was only thinkin' on Shoozie."

"Shoozie!" exclaimed the astonished divine; "what do you mean by Shoozie?"

"Oh, ye ken, sir," replied the matron, "that was a cuddie we had. She dee'd twa or three weeks syne, and she was a kindly beast; an' I just thocht whiles when I heard ye in yer raptur's the day it was her roarin', an' I fairly broke doon wi't."

It was customary long ago to speak of the topic of a sermon as its *ground* or *grund*, and the story is told of an old woman bustling into church rather late one day. The preacher, a young man, had commenced his sermon. The old dame, opening her Bible, nudged her next neighbour with the inquiry, "What's his grund?"

"Oh," rejoined the other, "the silly elf's lost his grund lang syne; he's just *soomin*!"

It was no use trying to throw dust in the eyes of such practical people.

Another plain-spoken dame said of a preacher of diminutive stature, who occasionally officiated in the church in which she was a regular hearer, and to whom she cherished some antipathy, "If there's an ill text in a' the Bible, that ugly wratch o' a creatur' is sure to tak' it."

A city congregation not long since presented their minister with a sum of money, and sent him off to the Continent for a holiday. Soon after, a gentleman, just returned from the Continent, meeting a prominent member of the congregation, said, "Oh, by the by, I met your minister in Germany. He was looking very well—he didn't look as if he needed a rest." "No," said the member calmly, "it wasna *him*, it was the congregation that was needin' a rest."

Shortly after a Congregational chapel had been planted in a small burgh in the North, an incident occurred which showed that the powers of its minister were appreciated in certain quarters. A boy named Johnnie Fordyce had been indiscreet enough to put a sixpence in his mouth, and accidentally swallowed it. Mrs. Fordyce, concerned both for her boy and the sixpence, tried every means for its recovery, consulted her neighbours, and finally, in despair, called in the doctor, but without result. As a last resort, a young girl present suggested that they should send for the Congregationalist minister. "The minister?" chorused mother and neighbours. "Ay, the minister," rejoined the girl. "My faither says if there's siller in onybody he'll tak' it oot o' them."

The following illustrates how careful a minister should be to fulfil his promises. A poor old deaf man, residing in Fife, was visited one day by the parish minister, who had been recently inducted. Talking with the spouse of the afflicted parishioner, the minister professed to be greatly interested in the old man's case, and promised before leaving that he would call regularly and pray with him. He, however, did not darken the door of their home again until about two years after, when happening to go through the street in which the old man lived, he found the wife standing at the door, and of course made anxious inquiry regarding her husband.

"Well, Margaret," said he, "how is Thomas?"

"Nane the better o' you," was the rather curt reply.

"How, how, Margaret?" inquired the minister.

"Oh, ye promised twa years syne to ca' and pray ance a fortnicht wi' him, and ye hae never ance darkened oor door sin' syne."

"Well, well, Margaret, don't be so short. I thought it was not so very necessary to call and pray with Thomas, for he's so deaf, you know, and couldn't hear me."

"Ay, but, sir," rejoined the woman, "*the Lord's no' deaf?*"

He was well answered.

That story suggests another which I have heard told by the worthy divine in whose experience it happened. He had on his "sick list" an old male parishioner, on whom he made frequent calls, and invariably read and prayed with the family before leaving. One day there were only the old man and the old woman in the house. The customary chapter was read, after which the divine engaged in prayer. On looking round at the conclusion of the latter, he was astonished to discover that the woman had disappeared. He had scarcely recovered from the bewilderment of the occasion, however, when she came timidly slipping through the doorway. "Hech, sirse!" she exclaimed, in a tone of surprise, "are ye dune already?" then added, by way of explanation, "Ye see, sir, the Kirkintilloch flute baund gaed by there a maument syne; oor Jamie's in't, an' I just ran oot to see the crood, thinkin' I wad be back again afore ye wad ken."

Here is a worthy companion story to the above. A country minister had occasion to call upon one of his parishioners who kept a toll-bar, and after some conversation he proceeded to pray with him. He had not uttered many words when he was interrupted by an exclamation from the tollman—"Wheest a minute, sir; I think I hear a cairt!" and out he went.

A Rev. Dr. Henderson of Galashiels in the course of his pastoral visitation, called on a widow with a large family, and asked how they all were, and how things were getting on. She said, "A' richt, except Davie; he's been troubled wi' a sair leg, and no fit for wark." The doctor could not remember which one Davie was, but did not like to hurt the widow's feelings by betraying his ignorance, and in his prayer he pled that David's affliction might be blessed to him. On going home, he said to his wife, referring to his call, "Which of the sons is David?"

"Hoot," she exclaimed, "Davie's no a son, Davie's the cuddie!"

It was the minister there. In the next story it was the other way about. A former minister in the parish of Kilspindie, in the Carse of Gowrie, in the course of his parochial visitation called at the house of a ploughman where the oldest boy, a lad of ten, had been severely coached by his mother in anticipation of the "visit," and with the hope of his making a good show. When, by and by, the minister took notice of the boy, "Ay," interposed the mother, "an' he can say his Carratches, too." "Indeed!" exclaimed the minister, still eyeing the lad, "how nice! Who made you?"

"God."

"Quite correct. Who redeemed you?"

"Christ."

"Right again. You're a clever little fellow, and [putting his hand on his head] who cut your hair?"

"The Holy Ghost," was the reply; and the interview terminated.

"Sir," said the long-haired lessee of a small farm in the North one day as he came up to the door of the Free Church Manse, "this is awfu' weather w' drooth; an' I ha'e come across to see if you wad put up a petition for a shooer o' rain, for my neeps are just perishin'."

"You are a member of the Established Church," said the clergyman addressed; "why not ask your own minister to intercede on behalf of your turnips?"

"It's no very likely he'll pray for rain for my neeps," was the blunt response, "when his ain hay's no in yet."

It is quite true that—

"If self the wavering balance shake,

It's rarely richt adjusted."

But perhaps this worldly-minded agriculturist wronged his minister. There have been many kind, generous souls among them. I remember, says Dr. John Brown, a story of a good, old Anti-Burgher minister. It was in the days when dancing was held to be a great sin, and was dealt with by the Sessions. Jessie, a comely, blythe, and good young woman, and a great favourite of the minister, had been guilty of dancing at a friend's wedding. She was summoned before the Session to be "dealt with"—the grim old fellows sternly concentrating their eyes upon her as she stood trembling in her striped short-gown and her petticoat. The Doctor, who was one of divinity, and a deep thinker, greatly pitying her and himself, said, "Jessie, my woman, were ye dancin'?"

"Yes," sobbed Jessie.

"Ye maun e'en promise never to dance again, Jessie."

"I will, sir; I will promise" (with a curtsey).

"Noo, what were ye thinkin' o', Jessie, when ye were dancin'?—tell us truly," said an old elder, who had been a poacher in youth.

"Nae ill, sir," sabbed out the dear little woman.

"Then, Jessie, my woman, *aye dance!*" cried the delighted Doctor.

It was capital!

When the Rev. Mr. (now the esteemed Dr.) Macgregor, of Edinburgh, settled in Glasgow as minister of the Tron Kirk, he had occasion, a few weeks after, to visit a family in one of the poorer districts, where he was as yet unknown to the eyes of his flock, although their ears had heard his name, and his personal appearance had become in some vague way familiar to their minds. He inquired of the goodwife whether the head of the house was at home, and, being informed that he was not, was kindly invited to await his arrival. This not occurring so soon as the goodwife had expected, she suggested to her visitor, who had not acquainted her with his name or station, that he should "gang oot an see the pigs," the mother-pig having brought into the world a fine litter, a few days before. This, of course, Mr. Macgregor cheerfully consented to do. The inmates of the sty having been duly inspected, and the virtues of the mother-pig extolled till the old woman's vocabulary refused to supply another adjective, she informed her visitor that "the young piggies had a' been named aifter different fouk;" according as their personal appearances seemed to offer points of resemblance. And she indicated this and that one, as the bearer of some well-known name, honoured or otherwise, until she came to the last one, a rather diminutive, but active specimen of the porcine breed. "An' this ane," said she to her unknown and attentive listener, "this wee black deev'luck, we ca' *Wee Macgregor o' the Tron*!"

"An' this ane," said she to her unknown and attentive listener, "this wee black deev'luck, we ca' *Wee Macgregor o' the Tron*!"

The genial Doctor himself has frequently told the above story with great and unaffected gusto.

The Christenin', the Waddin', the Catakeezin' (now an unknown institution), and the Burial—these were occasions which brought the occupants of the pulpit and the pew into the closest relationship, and from which many capital illustrations of the national humour and character have arisen.

Baptism, of course, sometimes had a different significance for different persons. "What is Baptism, John?" a minister, in the course of a public catechising, asked his beadle.

"Baptism?" answered John, scratching his head, "weel, ye ken, it's sometimes mair and sometimes less, but, as a general rule, it's auchteenpence to me and a shillin' to the precentor."

"Hoo mony o' the Elect will there be on the earth the noo, think ye, Janet?" said one old crone to another. "Ten?"

"Na: naething like it, woman."

"Hoots, Janet, ye think there's naebody good enough for heaven but yersel', and the minister."

"Deed," replied Janet, "I hae sometimes very grave doots aboot the minister."

Here was a more generous spirit. The late Dr. Wilberforce, while paying a visit at Taymouth Castle during the lifetime of the last Marquis of Breadalbane, a devoted adherent of the Free Church, was taken by Lady Breadalbane (*nee* Baillie of Jerviswoode) into one of the cottages on the estate occupied by an old Highland woman—a "true blue" Presbyterian—who was greatly pleased by the Bishop's frank and friendly manner. A few days afterwards the Bishop left the castle, and Lady Breadalbane paid another visit to her old friend, when the following conversation took place:—"Do you know who that was, Mary, that came to see you last week?" "No, my lady," was the reply. "The famous Bishop of Oxford," said her ladyship. On which the denizen of the mountains quietly remarked, "Aweel, my lady, he's a rale fine man; and a' I can say is, that I trust and pray he'll gang to heaven—Bishop though he be!"

"I hope you have made due preparation, and are in a fit state to have the Sacrament of Baptism administered to your child, John," said a minister to one of his parishioners, a ploughman, who had called at the manse in connection with a recent event in his domestic circle.

"Weel," said the ploughman, "I haena been ower extravagant in the way o' preparation, maybe. I'm a man o' sma' means, ye ken; but I've gotten in a bottle o' whisky and the best hauf o' a kebbuck o' cheese."

"Tuts, tuts!" interrupted the minister, "I do not mean preparation of the things that perish. Is your mind and heart in proper condition?"

"Do you mean that I'm no soond in the head?" queried the ploughman.

"No, I do not mean that at all," said the divine. "You do not appear to have an intelligent idea of the matter that has brought you here."

Then, after a minute's reflection, he continued—"How many Commandments are there, John?"

"I couldna tell ye jist exactly on the spur o' the meenit," said John, scratching his head, "but there's an auld beuk lyin' i' the hoose yonder, gin I had it here I could sune answer yer question."

"John," said the minister, "I am afraid you are not in a fit state to hold up your child for baptism."

"No fit to haud him up?" echoed the ploughman, starting to his feet, and posing in the attitude best calculated to display his great muscular form. "Me? Man, I could haud him up gin he were a bull stirk!"

And ludicrous incidents have occurred even in the supreme moment occupied by the ceremony of the baptism of a child, and when no one was very seriously to blame. In Paisley, some time ago, the father of a child was from home at the time of its birth, and was not expected to return for two or three months. The mother, desiring that the baptism of the child should not be delayed so long, was consequently obliged to present the infant herself, the ordinance being administered in private. The officiating clergyman was an old man, who, when in the act of dispensing the sacrament, asked the name by which the child was to be called. The mother, who had a thickness in her speech, politely said, "Lucy, sir."

"Lucifer!" exclaimed the old and irritable divine, in exasperated horror, "I shall baptise no child by the name of the Prince of Darkness, madam. The child's name is John."

But perhaps the very best specimen story on record is the well-known one which is associated with the name of Ralph Erskine, the father of the Scottish Secession Kirk, and which the late Robert Leighton, the poet, rendered so happily into rhyme under the title of "The Bapteezement o' the Bairn." Mr. Erskine was a most proficient performer on the violin, and so often beguiled his leisure hours with this instrument that the people of Dunfermline believed he composed his sermons to its tones, as a poet writes a song to a particular air. But to the story:—A poor man in one of the neighbouring parishes having a child to baptise resolved not to employ his own clergyman, with whom he was at issue on certain points of doctrine, but to have the office performed by some minister of whose tenets fame gave a better report. With the child in his arms, therefore, and attended by the full complement of old and young women who usually minister on such occasions, he proceeded to the manse of —, some miles off (not that of Mr. Erskine), where he inquired if the clergyman was at home.

"Na; he's no at hame the noo," answered the servant lass; "he's doon the burn fishing; but I can sune cry him in."

"Ye needna gie yersel' the trouble," replied the man, quite shocked at this account of the minister's habits, "nane o' yer fishin' ministers shall bapteeze my bairn."

Off he then trudged, followed by his whole train, to the residence of another parochial clergyman, at the distance of some miles. Here, on his inquiring if the minister was at home, the lass answered:

"Deed, he's no at hame the day; he's been oot since sax i' the mornin' at the shooting. Ye needna wait, neither; for he'll be sae dune oot when he comes back, that he'll no be able to say boo to a goose, lat-a-be kirsten a wean."

"Wait, lassie!" cried the man, in a tone of indignant scorn; "wad I wait, d'ye think, to haud up my bairn afore a minister that gangs oot at sax i' the mornin' to shoot God's creatur's? I'll awa doon to gude Mr. Erskine at Dunfermline; and he'll be neither oot at the fishin', nor shootin', I'm thinkin'."

The whole baptismal train then set off for Dunfermline, sure that the father of the Secession, although not now a placed minister, would at least be engaged in no unclerical sports to incapacitate him for performing the sacred ordination in question. On their arriving, however, at the house of the clergyman, which they did not do till late in the evening, the man, on rapping at the door, anticipated that he would not be at home any more than his brethren, as he heard the strains of a fiddle proceeding from the upper chamber. "The minister'll no be at hame," he said, with a sly smile to the girl who came to the door, "or your lad wadna be playin' that gate to ye on the fiddle."

"The minister is at hame," quoth the girl, "mair be token it's himsel' that's playin', honest man; he aye tak's a tune at nicht, afore he gangs to bed. Faith, there's nae lad o' mine can play that gate; it wad be something to tell if ony o' them could."

"*That* the minister playin'!" cried the man, in a degree of horror and astonishment far transcending what he had expressed on either of the former occasions. "If *he* does this, what may the rest no do? Weel, I fairly gie them up a' thegither. I have travelled this hale day in search o' a godly minister, an' never man met wi' mair disappointment in a day's journey. I'll tell ye what, gudewife," he added, turning to the disconsolate party behind, "we'll just awa' back to oor ain minister after a'. He's no a' thegither soond, it's true; but lat him be what he likes in doctrine, deil ha'e me, if ever I kenn'd him to fish, shoot, or play on the fiddle in a' his days!"

Weddings have been the occasion of much joy in the world, and are clustered around with capital stories. "Jeanie, lassie," said an old Cameronian to his daughter, who was asking his permission to marry, "mind ye, it's a solemn thing to get married."

"I ken that, faither," returned the sensible lass, "but it's a solemner thing no to be married."

"It's the road we've a' to gang," said the short-sighted old maid, solemnly, mistaking a passing wedding party for a funeral procession. So also seemed to think the heroine of the following anecdote and no *mistake* about it:—A clergyman, having three times refused to marry a man who had as often come before him drunk, on the third occasion said to the woman, "Why do you bring him here in that state?"

"Please, your reverence," said she, "he'll no come when he's sober."

The Rev. Dr. Wightman, of Kirkmahoe, was a simple-minded clergyman of the old school. When a young man, he paid his addresses to a lady in the parish, and his suit was accepted on the condition that it met with the approval of the lady's mother. Accordingly, the Doctor waited upon the matron, and, stating his case, the good woman, delighted at his proposal, passed the usual Scottish compliment, "'Deed, Doctor, ye're far ower gude for our Janet."

"Weel, weel," was the instant rejoinder, "ye ken best; so we'll say na mair aboot it." And he never did, although the social intercourse of the parties continued as before; and forty years after Doctor Wightman died an old bachelor, and the *affiancee* of his youth died an old maid. Ah, it's a solemn thing marriage!

A humorous old divine, who had strong feelings on the subject, was in the habit of prefacing the ceremony thus—"My friends," he would say, "marriage is a blessing to some, a curse to many, and a great risk to all. Now, do you venture?" And no objections being made—"Then let us proceed."

A clergyman, in marrying a couple, failed at the crucial part of the service to obtain any indication from the bridegroom as to whether he would accept the bride as his helpmeet. After a considerable pause, the bride indignant at the stolidity of her intended husband, pushed down his head with her hand, at the same time ejaculating, "Canna ye boo, ye brute?" That young lady should have been courted by the hero of the next story.

Some time ago a couple went to a clergyman to get united in the bands of wedlock. As the custom is, before pronouncing their doom, the minister asked the bridegroom if he was willing to take the young woman whom he now held by the hand to be his lawful wife. He nodded assent. The bride was then asked the same question.

"No sir," said she.

"What are your reasons," asked the worthy divine, "for drawing back after you have come this length?"

"Oh," replied she, hanging down her head, "I ha'e just ta'en a scunner at him."

They accordingly went away; but in about a week they returned. When the minister asked her if she now consented to take this man to be her husband,

"Yes, sir," was the answer.

He then asked the bridegroom if he was willing to take this woman to be his wife.

"No, sir," he replied.

"And what has come over you now?" inquired the minister, in a tone of surprise.

"Oh," said he, "I ha'e just ta'en a scunner at her."

And so away they went a second time without being married.

They came back a third time, however, in about a fortnight after, now both thoroughly resolved; but when the minister saw them coming, he hurried downstairs and shut the door, and, returning to his study, cried over the window to them—

"For gudesake, gae awa' hame, you twa, for I've ta'en a scunner at you baith!"

"Eh, minister, I maist think shame to come to ye," said an old dame, who had sought the clergyman's offices in this way on four previous occasions.

"What's the matter, Margaret, that you should think shame to come to me?"

"'Deed, sir, it's just this, I'm gaun to be married again."

"Well, Margaret, I do not see that you have any cause for shame in coming to me for such a purpose. Marriage, you know, is honourable in all."

"Nae doot, sir, nae doot. But eh! (bursting into tears) there never was surely ony puir woman fash'd wi' sic a set o' deein' men as I've had."

Another dame who had a similar experience in *husbandry*, took a brighter view of the situation. "Ay," she said, "first it was John Tamson, then it was Dawvit Soutar, syne Peter Anderson, then Tammas M'Farlane. Noo it's Willie Simpson; and eh! I wonder whase *dear lamb* I'll be next?"

The practice of house-to-house visitation and congregational catechising have yielded a host of anecdotes, one or two of which must suffice here. A country minister, accompanied by one of his elders, was visiting in the most outlying parts of his parish, and early in the afternoon arrived, after a long walk, at the house of a maiden lady, who kept a cow, a pig, and a few hens, etc. The house was so far removed from every other human habitation that anyone who reached it was in instant need of refreshment. On the arrival of her minister and elder, the good lady accordingly produced the kebbuck, a dish of milk, and a quantity of cakes. They were a welcome feast, for the visitors were famishing of hunger after their long and arduous walk. They therefore "laid their lugs amang" the eatables in a style which struck terror to the heart of their extra frugal hostess. By and by, and still "pegging away" at the pile of cakes and whangs of well-seasoned cheese, the minister looked over to Janet and remarked that he was very glad to see her in the church on Sabbath last, and asked her if she remembered the subject of his discourse.

"Ay, fine that," said she; "'twas the parable o' the loaves an' the fishes."

"Exactly, Janet," said the minister; "and what useful lesson did you derive from the exposition of the parable?"

"Weel, naething particular at the time, sir, but I was just sittin' thinkin' aboot it there a meenit syne."

"Well, Janet, that is very interesting; and what thought occurred to you a minute since in connection with the subject?"

"Weel, sir, I was just thinkin' that gin the elder an' you had been amang the multitude there wadna have been sae mony basketfu's left."

The answers vouchsafed in diets of catechetical examinations were often shrewd, if sometimes ridiculous. "What are the decrees of God?" was once asked of an old dame.

"'Deed, sir, He kens that best Himsel'," was the shrewd reply.

"Why did the Israelites make a golden calf?" was the question put to a little girl.

"Because they hadna as muckle siller as wad mak' a coo," she replied.

These examinations were invariably intimated from the pulpit, and the families in each district were invited to meet the minister on a certain day, at an appointed hour, and in a particular house. The farmers' wives, not better informed than the humble parishioners, yet considered themselves superior persons, and afraid lest they should be affronted by having a question put to them that they could not answer, the catechiser was frequently bribed by a basketful of eggs and a few pounds of fresh butter being sent over to the manse on the morning of the diet. Thus, a certain minister was intercepted whilst crossing a moor on his way to the house of meeting one day.

"Good morning, Janet," said the divine; "but are you not to present yourself at the diet of examination in the house of John Anderson, at noon to-day?"

"Ay am I, sir. Ou, deed, ay. But you see, sir, I just sent ower the lassie to the manse this mornin' wi' twa or three rows o' fresh butter and a curn eggs, d'ye see; an' I was just wantin' to say to ye, sir, that ye micht speir some easy question at me. It's no that I dinna read my Book, an' dinna ken, but I just get in a state o' the nerves, like, afore fouk, an' micht mak' a fule o' mysel'; an' that's the reason I wad like ye just to ask some very simple question when my turn comes."

"I'm surely obliged to you for your present, Janet," said the minister, "and, depend upon it, I shall be careful to give you a question that will be easily answered." So saying, he bade her good morning and rode on. Janet was forward in time; and when her turn came to be examined, the minister, remembering his promise, said—

"Janet Davidson, can you tell me which is the Seventh Commandment?"

Simple as the question would have been to many present, Janet could not answer it, and no voice responding, the question was repeated slowly and with emphasis on the words—*Seventh Commandment*. Janet cast a beseeching look at the minister, and in a half-reproving tone said—

"Eh, sir, after yon on the muir the day, I didna think ye wad hae askit me that question!"

The people looked to one another with astonishment, whereupon the minister prudently explained the whole matter.

When the venerable Ebenezer Erskine was minister of Portmoak, his brother, the equally well-known Ralph, afore-mentioned, paid him a visit. On his entering the manse Ebenezer exclaimed—

"Ralph, man, I'm glad to see you, ye hae come in gude time. I have a diet of examination to-day, and I have also important business to attend to at Perth. Ye'll tak' the examination, will ye, and let me gang to Perth?"

"With all my heart," said Ralph.

"Weel," said Ebenezer, "ye'll find a' my fouk easy to examine but ane, and him, I reckon, ye had better no meddle wi'. He has an auld-fashioned Scotch way o' answering a'e question by putting anither, an' he'll maybe affront ye."

"Affront me!" said Ralph indignantly. "Do you think he'll foil me wi' my ain weapons?"

"Aweel," said his brother, "I gi'e ye fair warning, ye had better no ca' him up."

The individual thus referred to was Walter Simpson, the village blacksmith, who at former diets of examination had proved himself rather troublesome to his minister. The gifted Ralph, indignant to the last degree at the idea of an illiterate blacksmith perplexing *him*, determined to encounter him at once by putting a grand, leading, unanswerable question. Accordingly, after putting a variety of simple preliminary interrogations to some of the senior members of his brother's congregation present, he cried out with a loud voice, "Walter Simpson."

"Here, sir," responded the smith.

"Now, Walter, attend," said the examiner. "Can ye tell me how long Adam continued in a state of innocence?"

"Oh, ay, sir; just till he got a wife," said Vulcan; "but can ye tell me how lang he remained innocent after that?"

"Sit down, Walter," said the discomfited divine, and proceeded to examine another.

"Can ye tell me how long Adam continued in a state of innocence?"

Scotch folks have each a mind of their own, which they respect. Still they are seldom found to be doggedly unreasonable. When it was proposed by the Secession congregation at Haddington to give *a call* to the afterwards celebrated Mr. John Brown, one of the adherents of the church expressed his decided opposition. Subsequent to his ordination, Mr. Brown waited on the solitary dissentient, who was threatening to leave the meeting-house. "Why do you think of leaving us?" mildly enquired Mr. Brown. "Because," said the sturdy oppositionist, "I don't think you a good preacher." "That is quite my own opinion," replied the minister; "but the great majority of the congregation think the reverse, and it would not do for you and me to set up our opinion against theirs. I have given in, you see, and I would suggest you might just do so too." "Weel, weel," said the grumbler, quite reconciled by the candidate's frank confession, "I think I'll just follow your example, sir." All differences were ended; and afterwards, than this same individual, the Rev. John Brown had no greater admirer in the town of Haddington.

Old Hackstoun of Rathillet one day said to Mr. Smibert, the minister of Cupar, who, like himself, was blessed with a foolish, or rather wild, youth for a son—"D'ye ken, sir, you and I are wiser than Solomon."

"How can that be, Rathillet?" inquired the startled clergyman.

"Ou, ye see," said Hackstoun, "Solomon didna ken whether his son was to be a fool or a wise man: but baith you and I are quite sure that our sons are fools."

These anecdotes and illustrations possess a value distinct from the rich ore of humour they reveal. They are redolent of the soil, and serve as "keek-holes" through which fitful glances are obtained of the manners and customs of the "rude forefathers of the hamlet," and the easy relationship which in bygone days existed between the occupants of the pulpit and the pew.

*Here endeth this lesson.*

# CHAPTER V
## THE OLD SCOTTISH BEADLE—HIS CHARACTER AND HUMOUR

The beadle, or betheral—frequently gravedigger, church officer, and minister's man all in one—bulks largely in every representative collection of the Scottish national humour and character—next to the minister here, indeed, as elsewhere—and furnishes the collector with his choicest specimens of Scotch wit and humour of the dry and caustic order. The type of beadle, of course, which fifty or a hundred years ago gave tone and character to the class, and has made them famous in story and anecdote, is now almost a defunct species. This being so, let us turn aside and review the "bodie" where he is preserved, "in his manner as he lived," in the many stories and anecdotes which have survived him. See him there! He is a shrewd, canny-going, scranky-looking individual. Fond of snuff, and susceptible to the allurements of a sly dram. He is proud of his office—the more solemn and conspicuous duties of which he performs with a dignity of deportment and solemnity of countenance which casts the minister almost hopelessly into the shade. He is heard to speak of "*me* and the minister;" and should there chance to come a young probationer to occupy the pulpit for a day, who appears flurried and nervous just before he is to ascend to the "place of execution," he (the preacher) will receive a kindly tap on the shoulder, and be warned not to let his feelings get the better of him. "I can never see a young chap like you gaun up into the poopit," he will continue, "without bein' reminded o' the first Sawbath that I took up the Bible. I shook like the leaf o' a tree! I dinna shak' noo: an' ye'll get ower yer nervousness, too, sir, wi' practice, just as I ha'e dune. I fand it the best plan—an' dootless sae will ye, gin ye'll try it—never to think aboot what ye're doin', nor wha's lookin' at ye, but just stap up the stair and gang through wi' the business as if you didna care a rap for a livin' sowl o' them."

His intimacy with the minister—the semi-private work he performs about the manse, and elsewhere, affording him an occasional keek behind the solemnity that doth hedge a clergyman—places him on easy conversation with his reverend master, and of this circumstance much of his humour is born and given to the world. The minister's condescendences towards him not unfrequently have had the effect of giving him an exaggerated notion of his own importance. His knowledge of what is going on at the manse makes him a welcome visitor at the houses of the gossiping members of the congregation; and Dean Ramsay tells a story which admirably illustrates this interesting phase of his character.

A certain country beadle had been sent round the parish to deliver notices at all the houses of the catechising which was to precede the preparation for receiving the Communion. On his return it was evident that John had partaken rather freely of refreshments in the course of the expedition. The minister rebuked him for his improper conduct. The beadle pleaded the pressing hospitality of the parishioners. The preacher would not admit the plea, and added, "Why, John, I go through the parish, and you do not see me return home fou', as you have done."

"Ay, minister," replied John, with an emphatic shake of the head, "but, then, ye're no sae popular in the parish as I am." The self-complacency of the reply could scarcely be surpassed.

It is told of another of the consequential breed that being asked by a member of the kirk—one of the humbler order—if he knew whether or not the minister was to be preaching himself on the approaching Sabbath, he dryly replied, "It's ill for me to ken a' that the minister intends doin'. Come ye to the kirk, an' whether the minister's there or no, ye'll see me in the poopit as usual, at ony rate."

"Indeed, sir," said Robert Fairgrieve, the beadle of Ancrum, one day to the minister, "Huz (us) that are offish-bearers (meaning the minister and himself) should be examples to the flock."

The self-same functionary when on his death-bed was visited by the minister, who was a little concerned to find him in a restless and discontented humour. On enquiring into the cause of his uneasiness, Robert replied, "Weel, sir, I was just mindin' that I have buried 598 fowk since I was made bedral o' Ancrum, and I was anxious, gin it were *His* will, that I micht be spared to mak' it the sax hunder."

When beadle meets beadle, as is the common practice with persons in other walks of life, they enter glibly into a free-and-easy criticism of their respective chiefs. One is admittedly "strong in prayer," whilst another is set aside as "weak in doctrine," and so forth.

"I think oor minister does weel," said one. "Man! hoo he gars the stoure flee oot o' the cooshions!"

"Stoure oot o' the cooshions!" sneered another. "If ye've a notion o' powerfu' preachin', come owre an' gie us a day's hearin'. Wad ye believe it?—for a' the short time yon man o' ours has delivered the Word amang us, he has knockit three poopits a' to shivers, an' has dung the guts out o' five Bibles!"

"The last minister I was wi'," said one, "had a great power o' water; for he grat, an' swat, an' spat like the very mischief."

"Well, Saunders," said a country clergyman to his beadle on Monday morning, "how did you like that minister who was preaching for me yesterday?"

"Oh, just very middlin' ways, sir," replied Saunders. "Just very middlin' ways. He was far owre plain and simple for me. I like a preacher that jummils the joodgement and confoonds the sense awee; and dod, sir, I never heard ony o' them that could beat yersel' at that."

Well said, Saunders! There are many people about who estimate a preacher much in the same fashion—measure his eloquence by his success in "jummlin' their joodgement" and "confoondin' their senses." They desire sermons so "deep" that they cannot see to the bottom of them; the more incomprehensible the preaching, the more profound the preacher is declared to be.

"Eh, he was grand the day!" said an old lady on her return from church.

"In what respect?" inquired her lord and master.

"Just terrible deep," said she. "I didna understand a word o't; but, eh! it was grand!"

"What makes you laugh, James?" inquired a country minister of his beadle one Sabbath in the Session-house between the preachings, as the humbler functionary stirred up the fire and "hottered and leuch," in a semi-suppressed manner. "It is unseemly, James. What is there to amuse you?"

The minister, it should be explained, had a reputation for giving his people what is well understood when described as "cauld kail het again."

"Eh, naething particular," said Jamie, still laughing. "I was only thinkin' o' something that happened when the kirk was skailin' a maument syne."

"What was it? Tell me about it."

"Weel, minister, dinna be angry wi' me," said Jamie, "an' I'll tell ye. Whether ye ken it or no, sir, ye're blamed for preachin' an auld sermon noo an' than, an' I think I rather got the better o' some o' them the day—some o' the kirk-fouk, I mean."

"How so, James?"

"'Deed, simply eneuch, an' I'll tell ye hoo. Just as soon as the hinmost psalm was finished, ye see, I gaed aff as usual an' opened first the West door, and syne ran round and opened the East door, and as I was comin' back round the kirk again, wha should I meet but Newmains, an' twa or three ither o' the farmers, an' by the way they were lauchin' an' nudgin' ane anither wi' their elbucks, I kent fine what they were ettlin' to say, so I tak's the first word wi' them, an' says I, 'Weel, lads,' says I, 'ye canna say that yon was an auld ane ye got the day, for it's no abune sax weeks since ye got it afore.' An' I think I got the better o' them, sir. An' that's hoo I canna help lauchin'."

The beadle of a northern city kirk was a pavior to trade, and the minister with whom he was regularly "yokit" every Sabbath coming up one day to where John was busily engaged laying causey, was struck with a fine simile, as he thought, and said, "John, you and I toil daily with the same object in view, namely, to *mend the ways* of our fellow-men. But, I am afraid, you make much better progress than I do."

"Ay," replied the pavior-beadle, dryly, "but maybe if ye was as muckle *on your knees* at your wark as I am, sir, you would come better speed."

A capital rejoinder.

One of the beadle's weaknesses is the "dram," as has been already hinted here, and as this must be taken on the sly, his defence must be strong, even though unscrupulous. Alexander M'Laughlan, a Blairgowrie beadle, had contracted a habit of tippling, and entering the Session-house one morning with the evidence of guilt in his breath, the minister deemed the occasion a fitting one on which to administer a reproof, and said—

"Saunders, I much fear that the bottle has become———"

"Aye, sir," interrupted the officer, "I was just about to remark that there was surely a smell o' drink amang's!"

In another case of the same kind, the defence was less equivocal.

"You have been drinking again, John," said the minister. "Why, John, you should really become a teetotaler."

"Do you never tak' a drap yersel', sir?" inquired John.

"I do; but, John, you must consider the difference between your circumstances and mine."

"Very true, sir," said John; "but do ye ken hoo the streets o' Jerusalem were keepit clean?"

"No, I am not sure that I do, John."

"Weel, then, I'll tell ye. It was just by ilka bodie keepin' their ain door-stane soopit."

The argument, doubtless, was not further continued on that occasion.

The minister of one of the Dundee parish churches had a beadle called Donald, who was a worthy and useful man. No fault could be found against him except his being too fond of a dram. At a meeting of the Session one night Donald was so unsteady in his gait that, to prevent an accident, one of the elders had to go to his assistance in lighting the gas, which could only be reached by a chair, or steps. The habit had become so marked of late that it was decided to have Donald "up." On his appearing, the minister, in his most impressive manner, said, "Donald, the Session has asked me to remonstrate with you on your intemperate habits, which seem to have become worse recently."

Donald, with as great a look of offended dignity as in the circumstances he could assume, replied, "I never takes more than what's good for me, shir; did you ever see me the—(hic)—worse of drink?"

The Session was not a little amused; but the minister, still keeping his gravity, said, "Well, Donald, we have pretty plain evidence to-night. And not very long ago I saw you clinging to a railing in the Nethergate, and, so that you might not know I saw you, I crossed to the other side of the street."

Drawing himself up to his full height, the beadle replied, "Well, you did wrong, shir—very far wrong; it was your duty, shir, to have stopped and admonished me." The minister was pleased enough to see Donald's back, as by this time it was very apparent the sympathies of the Session were with the accused.

We rarely find the beadle at loggerheads with the minister, however. He rather inclines to regard the minister's and his own interests as identical, and is disposed to be friendly and confidential. So confidential, indeed, that it is recorded of one that, when the minister was in a state of exasperation about something or other, John looked sympathisingly towards him and said, "Gin ye think that an aith wad relieve ye, sir, dinna mind me!"

"John," said a parish minister in Perthshire to his beadle not very long ago, "that Disestablishment cry is becoming serious. Dr. Hutton and his crew are apparently not to rest until they have us all put out of church and manse together. Why, I see there's to be a set of agitators from Glasgow and elsewhere to be holding a meeting in our very own parish this week." "Dinna ye bother yersel', minister," was the beadle's reply, "dinna ye bother yersel'. If the kirk continues to do her duty, the very gates o' hell will no prevail against her. We have Scripture for that. As an instance, sir. Ye mind o' yon five dissenters wha tried to put me oot o' the grave-diggin' twa years syne, *I've happit four o' them noo!*"

"Drunk again, John," said a north country minister one day to his beadle, meaning, of course, that John was clearly the worse of liquor.

"Don't mention't," replied John, with a bleary wink, "I'm geyan weel on mysel', sir."

"Drunk again, John," said a north country minister to his beadle (meaning, of course, that John was clearly the worse of liquor). "Don't mention't," replied John, with a bleary wink, "I'm geyan weel on mysel', sir."

"That's a damp, cold morning," said the minister, as he entered the Session-house, chaffing both hands and feet.

"Deevilish, sir, deevilish!" replied John, catching the *sense* perhaps, although the *sound* reached him imperfectly.

And, by the by, the word *sound* just reminds me of a very good beadle anecdote, and one which illustrates how expressive a monosyllable may sometimes be made. A certain country congregation had been hearing candidates, with a view to filling the pulpit. The third on the short leet, a young spark of a fellow, had preached, as it were, yesterday, and desiring to ascertain, not only what impression he had himself made, but also the esteem in which the members of the kirk held those who had preached before him, he sauntered around, looking for some suitable person to *sound* on the matter. In course of time he espied the beadle busily exercised in opening a grave, and, going towards the digger, he talked with him quietly for a time on matters likely to interest the rural inhabitant, and gradually arrived at the subject which was uppermost in his own mind.

"And what are the people saying about the candidate who preached first?" at length asked the budding divine.

"Soond!" replied John, throwing up a spadeful.

"And of the second one?" queried the preacher.

"*No* soond!" was the ready and emphatic answer.

"And do you know what opinion they entertain of myself?"

"*A'* soond!" snorted the beadle, and drove the spade into the loam with a thud that was even more eloquent than the words of his mouth.

Perhaps it was to this self-same functionary that a gentleman one day remarked—

"Ye hae been sae lang aboot the minister's hand, John, that I dare say ye could preach a sermon yersel' noo."

"Oh, na, sir," was the modest reply; "I couldna preach a sermon." Then, after a brief pause, he remarked, "But maybe I could draw an inference, though."

"Well, John," said the gentleman, humouring the quiet vanity of the beadle, "what inference could you draw from this text—'A wild ass snuffeth up the wind at her pleasure' (Jer. ii. 24)?"

"Weel," replied John, "the only naitural-like inference that I could draw frae it is just this, that she wad snuff a lang time before she wad fatten on't."

In a country parish in the Lothians the dwelling-house of the beadle was in close proximity to the manse, and both were on the summit of a hill overlooking the neighbouring village. The minister was greatly esteemed for his piety, and it was Sandy's ambition to be regarded as the one other *unco gude* man in the parish. They frequently foregathered and exchanged experiences and views, and always on the basis of their spiritual superiority to all their neighbours. During a certain Saturday night, a great storm of wind and snow had caused such drifts to accumulate about the doors of the villagers that when Sunday dawned all were prisoners within their dwellings except the minister and the beadle. Mr. Blank emerged from the manse, and stood on the hill-top surveying the scene. In a little while he was joined by

Sandy; and whether the minister could interpret the situation or not, the beadle had fully mastered its significance. "Gude mornin', Maister Blank," said Sandy; "ye mind what the Word says, 'He causeth His rain to fall upon the just and the unjust.'" Then slowly sweeping his outstretched arm over the imprisoned village, he added, with a peculiar emphasis, "But faith, sir, *the snow finds the sinners oot*."

Several capital examples of our subject's power of withering sarcasm have been already quoted, but the following would be difficult to rival:—

"Gin ye mention our local magistrates in yer prayers, sir," said the beadle of a small burgh town to a clergyman who had come from a distance to officiate for a day—"gin ye mention our local magistrates in yer prayers, dinna ask that they may be a terror to evil-doers, because the fack o' the maitter is, sir, the puir, auld, waefu' bodies could be nae terror to onybody."

To a notorious infidel, who gloried in his profanity, and was once denouncing the absurdity of the doctrine of original sin, a Falkirk beadle remarked, "It seems to me, Mr. H., that you needna fash yersel' aboot original sin, for to my certain knowledge you've quite as muckle ackual sin as will *do* for you."

An infidel citizen of an Ayrshire burgh built a handsome mausoleum for himself and family in the local cemetery. He spared no expense, and was rather proud of his family burial-place. Indeed, he closely superintended the operations of the workmen, and noted their progress. As he was going to the place one day, he met the beadle of the Secession kirk, and asked him if he had seen the new vault. "Ou ay," was all the answer he got. Nothing daunted, he proceeded to expatiate on the theme, and concluded by saying, "Yon's a gey strong place. It'll tak' us a' our time to rise out o' yonder at the last day."

"My man," said the beadle, "dinna gie yersel' ony trouble about *risin'*, for they'll maybe just ding the bottom out an' let ye gang *doun* instead."

They are generally found having a single eye to business, and one is reported to have rejoiced to hear that an epidemic had broken out in the parish; "for," said he, "I haena buried a livin' sowl for the last six weeks, binna a scart o' a bairn."

John Prentice of Carnwath put his plaint in a more pleasant form. "Hech wow!" he would say, when told of the death of any person. "Ay, man, an' is So-and-So dead? Weel, I wad rather it had been anither twa!"

A person once asked John Prentice if he considered himself at liberty to pray for his daily bread. "Dear sake, sir," he answered, "the Lord's Prayer tells us that, ye ken."

"Ay, but," said the querist, "do you think you can do that consistently with the command which enjoins us to wish no evil to our neighbours?"

"My conscience!" cried John, in astonishment, "the folk maun be buried!"

"Rin awa' hame, bairns," a well-known Perthshire beadle was in the habit of saying to such of the children as curiosity or playfulness had brought to the churchyard. "Awa' wi' ye! an' dinna come here again on yer ain feet."

Just after an interment one day in the same churchyard, and as the mourners were returning towards the gate, one of the party gave a cough, which caused the beadle to prick his ears, and, looking towards a friend who stood by, "Wha ga'e yon howe hoast (hollow cough)?" said he. "He'll be my way gin March!"

"I'm gettin' auld an' frail noo, Jamie," said a timorous and "pernickity" old lady one day to this same functionary; "there's a saxpence to ye to buy snuff. An' if I sud be ta'en awa' afore I see ye again, Jamie, ye'll mind an' lay me in oor wastmost lair."

"A' richt," said Jamie, "but there may be ithers i' the family that wad like the wastmost lair as weel as you, so, to save disappointment, ye'd better hurry up an' tak' possession."

The late Rev. Mr. Barty, of Ruthven, was a man brimful of humour, and many good stories are told of him. A vacancy having occurred in the office of gravedigger, one, Peter Hardie, made application for the appointment. The parish is small, consisting of five farms. The rate per head having been duly fixed, the minister and Peter had just about closed the bargain, when Peter, with an eye to self-interest, said, "But am I to get steady wark?" "Keep's a! Peter," answered Mr. Barty, "wi' steady wark ye wad bury a' the parish in a fortnicht!"

But the beadle sometimes meets with folks as inhumanly practical as himself.

"What's to pey, John?" asked a scrubby farmer of the sexton of Kilwinning, as the finishing touches were being given to the sod on the grave of the farmer's wife.

"Five shillin's," said John.

"Five shillin's for that sma' job? It's oot o' a' reason. Ye're weel pey'd wi' hauf-a-croon."

"She's doon seven feet," said John; "an' I've tell't ye my chairge."

"I dinna want to quarrel wi' ye here the day, John," said the farmer, gruffly; "so there's four shillin's, but I winna gi'e ye a fardin' mair!"

"See here!" said John, holding the money on the palm of his left hand just as he had received it, whilst he seized the handle of the spade in a businesslike way with the other, "doon wi' the ither shillin', or up she comes!"

Another was remonstrated with for making an overcharge. "Weel, you see," said the beadle, making a motion with his thumb to the grave, "him and me had a bit troke about a watch a dizzin o' years syne, and he never paid me the difference o't. Noo, says I to mysel', this is my last chance. I'll better tak' it."

"Ay, man, it's a bonnie turff," one is reported to have said. "It's a peety to see it putten doon on the tap o' sic a skemp!"

Of another deceased person another beadle said, "He was sic a fine child I howkit his grave wi' my new spade."

Not long ago a funeral party in the North on arriving at the kirkyard and placing the coffin over the grave, discovered that the latter was not long enough to admit of the interment. "Man, John," said the chief mourner to the beadle, "ye've made the grave ower short."

"It canna be," retorted John very gruffly, "I measured the coffin wi' my ain hand, and was very particular about it."

"Ye made a mistak' in the measuring, then, John," said the party, "or ye've gane wrang wi' the howkin'."

"*Me* wrang!" snorted the beadle, livid with rage; "see that ye haena brocht the wrang corp."

A physician in Dumfries, who was also a member of the Kirk-Session, meeting the beadle "the waur o' a dram," threatened to expose him.

"Man, doctor," said the gravedigger, with a twinkle in his eye, "I hae happit *mony* a faut o' yours, an' I think ye micht thole *ane* o' mine."

"Man, doctor," said the gravedigger, with a twinkle in his eye, "I hae happit *mony* a faut o' yours, an' I think ye micht thole *ane* o' mine."

The translation of the Rev. Donald Macleod from Linlithgow to Glasgow was deeply resented by the beadle, who also held the office of sexton. When Mr. Macleod first went to Linlithgow, the beadle took him into the graveyard, and, showing him the resting-places of his predecessors, said, "There's whaur Dr. Bell lies; and there's whaur Dr. Dobie lies; and there's whaur you'll lie if you're spared." As Mr. Macleod was taking his departure, the beadle said, "Weel, sir, ye're the first minister that was ever lifted out o' Linlithgow except to the grave."

In the memoir of the late Dr. William Lindsay Alexander there are some choice beadle anecdotes; and the following, which is identified with his first pulpit appearance in the congregation which had known him "man and boy," the rev. doctor himself told in a church meeting not very long before his death. "As well as I remember," he said, "I discharged the duty to the best of my ability. But, on coming down to the vestry, one of the worthy deacons came to me and said some very disparaging things about my sermon, saying plainly that this sort of thing would never do! Among other things he said it was too flowery. Saunders, the church-officer, who was in the vestry and was standing with his hand on the door, turned round and said, 'Flooers! an' what for no? What ails ye at flooers?' After the deacon went out I went up to Saunders and thanked him for taking my part. 'Weel, Maister Weelum, I jist didna like to see him ower ill to ye; but, atween oorsel's, he wasna far wrang, ye ken. Yon'll no dae!"

The Doctor one day told "Jimms," who had been gardener and minister's man at Pinkieburn when he (the minister) was a boy, that he had planned a new approach to the house, and intended to set about and have it made at once.

"Na, na, Doctor, that'll no dae at a'," Jimms sturdily exclaimed, when explanations of the plan had been laid before him.

"Well, but I have resolved to have it done," Dr. Alexander said, and quietly reminded Jimms that he was there to carry out orders.

"Nae doot, Doctor, in a certain sense that's true," was the prompt reply. "Still I'm here to prevent ye frae spoilin' the property."

When, however, the new walk was an accomplished fact, and approved of by the visitors, Jimms took his full share of the credit.

"Ou, ay," he would say, "nane o' yer landscape gardeners here. Me an' the Doctor, we managed it a'."

In course of time this "Jimms" went where all good beadles go, and his mantle fell on his successor, John Sloan. This worthy and the Doctor got on capitally together.

"There were never words atween me an' the Doctor," said Sloan. "I did my wark, and said straicht what cam' into my head, an' the Doctor liked it."

Sloan seldom volunteered advice, but when he did, it was always with good effect. On one occasion he found himself in the Deacons' vestry putting coals on the fire, when the subject under discussion was whether a service, at which a special collection was to be asked, should be held on Sunday afternoon or evening. Dr. Alexander had just said that he would prefer the afternoon, when Sloan paused for a moment, coal-scuttle in hand, and facing round, said, "The Doctor's richt. In the afternoon we'll ha'e oor ain fouk; at nicht there'll be a wheen Presbyterians—I reckon them at thruppence a dizzen!"

He did not wait to see the effect of his shot, but it ended the discussion.

"I don't think I should put on my gown to-day, John," said a country minister to his beadle, "the weather is so very hot. I will preach better without it."

"Put on the goun, sir," said John, "it mak's ye mair impressive like, an' ye need it a'."

In a congregation in the North the beadle had been systematically pilfering just as much of the church-door collection money as would keep himself in snuff. The acting elder habitually counted the money in the presence of the minister, put it in the box, turned the key in the lock, and left it there. By and by it was discovered that small sums were being regularly abstracted. Suspicion fell on the beadle. So one Sabbath after the minister had seen the elder count over the day's drawings, and place it in the box in the usual way, he returned to the Session-house after the Sabbath School was dismissed, and, counting over the money again, noticed that the usual small portion had disappeared. He accordingly summoned the beadle. "David," said the minister, "there is something wrong here. Some one has been abstracting the church money from the box; and you know that no one has access to it but you and I."

The minister thought he had the beadle thoroughly cornered, and that he would confess his guilt. But David cleared his conscience, and dumfoundered the minister by this strange proposal:

"Weel, minister," said he, "if there is a deficiency, it's for you and me to mak' it up 'atween us, and say naething about it!"

A highly respectable minister, who had no preaching gifts, was one day going to officiate for a country brother who was from home. The manse to which he was going was some miles from the railway station, and the minister's man, John, was in waiting with the conveyance for the stranger when the train arrived in the winter afternoon. John, after receiving him kindly, told him that he had some messages to do in the town close by the station, which would take him about half an hour, and that if he would go along to the hotel the landlord would give him a comfortable seat at the fireside till he was ready. The minister readily agreed, but when, instead of half an hour, considerably more than an hour elapsed before John appeared, he upbraided him when he came for his unnecessary delay, and threatened to report him to his master. At length John could stand it no longer, and said, "Weel, sir, if ye maun hae the truth, I was tell't by the maister to put aff at the toun till it was dark, so that the folk in the parish micht na see wha was to preach the morn."

When the Rev. Mr. Mitchell had been translated from a country parish to a church in Glasgow, a friend of his, visiting the old parish, asked the beadle how he liked the new minister.

"Oh," said the beadle, "he's a very good man, but I would rather hae Mr. Mitchell."

"Indeed," said the visitor; "I suppose the former was a better preacher?"

"No; we've a good enough preacher now."

"Was it the prayer of Mr. Mitchell, or his reading, or what was it you preferred him for?"

"Weel, sir," said the beadle, "if you maun ken the reason, Mr. Mitchell's auld claes fitted me best."

It is a truism that much depends upon the way in which a thing is done. A young spark of a fellow had been made a minister, neither very *wisely* nor very *well*, as we may in fairness suppose, for, being appointed to a country charge where the manse was situated at a considerable distance from the church, he very soon shocked the finer sensibilities of the lieges by driving tandem to and from the Sunday service—that is, having two horses yoked to his machine, the one running in front of the other. The like had never been seen nor heard of before. He would require to be spoken to about it at once. Driving of itself was tolerable, but *tandem* was out of the question. Accordingly, the elders laid their heads together, and one of them tackled the reverend gentleman on the question at the close of the service.

"Why, you drive to church yourself," said the minister to the elder.

"Ay, but in a very different manner frae that heathenish way that you do it," retorted the elder—"that *tandem* way."

"I see nothing more scandalous in driving horses tandem than running them abreast," coolly argued the minister; "but if you can convince me that there is, I will cease from doing it."

"I just dinna like it," said the elder, failing to discover a better argument at the moment.

"That's just it," sneered the minister. "You don't like it. It's a sheer case of conventionality and narrow-minded prejudice."

"Maybe it is. But it disna look weel," insisted the elder.

"Look! Look is nothing," returned the minister, "but a mere matter of taste."

"The elder's richt," broke in the beadle, who had been standing aside listening to all the argument. "Look has a hantle to do wi't. An' if ye'll aloo me, sir, I'll convince ye o' that by a very simple illustration. See ye here noo, sir. When ye pronounced the benediction twa or three minutes since, it lookit grand an' consistent-like when ye did it

*This way!*

But what gin ye had dune it

*That way?"*

The minister stood convinced, and never proposed tandem again as long as he lived.

Of a Durisdeer beadle it is told that having received from the minister—a comparative new-comer—the gift of a half-worn coat, he sidled to the door, and turning round gave him a lesson in the traditions of his office by explaining, "Mr. Smith used to gi'e me the waistcoat too."

The greatly esteemed Principal Caird was minister of Errol before he was appointed Professor of Divinity in Glasgow. While there the Doctor discovered the acoustic properties of the church to be by no means of the best, and his congregation being scanty, he suggested to the beadle that an improvement might be effected by boarding up one of the side aisles. "That may do very weel for you," replied the shrewd old Scotchman, "but what will we do for room if we should get a popular preacher to follow you?"

Robert Burns tells us that

"The fear o' hell's a hangman's whip

To haud the wretch in order,"

and the asseveration of the bard received favourable commentary at the instance of a sage country beadle not very long ago. The minister had for some time previously been favouring the free and easy theology which excludes belief in eternal punishment. He had, indeed, told his people from the pulpit that such an arrangement was not, in his opinion, consistent with the character and being of the Creator of the universe. From this point there was a marked falling off in the attendance at church on the Sabbath, and the preacher was, naturally, concerned.

"John," he said to the beadle one day between the preachings, "the people are not turning out to public worship nearly so well as they used to do."

"I dinna blame them for't," was John's dry reply.

"You what, John?"

"I dinna blame them for't, I'm sayin'."

"You do not blame the people for absenting themselves from divine service! Do you mean to insinuate, John, that my preaching is less able, less adequate to their needs, and——?"

"Yer preachin' may be a' ye wad claim for it, sir, an' I'll no argue wi' ye aboot it: but I say this, an' I'll stick till't, a kirk withoot a hell's just no worth a d—— docken."

'Twas coarse, but strong, and true.

In a Forfarshire parish, a number of years ago, the old beadle was an outstanding character even among his kind. The minister—a recent appointment—entered the churchyard one day accompanied by a gentleman friend—also a recent importation into the district—and approaching the beadle the following colloquy ensued:—

*Minister*—"This is Mr. So and So, John, he wishes to purchase a lair."

*Beadle*—"Imphm! Ou, ay. Just that. Is it for himsel'?"

*Gentleman*—"No. It's for my brother. He died last night."

*Beadle*—"Ou, ay. Weel it's a' the same to me, of course, ye ken; but d'ye ken hoo he wad like to lie?"

*Minister*—"What do you mean, John?"

*Beadle*—"Weel, ye see, there's some likes to lie wi' their feet to the east, some wi' their feet to the wast. There, just for instance, ahent ye, lies the auld minister an' his wife; him wi' his feet to the east, an' her wi' her feet to the wast. They were contrar' a' their days, an' they're contrar' yet."

In a short time a lair was selected, after which the minister enquired of John how long he had been about the place.

*Beadle*—"I've been howkin' awa' in this corner for mair than fifty year, sir."

*Minister*—"And I suppose you have buried one or more out of every house in the parish, John?"

*Beadle*—"Na', sir, na'. Thae folk o' Todhills there have run nearly twa tacks o' their farm, an' they havena' broken grund yet."

*Minister*—"Indeed, that's very remarkable, John, and old Todhills himself looks wonderfully hale and hearty still."

*Beadle*—"Hale an' hearty, ay, hale an' hearty eneuch, an' tichtenin' his grip on the warld every day. But folk sud live an' lat live, sir. I say, folk sud live an' lat live."

The minister and his friend thought John should take the same advice to himself, but preferred not to say so, and the interview terminated.

---

# CHAPTER VI
## HUMOUR OF SCOTCH PRECENTORS

Hand and personal labour of every kind in Scotland, as everywhere else, has in recent years been largely superseded by machinery, and no one can have failed to notice that even the office of "lettergae," or precentor, is a rapidly decaying institution in our midst. How rapid the progress of the decay is will be recognised from a consideration of the fact that, within the memory of many persons still alive, "reading the line" was the general custom in congregational praise. Then there was no such thing as an organ, or "kist o' whustles," in any Presbyterian kirk in the land, and choirs were the exception. In the North hymns were not mentioned, except with scorn and shaking of the head, and repeating tunes were regarded as a frivolity demanding extermination. By and by the repeating tune was tolerated, hymns were introduced here and there, choirs became the fashion; and thus far the precentor was a *sine qua non*. Ultimately the kirk doors were opened to the introduction of the organ, and precentors became known as "choirmasters" and "conductors of psalmody." Now the "whustles" are heard bumming in kirks, *bond* and *free*. "Whustle kirks" will very soon be the rule rather than the exception, and the precentor will, in the course of a few years, have become an almost unknown quantity. Some of us who have already cut our wisdom teeth may live to see him a totally defunct species. And yet, if we do, we will not behold the spectacle without acute twinges of regret, for many pleasing memories of the pleasantest period of our lives cluster around the familiar form of the village-kirk precentor as he appeared in the desk with clean-shaven chin, black "stock," stiffly-starched, high-rimmed linen collar, and ample shirt-front as white as the drifted snaw; and by the mildest effort of the imagination we can even now hear the familiar snap of his snuff-box lid, see him prime the one nostril, then the other, and hear the equally familiar dirl of the "pitchfork" on the book-board, and the reading of the line on the key-note of "Balermo," or "Devizes," "Coleshill," "St. Asaphs," or the "wild warbling measures of 'Dundee.'"

Of course it is just as the study of music progresses in Scotland, and the taste for the highly-refining art becomes general, that organs increase and precentors decay. It is to the olden times, however, when he who had a "fairish gude lug" and a thoroughly sound pair of lungs was, irrespective of musical education, elected to "fill the desk," that the humours of precenting almost exclusively belong. And, truly, of that time many a sufficiently funny and ludicrous story may be told.

The late and lamented David Kennedy, the eminent Scottish vocalist, began his career, as most people are aware, as a precentor in his native city of Perth, where his father before him held a similar office for many years in one of the larger Presbyterian kirks. Of the time of the elder Kennedy's precentorship, "Dauvit" remembered a well-known old character in Perth, an inveterate snuffer, who sang with all his might, and was in the habit of stopping short in the middle of a verse, blowing his nose in his red pocket-napkin, and, having carefully marked the place, would recommence where he left off, oblivious to the fact that the precentor and the rest of the congregation were two lines in advance of him. That man's singing resembled the dancing of a Perthshire ploughman I have heard of. This latter individual, who hobbled on the floor like a "hen on a het girdle," and never modulated the action of his limbs to fast or slow music, said he "maybe wasna a very elegant dancer, but he was awfu' constant."

Mr. Kennedy, also, when introducing one of his songs, used to tell a good story of the times when the minister did not choose his Psalms as at present, but the precentor simply went through the Psalm book, taking so many verses each time. The singer's father and some others, when lads, managed to take advantage of this custom to play a good practical joke on an old precentor. Gaining access to the vestry on the Saturday night they took his Psalm-book and, turning to the part which was to be used on the morrow, neatly pasted in the first page of the well-known ballad "Chevy Chase," the type in which the two books were printed being nearly similar.

On the day following, the precentor, as was the general custom in those days, read each line before singing it, and so managed to get to the end of the third line without noticing anything out of place:—

> "God prosper long our noble king,
>
> Our lives and safeties all;
>
> A woeful hunting once there did"—

Having reached the fourth line he read—

> "In Chevy Chase befall."

Muttering, "Hoots! I maun be turning blind," he adjusted his spectacles, and held the book close to his nose. Finding the exact words there, he gazed round him for a second as if he had doubts of his own sanity, and said, "Weel, freends, I am clean bambaized. I've sung the Psalms o' Dauvit for thretty year, but never saw 'Chevy Chase' mentioned in them before."

The feeling against repeating tunes approached to something like horror in certain parts of the country, even in the second and third decades of the present century, and I have heard my father tell how, when he was a young man, he accompanied a friend to the kirk in Logiealmond. The friend's father was an elder in the kirk in question, and he, the young man, was to occupy the precentor's desk for the day. In the course of the service he introduced a repeating tune, and the scene in the kirkyard at the "skailin' o' the kirk" made the occasion memorable. The young man's father had hurried out immediately after the benediction was pronounced, and placing himself at the cheek of the kirk door, as soon as the budding precentor appeared he seized him by the neck, threw him to the ground, and, belabouring him with hands and feet, he exclaimed—"You abominable scoundrel! if you dare again to profane the word of God in my hearing, I'll slay you with my own hands in the presence of the whole congregation!"

A precentor of age and experience was once as effectively corrected for the same practice. Thinking to steal a march on the minister, whose mind on the subject was well known, he started a repeating tune one day. As soon as his drift was evident the minister's hand was over the pulpit and his fingers among the "lettergae's" hair, and, "Stop, Dauvit! stop!" he shouted, "when the Lord repeats we'll repeat; but no till then."

Of course, then, even as now, repeating tunes had to be chosen with neat discrimination, as much of our sacred verse does not yield itself gracefully to such treatment. Repeats generally occur in the last line of a stanza, and the praise of a congregation has not infrequently been rendered ludicrous from the want of good taste and common-sense in the selection of tunes suited to the words, as well as to the sentiment of a psalm or hymn. To the well-known Hundredth Psalm a repeating tune has sometimes been applied, which, from a peculiarity in its arrangement, has rendered the line—"And for His sheep He doth us take"—thus, "And for His *sheep he'd*—And for His *sheep he'd*—And for His *sheep he'd*—oth us take." From the same indiscretion multitudes of people have been made to exclaim—"Oh! send down *Sal*—Oh! send down *Sal*—Oh! send down sal—va—tion to us," and solicit the privilege to "*Bow—wow—wow* before the throne." But surely the most ludicrous example of the kind ever produced was when the female voices in a choir had to repeat by themselves—"Oh! for a *man*—Oh! for a *man*—Oh! for a man—sion in the skies."

Occasions have also been made memorable by precentors from ignorance or accident launching into a tune in a different measure from the psalm. In this way a "lettergae" in a rural parish in the North, far from perfect in his profession, astonished the congregation one Sabbath many years ago. In the psalm which was intimated, the second line to be sung ended with the word "Jacob," said psalm being a common metre. The precentor, who sang "by the lug" and used no tune-book, went off on a peculiar metre tune, and not discovering the error until he had reached the word "Jacob," and then finding he was short of verbal material, he improvised for the occasion, and sang it "J—a—jay—fal—de—riddle—cob," and so on, as necessity demanded, until the verses were finished. On coming out of the church some of his neighbours approached him and said—

"O'd, yon was a new ane ye ga'e us the day, Geordie."

"Ay," replied Geordie; "yon's 'Kinnoull Hill,'" and away he went, avoiding further question as much as he could.

Geordie's *impromptu* was not disingenuous by any means, and his after-fencing was admirable; but he would have shown better discretion had he, when he discovered the incompatibility of the metres, acted after the manner of a well-known precentor of the same shire, lately deceased. This latter functionary was guided also more by the "lug" than the music-book, and in raising the psalm one day, even although he had hummed the tune to himself while the minister was reading the verses, his memory played him false at the critical moment of entering into action, and off he went on a tune the measure of which did not suit the psalm. The instant he discovered his error—which was at the end of the first line—he stopped, looked round the congregation—not a blush—and in a firm voice said, "I am wrong." Then he mused for a moment, caught up the tune he meant to sing, and away he went with it, and, as I have heard him tell, never sang with better "birr" in all his life. As he left the church his arm was touched by the factor's lady, a woman of rare intelligence and vivacity of manner, who exclaimed, "Now, Joseph, I see that a well-corrected mistake looks first-rate." So it does; and is often the making of a man. This Joseph was acknowledged to be the best "reader of the line"—that is, of reading each line on the key-note before singing it—within a radius of twenty miles. He only once "put his foot in it," so far as I have heard. It was in connection with the word "snow," to which he at first applied the wrong vowel sound, and in attempting to correct himself made it altogether "Snee-snaw-snow."

In connection with the practice of reading the line, I have heard several good stories. One of them is that a young man who looked even younger than he was, had been granted "a day in the desk" by the regular precentor of a country congregation. The first psalm given out was the fifth part of 119th, beginning "Teach me, O Lord, the perfect way;" and this line he declaimed with quite exceptional and inspiring eloquence. But on returning to sing it he failed to catch on the tune somehow. He read the line again; but, no, it would not go. Once more he tackled the subject by the "heft end," and exclaimed, "Teach me, O Lord, the perfect way." Still being unable to raise the tune, an old farmer in the church blurted out, "Dod, laddie, I'm thinking He has muckle need;" and rising to his feet, in response to a nod from the minister, he went off with the line and the tune both, much to the relief of the unfledged precentor. The next time that young man essayed to lead the praise in the same edifice, the service curiously enough opened with the 48th Paraphrase, the first line of which runs, "Let Christian faith and hope dispel;" and it was with him even as the words requested, for he disported himself to the complete satisfaction of all present.

The Rev. Sir Henry Moncrieff, Bart., was for some years minister of the parish of Blackford, prior to his translation to St. Cuthbert's in Edinburgh. During his incumbency at Blackford (about 1774), he had, as Doctor Rodgers tells, one Sabbath opened divine service by giving out a portion of the 71st Psalm, at the seventh verse. The conductor of the psalmody followed the practice then in vogue, and enunciated the opening line—

"To many I a wonder am."

Immediately the congregation seemed to be overpowered by an inclination to indulge in laughter, which, indeed, some were unable to restrain. The precentor faltered, but proceeded to read the line again. This tended only to increase the excitement; and while some quickly withdrew from the church, others concealed their faces under the pews, or buried them in their handkerchiefs. Sir Henry rose up, and, looking down at the precentor, called to him, "So you are a wonder, John; turn your wig." The oddity of the precentor's appearance with his wig misplaced, viewed in connection with his proclamation, had produced the mistimed merriment.

A precentor of humour, when Lord Eglinton's family were crowded out of sitting room in the kirk, exclaimed, "Stand back, Jock, and let the Eglinton family in;" then continued to read—

"Nor stand in sinners' way."

Dr. Chalmers attempted to abolish the practice of reading the line, and used to tell a story of an old woman in his congregation who stoutly maintained that the change was anti-scriptural. On being asked by the great preacher what was the scripture of which she regarded the change as a contravention, the good old dame at once replied by citing the text, "Line upon line," which, as she fancied, settled the matter.

It has been a common ambition among musical young men in country places to have "a day in the desk," and many sorrowful experiences might be related in connection therewith—experiences which would go to show that the late James Smith's account of "Barebones' First Day in the Desk" was not a severely overdrawn picture. Barebones' account is in "common metre," and the crisis of the occasion is thus graphically described:—

"Forth like a martyr then I went,
Quench'd were Hope's smould'ring embers;
And walk'd into a lofty church,
Well filled with country members.

With fear I saw each icy glance
That like a serpent stings;
Then mounted quickly to the desk,
And seemed to mount on wings.


Then when the psalm was given out,
I raised my fork on high
With energy of fierce despair,
And felt inclined to cry.

Again the line was thunder'd o'er,
Cold drops ran down my face;
A burning throb rush'd through my brain,
For I had lost the place.

I seized the first that came to hand,
And sang with deadly shudder!
'*Blessed is he that wisely doth*
*The poor man's case consider.*'

With knocking knees I slew *Montrose*,
And then 'mid some surprises,
I called at *York* and *Manchester*,
Then landed at *Devizes*!

At length *St. Lawrence* glided by,
'Mid stillness most unpleasant,
When suddenly a voice exclaimed—
'*Stop! that'll do at present!*'

I started, ceased, and looking round,
Beheld the congregation
Wild staring, with distended jaws.
In speechless consternation.

First one began to shake his head—
Another—and another;
Then, blinded with despair, I cried,
'*My mother! Oh, my mother!*'

Down from the desk I swiftly sprang,
And reached the vestry door;
Then rent the sable gown in twain,
And cast it on the floor."


In a rural village in Perthshire, a number of years ago, a tailor's apprentice, who was fain to thrill the congregation with a display of his vocal powers, failed even more conspicuously than Barebones aforesaid. This individual was allowed a "day," only after repeated entreaty, the habitual occupant of the "letteran" being dubious about the success of the venture. However, when sanction was at length given, the "Psalms" were early secured from the minister, and elaborate preparations ensued. Sabbath came, and on the last toll of the bell our hero emerged from the Session-house and stepped with jaunty and self-confident air into the desk in front of the pulpit. He was a sight to behold, and not soon to forget. Every hair was in its right place, and shone from the superabundance of scented pomade, and his whole demeanour was that of one who had come forth to conquer, or to die. While the first psalm was being read he kept sounding his pitchfork. As the time for rising drew near a nervous twitching of the mouth and eyes ensued, which was accompanied by sudden paleness of the features. Promptly as the minister sat down, however, he banged to his feet, once more struck the pitchfork on the book-board, once more sounded his *doh*. Then he raised his book—turned his eyes on the congregation—opened his mouth—and—and—no—not a sound would come. Perceiving the situation, the precentor, who was in his own family pew, opportunely threw his voice into the breach, and led off with the tune which he had previously directed should be sung to the first psalm. At the same moment his young substitute disappeared below the desk, and there he remained throughout all the rest of the service, and until every soul but himself and the beadle had quit the sacred edifice, the precentor having, as each successive psalm was given out, stood in his family pew and led the congregation. But, though baffled for the time being, Willie was not altogether discomfited, and before many months had passed he appealed for an opportunity to "redeem his character," as he put it. The request was by and by conceded, and he "stack" a second time. Again he essayed to "redeem his character," and once more the opportunity was afforded. This time it was to be "now or never," and no effort was to be spared to ensure success. He was himself thoroughly confident, as heretofore, and in marching proudly kirkwards he came up on the village wiseacre of the time, who was stepping leisurely in the same direction.

"Well, Mr. C—, I am going to redeem my character to-day," said Willie.

The old man stopped and looked reflectively.

"Ay! are ye gaein' to be precentin' the day, Willie?"

"Yes," replied Willie, proudly.

"Weel, then," said Mr. C—, "I'm gaein' hame;" and home he went.

He might have gone to church that day, however, for Willie came off with flying colours and, though he has precented many a year and day since, he has never had occasion again to "redeem his character."

But precentors have "stuck" after they have had years of experience, and I have heard of one in a country kirk who frequently pitched his tunes too high, and when he failed in his efforts to carry them through, he would stop and shake his head and exclaim, "It'll no do, chaps; we'll need to try't a wee thocht laicher."

Another, after repeated ineffectual attempts to raise the tune on a certain occasion, turned round, and looking up to the minister, exclaimed, "Dod, sir, that psalm'll no sing ava."

One who was suffering from cold occupied the desk so imperfectly that the minister whispered to him over the pulpit—

"What's the matter wi' ye, John?"

"'Deed, sir," replied John, "I'm fash'd wi' an unco kittlin' i' the paup o' my hass."

"A kittlin', do ye ca't?" exclaimed the minister, loud enough for all the congregation to hear him. "It soonds to my lug mair like the catterwaw o' an auld tam-cat."

And there have been humorous incidents connected with the praise of the Church for which the precentor could only be held directly responsible. Thus in the *Statistical Account* we read that, in the days of Mr. Cumming, the late Episcopal minister in the parish of Halkirk, in Caithness-shire, there was no singer of psalms in the church but the "lettergae" and one Tait, gardener in Braal. This Tait sang so loud, and with such a large open mouth, that a young fellow of the name of Inverach was tempted to throw a small round stone into his mouth, whereby his teeth were broken and his singing stopped at once, and he himself almost choked. Inverach immediately took to his heels; the service was converted to laughter; two of Tait's sons chased and overtook him; and the scene was closed with a desperate fight.

Precentors, like musical men generally, of course, have not suffered from an overstock of modesty. Dr. Blair used to tell the following anecdote of his precentor with a great deal of glee. Happening to preach one day at a distance, he next day met that official as he was returning home—

"Well," said the Doctor, "how did matters proceed yesterday at church in my absence?"

"'Deed," replied the man of song, "no very weel, I'm dootin': for I wasna there, Doctor, ony mair than yoursel'."

I have heard how the vanity of a choirmaster was effectually crushed. It was in a certain church in one of our large towns some years ago. The rev. Doctor had given out a well-known psalm, which he expected would be sung to the tune of *Martyrdom*. Instead of that it was sung to a new tune which none of the congregation knew, and the choir had thus the whole singing to themselves. When they had finished, the Doctor rose, with an angry look on his face, and remarked, "Since the choir have sung to their own praise and glory, we shall now sing to the praise and glory of God." Forthwith he began the words to the tune of *Martyrdom*, and the whole of the people joined with great warmth.

The reading of the proclamations, or marriage banns, etc., was long a duty which in country parish churches generally devolved on the precentor, and many sufficiently funny blunders was the result. In a small seaport town in the North, many years ago, when vessels left port, those of the crew who were members of the visible Church in the midst thereof were recommended publicly to the prayers of the congregation. Captain M'Pherson and his lady were prominent members, and the Sabbath succeeding the captain's departure on one occasion, the written intimation which was handed to the precentor read as follows:—"Captain M'Pherson having gone to sea, his wife desires the prayers of the congregation in his behalf." By the simple displacement of the comma after "sea," the people were told that "Captain M'Pherson having gone to see his wife, desires the prayers of the congregation in his behalf."

Precentors have sometimes received compliments which might be envied by those occupying higher places. The late Rev. Mr. M'Dougall, of Paisley, used to tell of having been accosted by a man on leaving some meeting, with—

"You're Mr. M'Dougall, I think?"

"Yes, I am. How do you happen to know me?"

"Oh! I'm whiles in your kirk."

"Do you live in Paisley?"

"No, I live in Gleska'."

"Then, I suppose you sometimes stay with friends in Paisley?"

"No, I just walk out on the Sundays."

"That's a long walk, surely?"

The minister was beginning to feel quite proud of his power of drawing a congregation, and said—

"Do you stay over the night after going to church?"

"No, I just walk back again."

"That is a very long walk."

"Oh, ay, it's a bit gude walk; but ye see I think a deal o' your precentor."

It was the minister here:—In a rural parish the old preacher felt out of sorts one Sabbath, and to provide a rest for himself before delivering the sermon, he gave out a long psalm to be sung, not taking into account the precentor's bad cold, which was a chronic complaint. The first four verses were finished not so badly, but at the fifth Tammas stuck, and no amount of tuning could get him started again. At last the minister had to get to his feet, and in no very pleasant mood. Accordingly, leaning over the pulpit, he addressed the precentor thus:—"Tammas, if ye mak' sic a wark about skirlin' out four verses o' a psalm noo, hoo do ye expect ye're to manage to sing through a' the ages o' eternity?"

The story of "The Foxes' Tails," so admirably elaborated to the dimensions of a public "reading" by Dr. Moxey of Edinburgh, I was accustomed to hear, more than twenty years ago, as having transpired between a country minister and his precentor, Sandy Johnston; and in this way. In the course of a twa-handed crack one day, the minister had ventured on some friendly criticism of Sandy's singing, whereupon Sandy retaliated by remarking that he thought the singing would compare favourably with the preaching any day.

"Don't let us quarrel, Sandy," said the minister; "we may each benefit by the other's criticism. Now, tell me candidly, what the chief faults of my preaching are?"

"Ou, I'm no sayin' I ha'e ony fauts till't, but just this, that I've noticed ye—weel—that is to say—ye exaggerate a wee."

"Well, Sandy, if I exaggerate the truth in the pulpit, I am certainly not aware of it."

"Ye do't a' the same, though," insisted the precentor.

"Sandy, I respect your opinion," said the minister, "but I am so satisfied that I am innocent of the charge you have preferred against me, that I now call upon you, if ever on any future occasion you shall hear me exaggerate in the pulpit, you will pull me up there and then, just by emitting a low, thin whistle."

Sandy agreed to this arrangement. Several Sabbaths passed, and nothing out-of-joint was said or heard. The precentor, however, still kept his "lug on the cock," and at length his patience was rewarded. Lecturing one day on that chapter of the Scriptures which describes Samson as catching three hundred foxes, tying them tail to tail, casting firebrands in their midst, starting them among the standing corn of the Philistines, and burning it down.

"My friends," said he, "you will be wondering in your minds how Samson could tie so many foxes tail to tail, for the best man in Scotland couldn't tie two of our foxes' tails together. Samson, however, was the strongest man the world has ever seen, and these Eastern foxes, travellers tell us, had very long tails—tails, indeed, forty and fifty feet long. [Precentor emits a low thin whistle.] I should have said," continued the preacher, "that—that—is the account given by the earliest travellers to the East, and that recent investigation had proved its inaccuracy, and that these foxes' tails could not have exceeded about twenty feet in length. [Sandy whistles again.] Twenty feet did I say," continues the minister, "yes! but the matter has very recently been commanding attention in scientific circles, and it is doubted whether foxes' tails, in any part of the world, ever at any time, exceeded ten or twelve feet in——" [Sandy whistles.] At this crisis, the minister strikes his book with his clenched fist, and leans over the pulpit and exclaims, "I'll tell you what it is, Sandy Johnstone, I'll no tak' anither inch aff thae foxes' tails tho' ye sit there and whistle till the day o' joodgment!"

"I tell you what it is, Sandy Johnston, I'll no tak' anither inch aff thae foxes' tails tho' ye sit there and whistle till the day o' joodgement!"

Yes! as already stated here, the Scotch precentor is a decaying institution; yet luckily for his peace of mind there are still a respectable number in the land who think with the old lady who remarked, "Organs, nae doot, mak' unco grand music; but, eh! it's an awfu'-like way o' spendin' the Sawbath!"

# CHAPTER VII
## HUMOURS OF DRAM-DRINKING IN SCOTLAND

"Leeze me on drink, it gie's us mair

Than either school or college:

It kindles wit, it waukens lear,

It pangs us fu' o' knowledge.

Be't whisky gill or penny wheep,

Or ony stronger potion,

It never fails, in drinking deep,

To kittle up oor notion

By night or day."

So sang Scotland's greatest, Scotland's sweetest poet; and whether in his heart of hearts he believed the sentiment which in those lines we find so vigorously expressed, he has undoubtedly reflected therein, for the enlightenment of his countrymen through succeeding ages, the popular notion of his own time regarding the potency of the "dram." In Burns' day, and for some time thereafter, happiness and whisky were regarded as almost synonymous terms; deep drinking was fashionable; and "the last beside his chair to fa'" was verily the hero of the social community. "We're happiest when we're fou," is a well-worn proverb. "We'll aye sit an' tipple owre a wee drappie o't," croons an old song-writer, evidently impressed with the conviction that a man could not be better occupied than in consuming malt liquors. "Freedom and whisky gang thegither—tak' aff your dram!" shouts Burns. Yes. But the same sweet singer has fervidly prayed—

"Oh, wad some power the giftie gi'e us,

To see oursel's as ithers see us."

And happily, whilst the *shout* is going in at the one ear and out at the other—is failing to command obedience—the *prayer* is gradually being answered. Old customs, like old prejudices, no matter how absurd they may be, die hard; but with the general advance of education in Scotland, and the dissemination of cheap and healthy literature, the people are becoming day by day more distinctly convinced of the many ludicrous absurdities connected with our social habits, particularly with the old-fashioned ideas relating to hospitality and conviviality, and with the practice of persistent and indiscriminate dram-drinking. A man may be merry nowadays without being "half fou," and yet not be considered "daft," and we have been realising that there are other ways of hospitably entertaining a friend than by filling him to the chin with whisky. Our dram-drinking tendencies have made us the butt of the Continental jokist, and no wonder. How utterly absurd the practice in general has been—in many instances how highly humorous! Your teetotal lecturer, I have often thought, dwells too frequently on the tragedy of the subject. It has a tragic side, no doubt, and a woefully pathetic one; but very much connected with it, like the antics of a half-tipsy individual, is ludicrously humorous, and needs only to be dangled before the eye of sober sense to render the persistent and indiscriminate participator more than half-ashamed of his connection with it. Let our active teetotallers instruct themselves fairly in the art of photography, and go around photographing respectably-dressed persons in their various stages of intoxication, afterwards circulating copies of the photos amongst the subject's friends, being careful not to neglect sending a few to the tippler himself, and they will do more service to the temperance cause in one month than perhaps all the labour of their lives has hitherto achieved. But to come directly to look at the humours of dram-drinking. What have been the facts of the case? Whisky has been made the cure for all diseases, and the "saw for a' sairs." Was Sandy cold, he took a dram to warm him. Was he hot, he took a dram to cool himself. Did he feel hungry, and the dinner not quite ready, he took a dram to appease his appetite. Did he not feel very hungry when dinner was set before him, he took a dram to sharpen his appetite, and another one after dinner to aid his digestion. Was he sad, he took a dram to make him "bear his heart abune." Was he merry, he took a dram to tone himself down, or to increase the jollity according as he might desire. Did he feel sleepy, a dram was called in to hold him wide-a-wake. Did he feel too wide-a-wake, he required a dram to induce sleep. Did he drink so much at night that he had a headache in the morning he required "a hair more of the dog that bit him," and so on. Was there a birth in the family, the dram had to circulate to handsel the young Scot. The "kirstenin'" had equal honour awarded it. The "waddin'," the "lyke-wake," the "burial," the "foondin'," the "hoose-heatin'," the "foy," the "maiden," and dozens of inevitable occasions demanded that the "grey-beard" should be filled and emptied within a brief space of time. Did Sandy buy a cow, he "stood a dram;" did he sell a cow he did the same. There is an old woman still living in Dundee who some years ago actually went and took a dram to herself because her cat had died. It was called in to solder every bargain, and the "luck-penny," and the "arle-penny," and the "Queen's-shilling" demanded in the enlistment of every soldier, meant just so much money to be spent in drink which should be consumed on the spot. Not of "Tam o' Shanter" alone might it be said that "ilka melder wi' the miller he drank as lang as he had siller; that ilka naig was ca'd a shoe on, the smith an' he got roarin' fou on." Two friends could not meet and part in town or country but there had to be a dram both given and taken, or the one would have suspected the other of entertaining a grudge towards him. It was the unequivocal pledge of friendship, and "surely you'll be your pint-stoup, and surely I'll be mine," was the spirit principle of their social creed. Were quarrels made over the dram they had to be settled over it also—

"For aye the cheapest lawyer's fee

'S to pree the barrel."

In houses of quality, as late as the end of last century, it was the custom to keep a household officer, whose duty it was to prevent the drunk guests from choking. Old Henry Mackenzie, the author of *The Man of Feeling*, Lord Cockburn tells, was once at a festival at Kilravock Castle, towards the close of which the exhausted topers sank gradually back and down on their chairs, till little of them was seen above the table but their noses; at last they disappeared altogether and fell on the floor. Those who were too far gone lay still there from necessity; while those who, like the *Man of Feeling*, were glad of a pretence for escaping, fell into a dose from policy. While Mackenzie was in this state he was alarmed by feeling a hand working about his throat, and called out, when a voice answered, "Dinna be fear'd, sir; its me." "And who are you?" "I'm the lad that lowses the graavats."

It was employed, I have said, as the cure for all diseases, and the "saw for a' sairs;" and the practice finds apt illustration in the story of a schoolmaster who had been appointed to "teach the young idea" in a sparsely populated country district. Sallying forth one day soon after his settlement in the neighbourhood to spy out the land, and discover whether or not he was within a day's march of any person of intelligence, he came up, after walking about two miles, to a man breaking stones by the roadside. Interrogating the workman as to the amenities of the locality in general, the dominie proceeded to make enquiries in particular, and said—

"How far distant is the nearest minister?"

"Ou, about four mile," said the roadman.

"Indeed. And how far are we from a doctor?"

"Ten mile an' a bittock, e'en as the craw flees," replied the roadman.

"Dear me, that's very awkward. How do you do when anyone turns suddenly ill?"

"Ou, just gi'e him a gless o' whisky."

"But if a glass of whisky has not the desired effect; what then?"

"We just gi'e him anither ane."

"But if two does not set him right?"

"Weel, just gi'e him three."

"But if neither three nor four either will cure him?"

"Weel, then, fill him fou, and put him till his bed."

"Yes; but if filling him fou does not even suffice?"

"Weel, just lat him lie in his bed and drink until he's better."

"Yes, yes, my friend, but if whisky administered to him in any quantity will not cure him?"

"Ou, weel, then, sir," gravely replied the roadman, "if whisky winna cure a man, he's no worth curin', an' may weel be latten slip."

Oh, they had sublime confidence in the "dram" as a revivifying agent, and no mistake about it! Indeed, it was regarded in some quarters as a necessity to existence. And "be carefu' o' the mercies" was a stock phrase relating to it. The Highlander, content to pray for "a mountain of snuff," wanted "*oceans o' whisky.*" It was called in to act as "an eye-opener," and to serve also as "a night-cap."

So regularly had a certain Scotch laird used it in the latter capacity, that once in his lifetime—so he said himself—he "got an awfu' fricht." "We ran short o' the mercies," said he, "and I had to gang to my bed sober. I dinna feel ony the waur the day; *but, Lodsake, man, I got an awfu' fricht.*"

A well-known Scotch laird of the old school, Dean Ramsay tells us, expressed himself with great indignation when someone charged hard drinking with having actually *killed* people. "Na, na," said he; "I never knew onybody that was killed wi' drinking, but I hae kenned some that dee'd in the training."

So have we all, laird—a great many! And yet the students have been numerous and persistent. That Highlander who, when the minister shook his reverend head towards him, and said, "Whisky is a bad, bad thing, Donald," replied, "Ay, sir, especially *bad* whisky," thought, no doubt, that he had made a concession in opinion that would greatly mollify his clerical mentor. Many of your tipplers possessed a rough and ready wit, and from that fact no little humour has sprung. A Perthshire blacksmith, whom I myself knew intimately, was once remonstrated with by the Free Church minister who lived near by anent his frequent and excessive indulgences.

"Was ye ever drunk, sir?" inquired the smith.

"No, Donald," said the minister, "I am glad to say I never was."

"I thocht as muckle," said the smith; "for, man, if ye was ance richt drunk, ye wad never like to be sober a' your days again."

"There's death in the cup!" exclaimed a violent teetotal lecturer as he rushed up to where an old farmer was carefully toning his dram with water from a huge decanter. More of the *pura* had flowed forth than was intended, and eyeing his glass critically, "Hech, an' I think ye're richt, freend," was the response, "for *I've droon'd the miller.*"

"There is good whusky, and there is better whusky," said an old Highlander, "but there never yet was bad whusky." Many Lowlanders act as if they held the same opinion.

"You're just a sot, man, John," once said a wife to her tippling husband; "ye ha'e drucken a hoose in your time."

"Ah, weel, Kate, I think its been a thack ane," was the reply; "an' there's some o' the stoure in my throat yet."

"It's an awful thing that drink," exclaimed a clergyman, when the barber, who was visibly affected, had drawn blood from his face for the third time.

"Ay," replied the tonsorial artist, with a wicked leer in his eye, "it mak's the skin tender."

Told that whisky was a slow poison; "It maun be awfu' slow, then," said an old veteran, "for I've toothfu'd an' toothfu'd awa' at it this saxty year, an' I'm aye livin' yet."

Neil Gow honestly declared that, when in a certain condition, "it wasna the length o' the road, but the breadth o't," that bothered him. Another, "wha leeward whiles against his will" was taking "a bicker," on being asked by a passing acquaintance if he was getting home, eloquently replied in the word, "Whiles."

"You are reeling, Janet," remarked a country parson, meeting one of his parishioners carrying more sail than ballast, as a preliminary to lecturing her on the evils of her conduct.

"Troth, an' I canna aye be spinnin', sir," returned she, casting anchor in the middle of the road, and leering blandly up into the face of her interrogator.

"You do not seem to catch my meaning clearly, Janet," continued the divine. "Do you know where drunkards go?"

"Indeed, they generally gang whaur they get the whisky cheapest and best, sir."

"Yes, Janet, but there is another place where they go. They go where there is weeping and wailing and gnashing of teeth."

"Humph!" sneered the case-hardened old sinner. "They can gnash teeth that have teeth to gnash. I hav'na had but a'e stump this forty year."

A Perthshire village tradesman, recently deceased, as a rule "took a drappie mair than was gude for him" when he visited the county town. Indeed, he occasionally got "on the batter" and did not return home until after the lapse of several days. Returning from one of these "bouts" his wife met him in the door with the question, "Whaur ha'e ye been a' this time?"

"Perth," was the sententious reply.

"Perth!" echoed the wife. "An' what was ye doin' sae lang at Perth? Nae mortal man could be doin' gude stayin' in Perth for three hale days on end."

"Awa! an' no haiver, woman," was the dry reply; "plenty o' fouk stay a' their days in Perth an' do brawly."

The parish minister, in reproving this same character warned him that there would be a day of reckoning for it all yet. "I wish a day may do it, sir," said the immovable Peter, "it'll tak' a day an' a hauf I doubt. Deed, a day an' a hauf, sir, ilka minute o't," and leisurely moved on.

One festive old Scot recently visited another in the English capital. They had not met before for many years, and a good deal of hot water and sugar joined by a corresponding quantity of "barley bree" was stowed away within their waistcoats before it was considered that full justice had been done to the occasion. By this time the night was well advanced, and the visitor began to speak of making tracks for his hotel, when a cab was accordingly called and brought to the door. Now came the supreme moment of parting, and the host having led his friend by the arm in devious fashion to the head of the stair, halted and solemnly addressed him. "John," said he, "I winna gang doon the stair mysel' for fear I mayna get up again. I'm real gled to have seen you, and we've had a grand nicht. Good-nicht, John, good-nicht; and mind your feet on the stair. And John, hark ye! when ye gang oot at the door you'll see twa cabs, but tak' the first ane—the tither ane's no' there."

John M'Nab, though withal an industrious crofter, got "roarin' fou" every time he went to Perth, which was once a fortnight or so, and like every other person who so conducted himself, found always some excuse for his behaviour, however far-fetched it might be. John could not have a glass, as his wife said, but "a' the toon boot ken, for he was ane o' the singing kind, an' waukened a' the country-side."

On the morning which succeeded one of his periodical "bursts," the minister happening to pass just as John was watering the cow at the burn a little beyond the door of his house, saw, as he thought, in the incident a fine opportunity for improving the occasion.

"Ah, John," said he, "you see how Crummie does. She just drinks as much as will do her good, and not a drop more. You might take an example of the poor dumb brute."

"Ah," said John, "it's easy for her."

"Why more easy for her than you, John?"

"Oh, just because it is. Man, there's nae temptation in her case."

"Temptation, John? What do you mean?"

"Weel, you see, sir, it's no the love o' the drink a'thegether that gars a body get the waur o't. It's the conveeviality o' the thing that plays the plisky. Ye see, sir, ye meet a freend on the street, an' ye tak' him in to gie him a dram, an' ye crack awa' for a while, an' syne he ca's in a dram, an' there ye crack an' ye drink, an' ye drink an' ye crack, an' dod, ye just get fou afore ye ken whaur ye are. It's easy for Crummie, as I said, she has naebody to lead her aff her feet, as ye may say. She comes oot here an' tak's her drink, an' no anither coo says Crummie ye're there. But, certes, sir, had Dauvit Tamson's coo just come to the ither side o' the burn a meenit syne, an' as Crummie was takin' her first toothfu', had flappit hersel' doon on her hunkers an' said, 'Here's to ye, Crummie,' I'll eat my bonnet if she wadna hae flappit hersel' doon on her hunkers an' said, 'Here's to *you*, Hornie.' An' there the twa jauds wad hae sitten an' drunken until they were baith blind fou. I tell you again, sir, it's the conveeviality o' the thing that plays the plisky."

And yet there are instances to show that some of those old tipplers repented somewhat of their folly. The celebrated teetotaller, the Rev. Dr. Ritchie, of Potterrow, Edinburgh, once went to form a teetotal society at Peebles, and a man and wife who heard the speeches were conscience-smitten, and after they went home the wife said—

"'Od, John, I think we'll hae to set doon our names to that *thing* yet."

"We'll gang to anither o' the meetin's yet afore we decide," said the husband.

Next meeting showed the picture of a young man ruined by drink, and the two went forward at the close to set their names down.

"But are we never to taste it ava'?" they asked simultaneously.

"Never," quoth the minister, "*unless for a medicine.*"

Nothing daunted by this the old couple took the pledge, and went home, taking a bottle of whisky with them—the which Janet stowed away in the ben-house press to wait on cases of emergency. More than a fortnight elapsed before drink was again mentioned by one to the other, when one night John complained of an "awfu' pain in his stammack," and suggested that it might not be safe to go to bed without taking just half a glass or so.

"O, man, John, it's a pity ye hae been sae lang o' speakin'," said Janet, "for 'odsake, I've had sae mony o' thae towts mysel' this auchtdays that there's no a drap o' yon to the fore."

An old woman, who was a rigid total abstainer, was very ill. The doctor told the nurse that she must give her a little toddy the last thing at night. So when night came the nurse said to her patient, "The doctor says ye maun tak' some toddy." "Oh, no, no!" whined the poor old body; "it's against my principle." "But," remonstrated the nurse, "the doctor says ye maun tak' it." "Aweel," replied the old woman resignedly, "I suppose we maun use the means; but mak' it strong, and gar me tak' it—gar me tak' it."

Tam Forsyth was one of those who went from bad to worse with the dram, and never repented of his folly. One night in going home the breadth of the road fatigued him so, that, coming to a quiet corner, he lay down, and was soon fast asleep. Some young fellows finding him lying snoring, resolved to have some fun out of the reprobate, so they gently removed him to a dark cellar. Getting some phosphorus, they rubbed it on their own and Tam's hands and faces, and then awakened their victim. Tam seeing the state those around him were in, inquired, fearfully—

"Whaur am I?"

"Ye're dead," said one of the young men.

"Hoo lang have I been dead?"

"A fortnicht."

"An' are ye dead, too?"

"Yes."

"Hoo lang have you been dead?"

"Three weeks."

"Then," said Tam, without a tremour in his voice, "you'll be better acquaint here aboot than me: there's a shillin', skirt awa' roond an' see if ye can get hauf a mutchkin, for I'm as dry's a wooden leg."

I have remarked on how strongly the practice of dram-drinking had established itself in the social life of Scotland. It is *the* sore spot in our national character—a distinct characteristic (happily on the wane)—and the inducements to participation have been often novel and therefore humorous. Well-to-do individuals long ago frequently gave instructions to their relatives likely to survive them to be sure and have plenty of whisky at their funerals. A Montrose tradesman, feeling the near approach of his dissolution, signalled his wife to his bedside and very gravely said, "Ye'll get in a bottle o' whisky, Mary, for there's to be sad cheenge here this nicht."

The association of the "dram" with our marriage festivities has been happily hit off by Robert Buchanan in "The Wedding of Shon MacLean," where "every piper was fou—twenty pipers together;" but surely the stupidity, the folly, the humour of dram-drinking to excess was never better illustrated than by Burns in the tale of "Tam o' Shanter." To have attributed such hair-lifting experiences to any sober Carrick farmer, as he "frae Ayr a'e nicht did canter," would have been absurd, and the author knew it. Such a phantasmagoria of "warlocks and witches in a dance" could be patent only to the heated imagination of a "bletherin', blusterin', drunken blellum," such as the poet has represented his hero to have been.

Of whisky the poet has said—

> "It makes a man forget his woes,
>
> It heightens all his joys;
>
> It makes the widow's heart to sing
>
> Though the tears are in her eyes."

And so it does; but it reduces all who imbibe it for such effects, mentally to the level of the ring-tailed monkey, and makes them cut capers as fantastic as were ever performed by the most agile "Jacko." To this showing let our further illustrations here tend.

A West country farmer on a certain moonlight night, setting out towards home from the market town where he had sat too long and drunk too deep, had reached the burn near to his own house, attempting to cross which by the stepping-stones he missed his footing and came down with a splash into the burn. Unable to raise himself beyond his hands and knees, he looked down into the clear water, in which the moon was vividly reflected. In this position, and with the water streaming from his forelock and beard he began to shout to his wife. "Marget! Marget!"

The good woman heard and distinguished the well-known voice of her husband, and rushed out crying, "Ho, John! My, John! Is that you, John? Whaur are you, John?"

"Whaur am I?" rejoined the voice from the burn. "Gudeness kens whaur I am, Marget, but I see I'm far abune the mune."

A country laird on one occasion sent his gardener, John by name, to his cellar to bottle a barrel of whisky, and cautioned him at the same time to be sure and drink one whole glass of the liquor before starting to the work, or else the fumes might go to his head and seriously affect him. John was a careful man, generally speaking, so took extra precautions, though these were not attended with satisfactory results. Entering the cellar the laird was astonished to find his trusted retainer staggering about stupidly in the place.

"Ah, John, John," exclaimed the laird, "you have not acted on my advice, I fear, and taken a dram before starting."

"Dram be hang'd!" blurted out John. "It's no a bit o' use. I hae ta'en nearly a dizzen o' them, an' I'm gettin' aye the langer the waur."

A Forfarshire agriculturist, somewhat given to the dram, coming home one evening fully "three sheets to the wind," took a seat by the fire, and, what with the heat and the fumes of the whisky he had imbibed, he soon became sick, and possessed of an irresistible desire to turn himself inside out. At his feet sat a "coal baikie," which for the nonce was occupied by a brood of young ducklings that had been deserted by their foster mother, and for the sake of preservation had been brought into the kitchen and placed thus near the fire. Into this utensil our hero deposited the cause of his internal derangement. And his good wife appearing on the scene, observing but unobserved, a minute or two later, she found her husband peering critically down into the "baikie," and muttering to himself—

"Eh! megstie me. It surely canna be possible. I mind weel eneuch o' eating that cheese, an' (hic) thae biscuits, an' the beef. An' I mind perfectly weel o' suppin' thae (hic) kail, an' the barley amon' them; but, in the name o' a' that's wonderfu', whaur in a' the world did I get (hic) thae young deucks!"

He learned next morning, doubtless, on the deafest side of his head.

Even so stern an institution as total abstinence (?) has its humorous side:—

An old "wifie," who had a weakness for whisky, had been prevailed upon to take the pledge.

Shortly afterwards she called upon a rather "drouthie neebor," who was not aware of her visitor's reformation.

The bottle was at once, as usual, produced, and the recent convert to total abstinence was sorely tempted.

She made, however, a gallant effort to remain true to principle, and, holding up deprecating hands, she said, "Na, thank ye, Mrs. Mitchell, I've ta'en the pledge. I have made a solemn vow not to pit han' or lip to gless again."

But then, seeing Mrs. Mitchell was about to remove the spirits, she hesitatingly said, "I daur say if you wad put a wee drappie in a *tea-cup* I could maybe tak' it."

A young countryman went a considerable distance to pay a visit to his uncle and aunt and cousins, who were reputed a family of strict teetotallers. During his first meal at his kinsman's table the young man commented on the absence of spirituous liquors.

"We are a' temperance folk here, ye ken," interrupted the old man. "No spirituous liquors are allowed to enter this house."

After dinner the old man went up stairs to take his customary "forty winks," the girls started off to Sunday School, and the boys lounged away to smoke in the stable. As soon as Aunt Betty found herself alone in the kitchen she put her initial finger to her lips, to enjoin silence on the part of her youthful nephew, and going to a dark nook in the pantry she drew therefrom a little black bottle, and filling a glass held it out to him, and said—

"Here, John, tak' a taste o' that. Our gudeman's sic a strict teetotaller that I daurna let him ken that I keep a wee drap in the hoose—just for medicine. So dinna mention it."

A few minutes later the old man cried from the stairhead, "Are you there, John?"

The nephew went upstairs, when the head of the house took him to his own bedroom, where he promptly produced a gallon-jar of whisky from an old portmanteau under the bed, and pouring out a hearty dram, said—

"Teetotalin' doesna prevent me frae keepin' a wee drap o' the 'rale peat reek' in case o' illness, or that; so here, lad, put ye that in your cheek; but (confidentially) not a word aboot it to your auntie, or the laddies."

Strolling out of doors soon after this second surprise, and entering the stable, the cousins beckoned their relative into the barn, where, after fumbling among the straw for a few seconds, they handed him a black bottle, with the encouraging words—

"Tak' a sook o' that, cousin, ye'll find it gude; but not a word to the old fouks, mind, for twa mair infatuated teetotallers were never born."

I have said that our drinking customs have made us the butt of the foreign "jokist." Here is the proof, in the following clever skit—a burlesque report of the celebration of St. Andrew's Day in Calcutta—which appeared some years ago in the columns of the *Indian Daily News*, under the title of—

### YE CHRONICLE OF SAINT ANDREW.

1. It came to pass in the year one thousand eight hundred and four score and one, in the City of Palaces, dwelt certain wise men from a far country beyond the great sea.

2. (In that year the rulers of the city did that which was right in their own eyes).

3. Now these wise men assembled themselves together, and they said one to the other, Go to, let us remember our brethren whom we have left.

4. For, behold, we be in a far country, and it shall come to pass that men shall say to us, Ye be nameless on the earth; ye have fled from the land of your nativity, because the land of your nativity is poor.

5. This thing, therefore, will we do; we will make a great feast, so that the nose of whomsoever smelleth it shall tingle, and we will call to mind the ancient days and the mighty deeds of our fathers.

6. So they appointed a day, and many were gathered together—a mixed multitude from the Land of Cakes and of Thistles, from the West and from the North, and from the Isles of the Sea.

7. And, behold, a great feast was prepared, and men in white raiment ministered unto them, and a ruler of the feast was appointed, and set in the midst.

8. And forthwith to each man was given a writing of the good things of the feast, and the writing was in a tongue no man could understand, for the language was the language of the *Crapaud*, which signifieth in the heathen tongue, a frog.

9. And some there were who pretended to know the writing, and the interpretation thereof; now these were hypocrites; for they knew but six

letters of the writing, and those letters were **HAGGIS**, and even this much was a great mystery.

10. And the dishes no man could number; the people ate mightily, as it were the space of one hour. And no man spoke to his neighbour till his inner man was comforted.

11. And while they ate, behold there drew near three mighty men of valour, clothed in many-coloured garments; and they bore in their arms musical instruments shaped like unto a beast of prey.

12. And they blew mightily upon what seemed the tail thereof, and straightway came there forth shrieks and sounds as if it were the howlings of the damned.

13. And the hearts of the people were comforted, for this is that wherein their great strength lieth.

14. And wine was brought in vessels, but the children of the North would have none of these; for they quenched their thirst with the Dew of the Mountain, which is the water of fire.

15. Then spake the wise men of the congregation unto them, and called to mind the ancient days and mighty deeds of their fathers. And the people rejoiced exceedingly.

16. Now it came to pass when they had eaten and drunk greatly, even unto the full, that the hinges of their tongues were loosened—yea, even the joints of their knees.

17. And the ruler of the feast fled to his home, and a third part of the multitude followed, and a third part remained, saying, We thirst; and a third part rose up to play.

18. And they played after the fashion of their country, and their movements resembled the peregrinations of a hen upon a girdle which is hot. Yet they seemed to think it pleasant, for they shouted with joy.

19. Now, as for them that were athirst, behold, their drinking was steady, but their limbs were not so; yea, they also shouted for joy and sang amazingly.

20. And they answered one to another, and said that, notwithstanding the crowing of the cock or the dawning of the day, they should still partake of the juice of the barley. So they encouraged one another with these words.

21. Now it came to pass that, as they sat, one came and said he had seen a strange fire in the sky, but what it was he could not tell.

22. And some said, It is the moon; and others said, It is the sun; and some said, Doth the sun rise in the west? and others said, This is not the west, but the east; and some said, Which is it, for we perceive two in the sky.

23. And one said, I see nothing. Now the name of that man was Blin' Foo. He was the son of Fill Foo, and his mother's name was Haud Foo; and his brethren—Bung Foo, Sing Foo, Greet Foo, and Dam Foo—were speechless.

24. Then each man bade his neighbour farewell, embracing and vowing eternal friendship, and some were borne home by men in scanty raiment, and others in carriages which jingled as they went; and others drove their own chariots home, and saw many strange sights, for they found grass growing and ditches in the midst of the way where they had not perceived them before.

25. And it came to pass that in the morning many lamented, and took no breakfast that day; and the men in white raiment brought unto them many cunningly-devised drinks, yea, pick-me-ups, for their tongues clove unto the roofs of their mouths, and the spittle on their beard was like unto a small silver coin, even a sixpence.

26. But, when they thought on the previous day, they rejoiced again, for they said, Our brethren whom we have left will hear of it at the Feast of the New Year, and they will remember us and bless us, and our hearts and hands shall be strengthened for our labour here.

That is quite delicious! And now we will allow George Outram to close the chapter with his inimitable poem:—

DRINKIN' DRAMS,

OR, "THE TIPPLER'S PROGRESS."

He ance was holy

An' melancholy,

Till he fand the folly

O' singin' psalms;

He's now as red's a rose,

An' there's pimples on his nose,

An' in size it daily grows,
By drinkin' drams.


He ance was weak,
An' couldna eat a steak
Without gettin' sick,
An' takin' qualms;
But now he can eat
O' ony kind o' meat,
For he's got an appeteet,
By drinkin' drams.

He ance was thin,
Wi' a nose like a pen,
An' hands like a hen,
An' nae hams;
But now he's roond an' ticht,
An' a deevil o' a wicht,
For he's got himsel' put richt
By drinkin' drams.

He ance was saft as dirt,
An' as pale as ony shirt,
An' as useless as a cart
Without the trams;
But now he'd face the deil,
Or swallow Jonah's whale—
He's as gleg's a puddock's tail,
Wi' drinkin' drams.

Oh! pale, pale was his hue,

An' cauld, cauld was his broo,
An' he grumbled like a ewe
'Mang libbit rams;
But now his broo is bricht,
An' his een are orbs o' licht,
An' his nose is just a sicht,
Wi' drinkin' drams.

He studied mathematics,
Logic, ethics, hydrostatics,
Till he needed diuretics
To lowse his dams;

But now, without a lee,
He could mak' anither sea,
For he's left philosophy,
An' ta'en to drams.

He fand that learning, fame,
Gas, philanthropy, an' steam,
Logic, loyalty, gude name,
Were a' mere shams;
That the source o' joy below,
An' the antidote to woe,
An' the only proper go,
Was drinkin' drams.

It's true that he can see
Auld Nick, wi' gloatin' e'e,
Just waitin' till he dee
'Mid frichts an' dwams;

But what's Auld Nick to him,
Or palsied tongue or limb,
Wi' glass filled to the brim,
When drinkin' drams.

# CHAPTER VIII
## THE THISTLE AND THE ROSE

Fifty years ago native opinion generally would, I believe, have corroborated the statement of the inspired *Shepherd* of the "Noctes," that "the Englishers are the noblest race o' leevin' men—except the Scotch." That very decided compliment, notwithstanding, however; and even although nowadays so many Scotchmen are fain to emulate the Cockney speech and fashion in all things, it is putting the case in the mildest terms to say that, up to and even beyond the period indicated, there had never been much love lost between the denizens of the sister nations, Scotland and England. On all pre-eminent occasions, subsequent to the Union, to the credit of both be it often told, their cherished antipathies—trifles mayhap at the best—have magnanimously been allowed to lapse for the time being, and "shoulder to shoulder, knee to knee," John Bull and Sandy Cawmil, aided and abetted at all times by their brow-beaten half-brother Paddy, have presented a brave and unbroken front of steel to the enemies of their United Kingdoms. But, the conflicts over—the sword sheathed—the old animosity, the chronic jealousy, has again and again manifested itself between the Thistle and the Rose. Into the causes of this little estrangement in friendly feeling which so long obtained, but has now almost entirely disappeared, though some of them are obvious, we shall not trouble ourselves here particularly to inquire, but will rather review some of their effects as they are illustrated in the records of the many witty skirmishes which have taken place here and there between them, and in which the Thistle has fairly justified its popular motto of "*Nemo me impune lacessit*!" Yes! and surely it is remarkable—is an extraordinary circumstance, indeed, when viewed in the light of the fact that the English deny to the Scotch any idea of wit—that in nearly every witty encounter that has taken place between them Sandy has had the best of it. They are "a noble race o' leevin' men," as the *Shepherd* averred. But, no, blustering John Bull is no match for canny Sandy Cawmil. He would have delighted in coercing him—would have given his right hand to have been able to say, "Sandy, *you must*." But, as the late David Kennedy, the Scottish singer, used to put it, when introducing the song of "Scots wha hae," "*must* was buried at Bannockburn." And thenceforth, whilst strife with the sword had ceased between them, "a wordy war"—a war of wit and ridicule—long obtained instead. It has been a favourite sarcasm of John that the finest view in all Scotland to the eye of the Scot is the road that leads from it into England. To which Sandy has made the withering reply, "There's nae doot, John, a hantle o' us hae fund oor way to Lunnon, but it's been gude for you as it's been gude for us, for everybody kens ye wad be *puir things withoot's*." Notable features in the characteristics of the two are these, that each has been inclined to over-estimate himself and to under-estimate his neighbour. In the opinion of many a living London Cockney, a Scotsman is a being only slightly superior to a Red Indian savage. 'Arry entertains in all seriousness the conviction that every home-bred Scotsman is red-headed; and that we all wear kilts, play on the bagpipes, drink whisky *ad lib.*, snuff, and feed exclusively on kail-brose and bannocks of barley meal. Sandy, on the other hand, has regarded himself individually as the ideal *man*—the noblest work of his Creator—and has declared the English to be "maybe no sae very bad considerin', but even at the best neither mair nor less than a parcel o' upsettin', ignorant, pock-puddin's." It has been English money in general, but Scotch brains in particular, he has asserted time and again, that have made London what it is. "All the brightest intellectual luminaries of your London firmament," he has told John Bull, "have been nursed and reared amid the hills o' Bonnie Scotland."

"What of Shakespeare?" John has asked. "You don't claim him as a Scotchman, do you?"

"No; oh no," Sandy has replied, "I'll no say that Shakespeare was a Scotchman; although the way ye brag o' him ye seem to think he was maist clever eneuch to be ane."

And as in the opinion of the typical Scotsman there is no man to equal a Scotsman, so there is to his mind no land on earth like his own Scotland. He may have wandered far away from it, but distance only made his heart grow fonder, and lent enchantment to the view. And, as almost every Scotsman is a poet, if he took to sing its praises he would do so with such enthusiasm as is revealed in these lines:—

> "Land of chivalry and of freedom,
>
> Land of old traditional fame,
>
> May thy noble sons and daughters
>
> Long uphold thy honoured name.
>
> Land where foreign foe ne'er ventured,
>
> Land where tyrant never trod,
>
> Land whose sons are ever foremost,
>
> Treading nobly life's high road.
>
> Land of simple-hearted kindness,
>
> Land of patriotic worth,
>
> May thy virtues ever flourish,

> Hardy clansmen of the North!
>
> Land where rest in silent chambers
> Ashes of our honoured sires,
> May their memories long be cherished
> Round our humble cottage fires."

To the critical eye of John Bull the scene would appear different; and could he have sung as pithily in the vernacular speech of Auld Scotland, his vocal description would have been thus severely censorious—

> "Land of ancient bloody tyrants,
> Sneaking traitors deep and sly;
> Land of thieving 'Heclan' teevils,'
> Kilted rogues and stolen kye.
>
> Land o' bribes and kirks and bastards,
> Saints and lasses awfu' frail.
> Drunkards, shebeens, godly deacons,
> Parritch, thistles, brose, and kail.
>
> Land o' canny, carefu' bodies—
> Foes to a' ungodly fun;
> Those wha sum up man's whole duty—
> Heaven, hell, and *number one*.
>
> Land of droning psalms and sermons,
> Pauky wit and snuffy bores;
> Fair fa'n chields so fond o' country
> That they leave it fast in scores."

And when each had had his fling the true account would be found about midway between the two. But, oh! John did like to get a hair in Sandy's neck; and does so still. Nothing delighted Dr. Johnson, the eminent lexicographer, more. He had the meanest opinion of the Scotch, it is well known, and never missed an opportunity of casting ridicule upon them. Thus, when compiling his famous Dictionary, he defined the word *oats* as "food for men in Scotland and for horses in England." The definition afforded unmixed delight to the English mind, until, by and by, it was "cast in the teeth" of a witty Scottish Lord, who retorted with—

"Yes; and where will you find such men and such horses?"

Since then, the fun of it has not been quite so apparent. But the Doctor frequently met his match, and got paid back in his own coin. Soon after his return from Scotland to London, a Scotch lady resident in the capital invited him to dinner, and in compliment to her distinguished guest ordered a dish of hotch-potch. When the great man had tasted it, she asked him if it was good, to which he replied, with his usual gruffness, "Very good for hogs, I believe!"

"Then, pray," said the lady, "let me help you to a little more;" and she did.

Of course John Bull had never been loquacious to any great extent on the subject of Bannockburn; and Sandy, I suppose, remembering Flodden, has not reminded him too frequently of the incident. Occasions have arisen, however, when enlightenment was necessary. Thus, when, many years ago, a little company of Englishmen were travelling by railway between Glasgow and Stirling, having an old Scotchman and his wife as fellow-travellers, the weather being wet, they abused the Scottish climate, "the doocid weathaw, you know," and everything Scotch to their hearts' content. Latterly one of them asserted that "no Englishman could ever settle down in such a region." By this time the train was emerging from Larbert station, and—

"Nae Englishman sattle doon in this region?" echoed the old Scotsman, who had hitherto not spoken. "Toots, man, ye're haiverin' nonsense. I'll let ye see a pairt alang the line-side a bit here, whaur a gey wheen o' yer countrymen cam' mair than five hunder year syne, and they're no thinkin' o' leavin't yet, tho' they maun be gey weel *sattled doon* by this time."

"Where is that?" asked several of the Englishmen at once.

"Bannockburn!" replied the Scot, and "silence deep as death" fell on the little company.

A similar reminder was more delicately given when two English tourists a few years ago visited the scene of what has been aptly termed "the best day's work ever performed in Scotland." A local cartwright pointed out with intelligence the positions of the contending armies; the stone where Bruce's standard was fixed, and other features of interest; and the visitors before leaving pressed their informant's acceptance of a small money gratuity.

"Na, na," replied the native with noticeable pride, "put up yer siller, I'll hae nane o't. *It's cost ye eneuch already.*"

Speaking of Flodden, Sir Walter Scott was wont to tell a good story of a Scotch blacksmith whom he had formerly known as a horse doctor, and whom he found at a small country town South of the Border, practising medicine among the natives, with a reckless use of "lowdomar and calomy," and who apologised for the mischief he might do by the assurance that it "would be a lang time afore it *made up for Flodden!*"

Nothing galls the national pride of the true-blue Scot more than the liberties that have been taken with that article of the Union which expressly declared that Britain should be the only recognised designation of the United Kingdoms of Scotland and England. The Queen of England, the English Ambassador, the English army, the English fleet, and similar expressions still in common use, despite the courageous and persistent protests of the Rev. David Macrae, and others, are therefore terms particularly offensive to a sensitive Scottish ear. A striking instance of this feeling occurred at the Battle of Trafalgar. Two Scotsmen, messmates and bosom cronies, from the same little clachan, happened to be stationed near each other when the now celebrated signal was given from the Admiral's ship—*England expects every man to do his duty.*

"No a word o' puir Auld Scotland on this occasion," dolefully remarked Geordie to Jock.

Jock cocked his eye a moment, and turning to his companion—

"Man, Geordie," said he, "Scotland kens weel eneuch that nae bairn o' hers needs to be tell't to do his duty—*that's just a hint to the Englishers.*"

A North country drover once, returning homewards, after a somewhat unsuccessful journey to the South, was, in consequence, not in very good humour with the "Englishers." On reaching Carlisle he saw a notice stuck up offering a certain sum to any one who could do a piece of service to the community by officiating as executioner of the law on a noted criminal then under sentence of death. Sandy herein perceived an opportunity of making up for his bad market; and comforted and encouraged that he was a perfect stranger in the town, he undertook the office, hanged the rogue, and got the fee. When moving off with the money, he was twitted with being a mean, beggarly Scot, doing for money what no Englishman would.

"'Deed," replied Sandy, with a wicked leer in his eye, "I would hang ye a' at the same price."

A Scotch family lately removed to London, wished to have a sheep's head prepared as they were accustomed to it at home, and sent a servant to the butcher's to procure one. She was a Scotch lassie, and on entering the shop—

"My gude man," said she to the butcher, "I want a sheep's head."

"There's plenty of them there," said he; "choose which you will."

"Na," said she, "but there's nane o' thae that will do; I want a sheep's head that will sing" (singe).

"Go, you idiot," said the butcher, "who ever heard of a sheep's head that could sing?"

"Why," replied the girl in wrath, "an' it's you it's the eedyit, I'm thinkin'; for ony sheep's head in Scotland can sing; but I jalouse yer English sheep are just as grit fules as their owners, and they can do naething as they ocht."

A Scotch gentleman, visiting some friends in England, displayed in conversation such contempt for the memory of England's most illustrious sons that one of the family resolved to pay him off in his own coin. He therefore took down a steel engraving of John Knox, which adorned the dining-room wall, and hung it up in a lumber room. The Scotsman, missing the picture, asked what had become of it. "We no longer consider your Reformer worthy of a place here," said his friend, "therefore we have hung him up in a dark closet."

"You could not have done better," said the Scotsman. "I consider the situation very appropriate; for if ever a man could throw light on a dark subject, that was the man."

Another Scot being in England at the time the nightingales were in song, was invited by his host one evening to come and hear one singing. As the nightingale is never heard in Scotland it was considered this would prove a rare treat to the Scotsman. After listening for a considerable time to the beautiful melody, and becoming somewhat impatient at hearing no expression of surprise or pleasure from his Scottish guest, the Englishman asked if he was not delighted. "It's a' very gude," replied the canny Scot, "but I wadna gie the *wheeple o' a whaup* for a' the nightingales that ever sang!"

Shortly after the accession of James I., when Scotch gentlemen were beginning to feel a little more at home than formerly in London, Lord Harewood gave a dinner party, to which there were invited a large number of courtiers and officers—both civil and military. The feast was ended, and with the flow of wine the company prepared for a corresponding flow of wit and jollity. After the bottle had circulated a few times, and the spirits of the assembly had begun to rise, General S——, an English trooper of fame, and a reckless *bon vivant*, arose and said, "Gentlemen, when I am in my cups, and the generous wine begins to warm my blood, I have an absurd custom of railing against the Scotch. Knowing my weakness, I hope no gentleman of the company will take it amiss."

He sat down, and a Highland chief, Sir Robert Bleakie, of Blair Athol, presenting a front like an old battle-worn tower, quietly arose in his place, and with the utmost simplicity and good-nature remarked, "Gentlemen, I, when I am in my cups, and the generous wine begins to warm my blood, if I hear a man rail against the Scotch, have an absurd custom of kicking him at once out of the company. Knowing my weakness, I hope no gentleman of the company will take it amiss."

It need scarcely be added that General S— did not on that occasion suffer himself to follow his usual custom.

And despite the heavy odds against him there have yet been times when Sandy stood in high favour in high quarters in the English capital. Thus in the year 1797, when the Democratic notions ran high, the King's coach was attacked as His Majesty was going to the House of Peers. A gigantic Hibernian on that occasion was conspicuously loyal in repelling the mob. Soon after, to his no small surprise, he received a message from Mr. Dundas to attend at his office. He went, and met with a gracious reception from the great man, who, after passing a few encomiums on his active loyalty, desired him to point out any way in which he would wish to be advanced, His Majesty having particularly noticed his courageous conduct, and being desirous to reward it. Pat scratched and scraped for a while, as if thunderstruck—

"The devil take me if I know what I'm fit for."

"Nay, my good fellow," cried Henry, "think a moment, and do not throw yourself out of the way of fortune."

Pat hesitated another moment, then smirking as if some odd idea had taken hold of his noddle, he said—"I tell yez what, mister, make a Scotchman of me, and, by St. Patrick, there'll be no fear of my getting on."

The Minister gazed a while at the *mal-apropos* wit—"Make a Scotsman of you, sir, that is impossible, for I cannot give you prudence."

Prudence is just what Paddy has always lacked, and what to all appearance he is never to learn. Had it been a special characteristic of John Bull, it would have saved him from many a *coup* he has received at the instance of his cautious and calculating brother Sandy, the following among the rest. A stout English visitor to one of the fashionable watering-places on the West Coast some years ago was in the habit of conversing familiarly with Donald Fraser, a character of the place, who took delight in talking boastfully of his great relations, who existed only, the stranger suspected, in the Highlander's own lively imagination. One day, as the Englishman was seated at the door of his lodging, Donald came up driving a big fat boar.

"One of your relations, I suppose, Donald?" exclaimed the visitor, chuckling, and nodding his head in the direction of the "porker."

"No," quietly retorted Donald, surveying the proportions of his interlocutor, "no relation at all, sir, but just an acquaintance, *like yoursel'*."

"My late esteemed friend, Mr. John Mackie, M.P. for Kirkcudbrightshire," writes the garrulous and entertaining author of *Reminiscences of Fifty Years*, "used to describe an extensive view which one of his friend's hills commanded. This he never failed to call to the attention of his English visitors when the weather was clear. Willy the shepherd was always the guide on such occasions, as he knew precisely the weather that would suit.

"One forenoon an English friend was placed under Willy's charge to mount the hill in order to enjoy the glorious view. 'I am told, shepherd, you are going to show me a wonderful view.' 'That's quite true, sir.' 'What shall I see?' 'Weel, ye'll see a feck o' kingdoms—the best o' sax, sir.' 'What the deuce do you mean, shepherd?' 'Weel, sir, I mean what I say.' 'But tell me all about it.' 'I'll tell you naething mair, sir, until we're at the tap o' the hill.' The top reached, Willy found everything he could desire in regard to a clear atmosphere. 'Noo, sir, I houp ye've got guid een?' 'Oh, my eyes are excellent.' 'Then, that's a' richt, sir. Noo, div you see yon hills awa' yonder?' 'Yes, I do.' 'Weel, sir, those are the hills o' Cumberland, and Cumberland's in the kingdom o' England; that's a'e kingdom. Noo, sir, please keep coont. Then, sir, I maun noo trouble you to look ower yonder. Div ye see what I mean?' 'I do.' 'That's a' richt. That's the Isle o' Man, and that was a kingdom and sovereignty in the families of the Earls o' Derby and the Dukes o' Athol frae the days o' King David o' Scotland, if ye ken onything o' Scotch history.' 'You are quite right, shepherd.' 'Quite richt, did you say; I wadna ha'e brocht ye here, sir, if I was to be wrang. Weel, that's twa kingdoms. Be sure, sir, to keep coont. Noo, turn awee aboot. Div ye see yon land yonder? It's a bit farrer, but never mind that, sae lang as ye see it.' 'I see it distinctly.' 'Weel, that's a' I care aboot. Noo, sir, keep coont, for that's Ireland, and mak's three kingdoms; but there's nae trouble aboot the neist, for ye're stannin' on't—I mean Scotland. Weel, that mak's four kingdoms; div you admit that, sir?' 'Yes, that makes four, and you have two yet to show me.' 'That's true, sir, but dinna be in sic a hurry. Weel, sir, just look up aboon yer head, and this is by far the best o' a' the Kingdoms: that, sir, aboon, is Heaven. That's five: and the saxth kingdom is that doon below yer feet, to which, sir, I houp ye'll never gang; but that's a point on which I canna speak wi' ony certainty.'"

I have said that the Scotch and English are each inclined to over-estimate themselves and under-estimate their neighbours; but to this should be added the fact, that the canny craftiness of Sandy—his characteristic prudence—has shown him how much he might gain by familiarising himself with all John's ways, and this he has done, whereas John has thought it sufficient to assume a knowledge of Sandy's affairs, even although he possessed it not. And this contemptuous assumption of knowledge has led to some sublime blundering on John's part. We scarcely expect our Cockney brethren to be familiar with our Northern tongue, or even to have very much sympathy with it. Yet, while they actually do not know it, and readily express contempt for it, they still continue to affect a knowledge, and so, to apply a well-known Irishism, "seldom open their mouth on the subject but they put their foot in it." Thus, not very long ago, one Cockney told another that he had learned a beautiful Scotch song, and would write out for him a copy of the words. The song was, "The Lass o' Gowrie," and the first two lines came from his pen as follows:—

"'Twas on a summer's afternoon,

A *week* before the sun went doon."

The prospect of such a long continued spell of daylight in Scotland proved too much for the risible susceptibilities of the party who looked over the writer's shoulder, and the pen had to be thrown aside, amid a roar of laughter. Not many years ago I myself saw the printed programme of a London Scottish concert, an item in which appeared as

"Ye Banks and *Brays* of Bonnie Doon,"

and I thought what an *ass* he must have been who prepared the "copy"! *Punch*—I think it was *Punch*—once made one Scotsman threaten to give another "A richt gude Willie-waucht in the side o' the head." Great dubiety existed in the London journalistic mind some time ago about the signification of the phrase, "The Land o' the Leal,"—was it the poetical designation of Scotland, or Heaven? "Old long since ago," and "Scots with him" are Anglicised Scotticisms as familiar as proverbs. But surely the very funniest results from Cockney intermeddling with things Scotch that ever appeared are to be found in a cheap edition of Burns's poems, which was issued some time since by John Dicks, the well-known Strand publisher. From this copy it is made apparent that Tam o' Shanter was not the hero of Burns's humorous masterpiece at all, but one Tam Skelpit—*vide* the following lines:—

"Tam Skelpit on through mud and mire,

Despising wind and rain and fire."

Then the family name of the householder immortalised in the "Cottar's Saturday night," according to this Cockney edition, was not Burns, as is popularly believed in Scotland, but *Hafflins*. The revelation appears in these lines:—

"The wily mother sees the conscious flame

Sparkle in Jenny's e'e and flush her cheek,

Wi' heart-struck anxious care inquires his name;

While Jenny Hafflins is afraid to speak;

Weel pleased the mother hears it's nae wild, worthless rake."

Tam Skelpit and Jenny Hafflins! My conscience! What next? Well, a cursory glance finds such improved readings as these (I will italicise the improvements):—

"The heapit *happier's* ebbing still."

"I held *awe* to Annie."

"They reeled, they set, they crossed, they *cleckit*."

"And *well* tak' a cup o' kindness yet."

"Or wake the bosom-*smelting* throe."

And there are many other blunders quite as ludicrous. Experience is a severe school, and when the Scotch becomes the universal tongue John Bull will perceive this; but perhaps not before.

A very humorous instance of the almost incomprehensibility of things Scotch by the English mind occurred during one of the earlier visits of the Royal Family to Balmoral. The late Prince Consort, dressed in a simple manner, was crossing one of the Scottish lochs in a steamer, and was curious to note everything relating to the management of the vessel, and, among other things, the cooking. Approaching the galley, where a brawny Scot was attending to the culinary matters, he was attracted by the savoury odours of a dish of hotch-potch which Sandy was preparing.

"What is that?" asked the Prince, who was not known to the cook.

"Hotch-potch, sir," was the reply.

"How is it made?" was the next question.

"Weel, there's mutton intill't, and neeps intill't, and carrots intill't, and——"

"Yes, yes," said the Prince, "but *what* is intill't?"

"Weel, there's mutton intill't, and neeps intill't, and——"

"Yes, I see; but what *is* intill't?"

The man looked at him, and, seeing that the Prince was serious he replied—

"There's mutton intill't, and neeps intill't, and——"

"Yes, certainly, I know," still argued the Prince; "but what is *intill't—intill't?*"

"Gudesake, man," yelled the Scotsman, brandishing his big ladle, "am I no thrang tellin' ye what's intill't? There's mutton intill't, and——"

Here the interview was brought to a close by one of the Prince's suite, who fortunately was passing, explaining to His Royal Highness that "intill't" simply meant "into it," and nothing more!

An incident of a somewhat similar nature, and even more humoursome than the above, which was happily paraphrased by the late Robert Leighton, the Scottish poet, under the title of "Scotch Words," occurred to an English gentlewoman, a number of years ago, in the course of a brief tour "here awa'." One night she rested at a respectable inn in a country village, and on being shown to her bedroom by the rustic chambermaid, the question was put to her—

"Would you like to have a het crock in your bed this cauld nicht, mem?"

"A what?" asked the lady.

"A pig, mem. Shall I put a pig in your bed to keep you warm?"

"Leave the room, young woman!" was the indignant response, "your mistress shall hear of your insolence."

"Nae offence, mem," insisted the lassie, "it was my mistress that bad me speir: and I'm sure she meant it a' in kindness."

The lady looked in the girl's face, and now satisfied that no insult was intended, said, in a milder tone, "Is it common in this country, my girl, for ladies to have pigs in their beds?"

"Ay, and gentlemen ha'e them too, mem, when the weather's cauld."

"But you would not surely put the pig between the sheets?"

"If you please, mem, it would do maist gude there."

"Between the sheets? It would dirty them, girl. I could never sleep with a pig between the sheets."

"Nae fear o' that, mem! You'll sleep far mair comfortable. I'll steek the mouth o't tightly, and tie it up in a poke."

"Do you sleep with a pig yourself in cold weather?"

"Na, mem, pigs are only for gentry like yersel' wha lie on feather beds."

"How do you sleep, then?"

"My neebor lass and I just sleep on cauf."

"What! you sleep with a calf between you?"

"Ou, no, mem, ye're jokin' noo. We lie on the tap o't."

When the two came to perfectly understand each other history deponeth not.

Dean Ramsay tells an amusing story of a Stirlingshire farmer's visit to a son, engaged in business in Liverpool. The son finding the father rather *de trop* in his office, one day, persuaded him to cross the ferry over the Mersey, and inspect the harvesting, then in full operation, on the Cheshire side. On landing, he approached a young woman reaping with the sickle in a field of oats, when the following dialogue ensued:—

*Farmer*—"Lassie, are yer aits muckle bookit the year?"

*Reaper*—"Sir?"

*Farmer*—"I am speirin' gif yer aits are muckle bookit the year?"

*Reaper* (in amazement)—"I really don't know what you are saying, sir."

*Farmer* (in equal astonishment)—"Gude—save—us—do ye no understand gude plain English? Are—yer—aits—muckle—bookit?"

He might as well have asked the road to Stronachlacher, Auchtermuchty, Ecclefechan, or Ponfeigh. The reaper decamped to her nearest companion declaring him a madman; while the farmer shouted in great wrath, "They are naething else than a set o' ignorant pock-puddin's."

"My girl," enquired a Cockney tourist of a Scotch lassie whom he met tripping lightly barefoot, "is it the custom for girls to go barefooted in these parts?"

"Pairtly they do," she replied, "and pairtly they mind their ain business."

"My girl," enquired a Cockney tourist of a Scotch lassie whom he met tripping lightly barefoot, "is it the custom for girls to go barefooted in these parts?" "Pairtly they do," she replied, "and pairtly they mind their ain business."

The dour, plodding, persevering nature of the Scot, by virtue of which he has often prevailed over his less crafty English brother, is well exemplified in the following little narrative, which humorously describes the opening of a large mercantile business between the West of Scotland and the English capital:—

A West country Scot, who had engaged in the manufacture of a certain description of goods, then recently introduced into that part of the country, found it necessary, or conjectured it might be profitable, to establish a permanent connection with some respectable house in London. With this design he packed up a quantity of goods, equipped himself for the journey, and departed. Upon his arrival he made diligent enquiry as to those who were likely to prove his best customers, and accordingly proceeded to call upon one of the most opulent drapers, with whom he resolved to establish a regular correspondence. When Saunders entered the shop in question he found it crowded with customers, and the salesmen all bustling about making sales, and displaying their wares to prospective purchasers. Saunders waited what he considered a reasonable time, then in a lull of the business, laid down his pack, his bonnet, and staff, upon the counter, and enquired for "the head o' the hoose."

One of the clerks asked him what he wanted.

"I'm wantin' to see gin he wants ocht in my line," was the answer.

"No!" shouted the foreman.

"Will ye no tak' a look o' the gudes, sir?" inquired Saunders.

"No, not at all; I have not time. Take them away."

"Ye'll maybe find them worth your while; and I dootna but ye'll buy," said Saunders, as he coolly proceeded to untie his pack.

"Go away, go away!" was reiterated half a dozen times with great impatience, but the persevering Scotsman still persisted.

"Get along, you old Scotch fool," cried the foreman, completely out of temper, as he pushed the already exposed contents of the pack off the counter. "Get along!"

Saunders looked up in the individual's face with a wide mouth and enlarged pair of eyes, then looked down to his estate that lay scattered among his feet, looked up again, and exclaimed—"And will ye no buy ocht? But ye dinna ken, for ye haena seen the gudes," and so saying he proceeded to replace them on the counter.

"Get out of the shop, sir!" was the peremptory and angry command which followed this third appeal.

Saunders, with great gravity and self-possession, said—"Are ye in earnest, freend?"

"Yes, certainly," was the reply, which was succeeded by an unequivocal proof of sincerity on the part of the person who made it, when he picked up Saunders's bonnet and whirled it into the street. The cool Scotsman stalked deliberately and gravely in quest of his Kilmarnock headgear, and after giving it two or three hearty slaps upon the wall outside the door, he re-entered very composedly, wringing the muddy moisture out of it, looked over to the person who had served him so meanly, and said, with a genuine Scotch smile—"Man, yon was an ill-faured turn; you'll surely tak' a look o' the gudes noo?"

The master draper himself, who was standing all the while in the shop admiring the patience and perseverance of the old man, and feeling a little compunction for the unceremonious manner in which he had been treated, came now forward, examined the contents of the pack; found them to be articles he stood in need of; purchased them; ordered an additional regular supply; and thus laid the foundation of an opulent mercantile house that has now flourished for several generations.

The subjoined well-known and diverting story may not inappropriately conclude this chapter—

### THE PROFESSOR OF SIGNS, OR TWO WAYS OF TELLING A STORY.

King James the Sixth, on removing to London, was waited upon by the Spanish ambassador, a man of erudition, but who had an eccentric idea in his head that every country should have a Professor of Signs to enable men of all languages to understand each other without the aid of speech. The ambassador lamenting one day, before the king, this great desideratum throughout all Europe, the king, who was an *outré* character, said to him, "I have a Professor of Signs in the most northern college in my dominions, viz., at Aberdeen; but it is a great way off—perhaps 600 miles."

"Were it 10,000 leagues off, I shall see him," said the ambassador, and expressed determination to set out *instanter*, in order to have an interview with the Scottish Professor of Signs.

The king, perceiving he had committed himself, wrote, or caused to be written, an intimation to the University of Aberdeen, stating the case, and desiring the professors to put him off, or make the best of him they could. The ambassador arrived, and was received with great solemnity. He immediately inquired which of them had the honour to be Professor of Signs, but was told that the professor was absent in the Highlands, and would return nobody could say when.

"I will," said he, "wait his return though it were for twelve months."

The professors, seeing that this would not do, contrived the following stratagem:—there was in the city one, Geordie, a butcher, blind of an eye—a droll fellow with much wit and roguery about him. The butcher was put up to the story, and instructed how to comport himself in his new situation of "Professor of Signs," but he was enjoined on no account to utter a syllable. Geordie willingly undertook the office for a small bribe. The ambassador was then told, to his infinite satisfaction, that the Professor of Signs would be at home next day. Everything being prepared, Geordie was gowned, wigged, and placed in a chair of state, in a room in the college, all the professors and the ambassador being in an adjoining room. The Spaniard was then shown into Geordie's room, and left to converse with him as best he could, the whole of the professors waiting the issue with considerable anxiety. Then commenced the scene. The ambassador held up one of his fingers to Geordie; Geordie held up two of his. The ambassador held up three; Geordie clenched his fist and looked stern. The ambassador then took an orange from his pocket, and showed it to the new-fangled professor; Geordie in return pulled out a piece of barley cake from his pocket, and exhibited it in a similar manner. The ambassador then bowed to him, and retired to the other professors, who anxiously inquired his opinion of their brother.

"He is a perfect miracle," said the ambassador, "I would not give him for the wealth of the Indies."

"Well," exclaimed one of the professors, "to descend to particulars, how has he edified you?"

"Why," said the ambassador, "I first held up one finger, denoting that there is one God; he held up two, signifying that there are the Father and Son. I held up three, meaning Father, Son, and Holy Ghost; he clenched his fist to say that these three are one. I then took out an orange signifying the goodness of God, who gives His creatures not only necessaries, but the luxuries of life; upon which the wonderful man presented a piece of bread, showing that it was the staff of life, and preferable to every luxury."

The professors were glad that matters had turned out so well; and having got quit of the ambassador, they called in Geordie to hear his version of the affair.

"Well, Geordie, how have you come on, and what do you think of yon man?"

"The scoundrel," exclaimed the butcher, "what did he do first, think ye? He held up a'e finger, as muckle as to say, you have only a'e e'e! Then I held up twa, meaning that my ane was as gude as his twa. Then the fellow held up three o' his fingers, to say that there were but three een between us; and then I was so mad at the scoundrel that I steeked my neive, and was gaun to gi'e him a whack on the side o' his head, and would hae done't too, but for your sakes. He didna stop here wi' his provocation; but, forsooth, he took out an orange, as much as to say, your puir, beggarly, cauld country canna produce that! I showed him a whang of a bere bannock, meaning that I didna care a farthing for him nor his trash either as lang as I had this! But, by a' that's gude," concluded Geordie, "I'm angry yet that I didna break every bane in his sun-singit, ill-shapen body."

Two sides of a story could not be more opposed to each other, and nothing could better illustrate the burly innocent humour of the Scottish character.

# CHAPTER IX
## SCREEDS O' TARTAN—A CHAPTER OF HIGHLAND HUMOUR

Differing from the Lowland Scotch in personal appearance, in language, in style of dress, and in other respects, the Highlander's humour also presents characteristics which are distinctively local. Though often rich, for example, it is never boisterous, never sparkling—is rarely spontaneous—but is nearly always slow, sly, severe, and insinuative. For, slow in muscular action, Donald is slow in mental action also. He has to be stimulated or induced to physical activity; and, naturally of a serious cast of mind, his humour, in its richest ore, comes out nearly always as the result of provocation. But rouse his Highland blood by insult—and a word will do it sometimes—or awaken his drowsy wits by banter, then get out of the reach of both his arms and his tongue instanter, for his hand is heavy, his eye is sure, and his speech is a hurricane. Much of what passes for Highland humour, as everybody knows, arises from the difference which exists between the Gaelic and the English and the Scottish idiom; and from the efforts of the semi-educated or non-educated Gaelic-speaking Highlander to express himself in English, or in the colloquial tongue of the Lowland Scot. The English language, "as she is spoke" by the Scottish mountaineer—felicitous examples of which we find in the lighter writings of John Donald Carrick, the first editor of "Whistle Binkie," in Sandy Roger's song of "Shon M'Nab," in Alexander Fisher's song, "Ta Offish in ta Mornin'," and "Ta Praise o' Ouskie," and in the old ballad of "Turnumspikeman"—is fearfully and wonderfully made. He transposes his tenses; calls yesterday "to-morrow," and to-morrow "yesterday." He confuses his genders; calls everything "she," except his wife and the cat, and these he calls "hims." He makes his nouns qualify his adjectives, and places the cart before the horse in every second sentence. "Ze can never learn zat tamn English langvidge," once exclaimed a French student in despair. "Ze spell von vord A-S-S, zen ze bronounce it DONKEY." Synonyms equally vex the spirit of the Scottish Highlander. Thus Donald Roy M'Vean, when interrogated in regard to the quality of his potato crop, provided amusement to the Lowlanders around him by replying—"They are just ferry goot, inteed, but fery *seldom* whatefer." Another fertile source of amusement is found in the difficulty with which the unkempt Highlander adapts himself to the usages of low country, and, particularly, to city life. A happy depiction of his *speech* and *behaviour* in such a circumstance is found in Rodger's familiar song of "Shon M'Nab," already referred to. On coming to Glasgow, "Shon" said—

"Ta first thing she pe wonder at,

As she came doun ta street, man,
Was mans pe traw ta cart himsel',
Shust 'pon his nain twa feet, man.
Och on! och on! her nainsel' thought,
As she wad stood and glower, man;
Poor man, if they mak' you ta *horse*—
Should gang 'pon a' your *four* man.

And when she turn ta corner round,
Ta black man tere she see, man;
Pe grund to music in ta kist,
And sell him for pawpee, man.
And aye she'll grund, and grund, and grund,
And turn her mill aboot, man:
Pe strange! she will put nothings in,
Yet aye teuk music out, man."

There are some choice specimens of Donald's English extant, and, before passing on to the richer ore of his natural humour, it will be worth while to glance at a few. First, there is the famous Inveraray proclamation, which I do not remember to have seen in print, but which, when a boy, I learned from the lips of a droll old man in Central Perthshire. It is a unique production, but is said to have actually been delivered at the Market Cross of Inveraray towards the close of the last century. Here it is—

"Ta-hoy!—a tither ta-hoy!—three times ta-hoy!—and ta-hoy! Wheesht!! By command of Her Majesty King Sheorge and Her Grace ta Tuke o' Argyll! Any persons found fishing abune ta loch or below ta loch, afore ta loch or ahent ta loch, in ta loch or on ta loch, roun ta loch or about ta loch, will pe persecuted with three persecutions—First she'll pe troon'd, and syne she'll pe hang'd, and ten she'll pe prunt; and if she'll come back any more she'll pe persecuted with a far worse persecution tan all that. Got save the King and Her Grace ta Tuke o' Argyll!"

If we admit the above to be *bona-fide*, we can scarcely doubt the genuineness of the following prayer, which is said to have emanated from a contemporary of the Inveraray bellman:—

"Gracious Providence! Bless all ta Macdonalds, and ta Macdonalds' children, tere sons' sons and tere daughters' daughters, for a thoosand years langsyne. Be gracious to send us mountains of snuff and tobacco, and send us oceans of whisky—ta very finest of whisky! Oh, yes! And send us hills of potatoes, and breads and cheeses as big as all ta Howe of Strathmore. And, moreover, likewise, send us floods of water, tat tere may pe grass for plenty to man and beast, and some to spare to ta poor of ta parish. Send us guns and pistols as more as ta sea and ta sand-shore; and swords, too, likewise, to kill all ta Grants and ta Macphersons for evermore. Bless ta wee stirk, and mak' him a big coo pefore Martinmas. Bless ta wee soo, too, and mak' him a big boar likewise. Oh, yes! Put the strength of Samson into Donald's arms, and send us parley, kail, and corn prodigious. Bless all ta pairns—Duncan and Rory and Flora, and you, Donald, and you, Lauchie, and you, Peter; and glorious, yours for evermore."

I do not ask any one to swallow the above, minus the proverbial "grain of salt." I like to take it that way myself. And yet there are well-authenticated instances and occasions revealing deliverances quite as ludicrous and absurd. Witness the following fragment of a pulpit homily which appears in Hugh Boyd's admittedly veracious *Reminiscences of Fifty Years*, and which the recorder appears to have heard himself, or received on highly credible authority:—

"Ah, my friends," exclaimed the preacher, "what causes have we for gratitude! Oh, yes! for the deepest gratitude! Look at the place of our habitation. How grateful should we be that we do not leeve in the far North, Oh, no! amid the frost and the snaw, and the cauld and the weet, Oh, no! where there's a lang day the a'e half o' the year, Oh, yes! and a lang nicht the tither, Oh, yes! That we do not depend upon the aurawry boreawlis, Oh, no! That we do not gang shivering aboot in skins, Oh, no! snookin' amang the snaw like mowdiewarts, Oh, no, no! And how grateful should we be that we do not leeve in the for Sooth, beneath the equawter, and the sun aye burnin', burnin'. Where the sky's het, Ah, yes! and the earth's het, and the water's het, and ye're burnt black as a smiddy, Ah, yes! Where there's teegurs, Oh, yes! And lions, Oh, yes! And crocodiles, Oh, yes! And fearsome beasts growlin' and girnin' at ye amang the woods. Where the very air is a fever, like the burnin' breath o' a fiery drawgon; that we do not leeve in these places—Oh, no, no, no, no! But that we leeve in this blessit island of ours, call't Great Britain, Oh, yes, yes! and in that part of it named Scotland, that looks up at Ben Nevis—Oh, yes, yes, yes! Where's neither frost, nor cauld, nor wund, nor weet, nor hail, nor rain, nor teegurs, nor lions, nor burnin' suns, nor hurricanes, nor——"

"Here," says the narrator, "a tremendous burst of wind and rain from Ben Nevis blew in the windows of the kirk, and brought the preacher's eloquence to an abrupt conclusion."

Highlanders have the habit when talking their English, so-called, of interjecting the personal pronoun "he" when it is not required—such as "the doctor he has come," or "the postman he is going"—and often in consequence a sentence or an expression is rendered sufficiently ludicrous, as the sequel will show. A reverend and pious gentleman once began his discourse thus:—"My dearly beloved brethren, you will find the subject of our observations this afternoon in the First Epistle General of Peter, the fifth chapter and the eighth verse, and in these words, 'The devil, as a roaring lion, walketh about, seeking whom he may devour.' Now, my brethren, with your leave, we will divide the subject of our text into four heads. First, we shall endeavour to ascertain *who the devil he was*. Secondly, we shall inquire into his geographical position—namely, *where the devil he was going*. Thirdly—and this is of a personal character—we will ask ourselves *who the devil he was seeking*. Fourthly, and lastly, my beloved brethren, we shall endeavour to solve a problem that has never been solved to this day—namely, *what the devil he was roaring at*."

Recently a Highland policeman, not many weeks imported from the island of Jura, approached to where a number of young men were standing in a knot on the pavement of one of the busier streets of the Western metropolis, and pushing them somewhat roughly, exclaimed, "If you'll be going to stand here, my lads, you'll have to be moving about."

"Is this not a free country?" demanded one of the fellows, somewhat sharply.

"This is not ta country at all, you tam sheep's head," shouted the now enraged member of the law, "this is one of the largest cities in the town of Glasgow!"

But if Donald's *uttered* speech is sometimes ludicrous, what are we to say concerning some specimens which we have seen of his *written* address! The *Glasgow Herald* a number of years ago gave its authority for the following being a *verbatim* copy of a letter which, a short time previously, had been received by a local coal-agent, the writer's name alone being mercifully withheld from publication:—

"Turbert,<br>27 February, 180074

"Sur,—I was understand that you was a cole pit. i was want to knew what was your monish for to supplie coal to be deliver to turbert at the Quay most nearust to the city of turbert loch fine side was I used to got my coal from a agent at Greenock but he was charge me a great dale much more than i was understand he was pae for them and though am always used to was a onest man i was not have many monish to spare, and was wish to have as chape a prise as I could got. I was tuk 2 cargos as wad full a smak about 20 tons twice as more every week to land on thursdae, and the monish wood be sented to you wunst every fridae by the agint of the bank a very dacent man and his wife too and has aulways pai his way and never was spoke an ill about any man as I was knew before, if you will rite your price to me the smallest you can took I will rite you a answer when the day after will come.

"I was like to deal with a highlandman, and always did use to like very more aul the Campbell's, my wife's cuisin's faither's uncle was a Campbell—a very civil lad as was a fishing smak and was made a dale of monish and was lefe a legacie to my wife who will be glad to see you with myselfe and gave you a bed if you was kum and spoke the prise you wood tuke for the coles and save you the trubel of wrighting a letter to was to tell the prise of the coles.

"If U cannot come ureself write to —— ——.

"I was got my son Lachie was a goot riter to rite the name of your shop in Glesco. He would tuke a place if you could get him wan."

Not long ago a stalwart west country Highlander was describing to a company of Lowlanders the wonderful power and facility in drawing possessed by his brother Donald, "Hooch ay," he said, "he'll juist tak' a bit cawk (chalk) the size o' her thoom's nose, and he'll draw a man *there*, and a horse *there*, and you couldn't tell which was which." The company laughed. "Ay," continued the speaker in a more impassioned vein, "and he wad tak' a piece o' cawk, and he wad draw a horse *there* and a cart *there*, and you *couldn't* tell which was which. They was *juist beautiful!*"

We have so far here been looking at Donald's humour on its least favourable side; having been viewing it, so to speak, in the garb of the Sassenach only. Let us now glance at a few examples in full Highland costume. And here at once is an instance showing rare shrewdness and wit combined. A Highland piper having a pupil placed in his hands by his chief, and not knowing the notes of music—the semibreves, minims, crotchets, and quavers, etc.—by the proper designations, although he knew each one by head mark, and its musical value very well, set to work in this way.

"Here, Donald," said he, "took your pipes, my goot lad, and blow a blast."

Donald did as requested.

"So, so!" exclaimed the old man, "tat iss very well blown, inteed—just beautiful. But what is sound, Donald, without sense? Just so. You may blow for ever without making a tune of it if I do not tell you how ta queer things on ta paper are to help you. Look here, lad. You see tat big fellow with ta round, open face (pointing to a semibreve between the two lines of a bar), he moves slowly from tat line to tis while you beat one with your foot and give a long blast. Now you put a leg to him. You make two of him, and he will move twice as fast. If you blacken hims face he will run four times faster as ta fellow with ta white face; but, besides blackenin' hims face, if you will bend hims knees, or tie hims legs, he will hop eight times faster as ta white-faced fellow I showed you ta first time. And now whenever you blow your pipes, Donald, remember tis, the tighter you will tie tese fellows legs ta faster they will run, an' ta quicker they will be sure to dance."

There is a characteristic story which Highlanders themselves delight to tell, to the effect, that, once upon a time, when one of their countrymen was passing a farm-steading, the dog attached thereto came rushing and barking towards him, and latterly added injury to the insult which had been offered by inserting its fangs in the naked calf of one of the brawny Celt's legs. Maddened by the pain, the Highlander seized a hayfork which happened to be conveniently near, and with one fell thrust transfixed the snarling tyke to the earth. The howls of agony quickly brought the farmer on the scene, who, on seeing his favourite collie writhing on the ground, exclaimed in wrath, "Why the devil did ye no tak' the other end o' the fork to the dog, you stupid ass?" "And why the dog did the deevil no tak' his other end to me, you stupid ass yourself?" the Highlander replied.

It is the Ettrick Shepherd, I think, who tells of two Highlanders who set out on a reiving expedition to steal the litter of a wild sow, which lay in a narrow-mouthed cave. Seizing the opportunity of Madame Grumphie's absence, one of the men crept in, and the other kept a watch at the mouth. Presently, down the hillside came the distracted and angry sow, and rushed with menacing tusks towards her den. The guard, as she slipped into the passage, had just time to lay hold of her tail, give it a firm twist round his strong hand; and, throwing himself down and setting his feet against the sides of the den, he held her fast. The Highlander in the cave was too much engaged with the screaming little pigs to hear the tussle going on outside; but finding himself in darkness, he called out to his mate, "Donald, fat the deil's the maitter? I canna see." Donald, who by this time had found a pig's tail a most uneasy tenure, and who had no wind left for explanations, briefly but significantly answered, "Gin the tail breaks, Dougal', my lad, you'll see fat's the maitter."

"Hillo, Donald!" exclaimed one Highlander to another, as they met on a country road recently, "what are you doing here at all? I socht you was always with M'Lachlan down in the Glen."

"So I was a long time with M'Lachlan too," replied Donald, "but I have left him, whatever."

"Why did you leave him? He's a good master I'm sure."

"Hooch, ay, a good master enough; but I left him about the salt beef."

"Did you not like salt beef?"

"Hooch, ay, I like salt beef well enough."

"Did you get too much salt beef?"

"This is how it was, you see. There was a cow that died, and he salted the cow, and we got nothing but salt cow as long as she lasted. And I like salt cow well enough. But then there was a sheeps that died, and he salted that too, and we got nothing but salt sheep as long as she lasted; and I like salt sheeps well enough. But some time after there was a pig that died, and he salted her too, and we got nothing but salt pig as long as she lasted. And I like salt pigs well enough. But just when the pig was nearly all done, one day his grandmother died, and he comes out to the stable, and says he, 'You'll have to go away for a stone of salt, Donald.'

"'Hooch ay,' thinks I to myself, 'my man; but if you'll thought that I was going to eat your grandmother you're very far mistaken,' and I never says a word to him at all, but just comes away."

Highlanders make good soldiers, good policemen, and faithful watchmen and shepherds. Forgathering with one tending his sheep on the verdant slopes of a Northern mountain one day, a company of English tourists thought to have some entertainment at his expense, and began by remarking that he seemed to be enjoying himself.

"Ou, ay," said the shepherd, "I'm shoost lookin' aboot me here."

"And what are you looking about you for?" inquired another.

"Oh, shoost because it's a fine view from this side o' the hill."

"Yes, but what can you see from here?"

"Well, if there was no mist ta day I would see ta town, and ta boats on ta loch, and many more things, whatever."

"I suppose you can see a great distance from here on a clear day?" remarked one.

"Oh, yes, shentlemen, a great distance, indeed," said the shepherd.

"I suppose, on a clear day now, you can see London from this extreme altitude?" exclaimed one of the Cockneys, quizzing the countryman, and nudging his companions.

"Och, ay, and much further than that too," replied the shepherd, who had perceived the nudge.

"Farther than London?" gasped two of the somewhat alarmed tourists.

"Ay, to be shurely, and further than America too," replied the Highlander.

"Farther than America?" shouted all the Cockneys together. "Impossible!"

"It's shoost true what I tell you whatever," said Donald; "but if you'll won't believe me, shoost sit doon there, and took out your flasks and took a dram, and wait for twa oors and more, and if the mist will clear awa' you will see the *moon* from here."

We may suppose that the next shepherd who came in the way of these tourists would not be unduly interrogated.

A Highland lassie whom I have heard of was not quite so successful in an encounter with the Sassenach postmaster. She had gone to the Post Office to take out a money order.

"Where is your order to go?" demanded the clerk, with the snappishness which only Post Office officials can command, and which roused the inflammable blood of the young countrywoman of Helen Macgregor.

"What you'll ask for? You'll look your book, and you'll saw there," the girl tartly replied (she had got an order a short time previous).

"I must know where your order is to go to," said the clerk, firmly.

The girl goes to the door and brings in a companion who explained that the order was for Tobermory.

"Who is to get the order?"

"My mother, to be surely."

"What is your mother's name?"

"My mother's name is Mrs. M'Tavish."

"What is your mother's Christian name?"

"What you'll want to know whether my Christian be a mother or not?" demanded the girl, now in a perfect rage with anger. "My mother be a good

Christian woman, and will go to the Free Church in Tobermory every Sabbath, which is maybe more than you'll do."

"I don't want to know anything about what church your mother goes to; I only wish to know her Christian name," now, somewhat mildly, explained the clerk.

"My mother's name is Mrs. M'Tavish," replied the girl, "and she's the decenter married womans than you are, and I'll not tell any mans born any more, whatever," and off she marched in the very highest dudgeon.

Donald is proud of his native heath, proud of his native dress, proud of his name and clan, proud of everything pertaining exclusively to his native hills. He claims for the Gaelic that it is not only the best but one of the oldest languages in the world. He would not like to say just *the* very oldest. The humorous poet no doubt has asserted that—

> When Eve, all fresh in beauty's charms,
>
> First met fond Adam's view,
>
> The first word that he'll spoke to her
>
> Was "*Cia mar a tha thu an duidh?*"

"But did you'll opserve," says Donald, "if it was ta Gaelic that was spoket in ta Garden of Eden, maybe they'll say ta Teevil was a Hielandman, and she wouldn't like that to pe at all, whatever!"

I have said that the Highlander is proud of his name and clan, and there are stories that reveal to what extent.

"Did you'll know what day this is, Donald?" inquired one Celt of another, on the morning of a certain national occasion which will come out in the sequel.

"Hooch, ay," replied Donald; "it's just ta day after ta morn, Dugald."

"Yes, Donald, to be shurely," replied his friend. "But did you'll forgot this was ta day ta Queen's dochter was to be married to ta Tuke o' Argyll's son—ta Marquis o' Lorne?"

"Ay, ay, did you'll told me that? Well, well, it's the prood, prood mans ta Queen will be this day."

On the occasion aforesaid there was, of course, great national rejoicing, and the town of Inverness was, like every other municipality, illuminated at night.

"Dear me, Donald," exclaimed one local shopkeeper to another, as he issued from his own door, "did you ever behold the likes of that? There's five-fourths of the whole town under luminations this nicht!"

"Toots, man, Angus, I'll thought that you know better than spoke like that," replied his neighbour. "A fourth is a quarter, and five quarters would be more than the whole."

"Och, Donald Fraser, my lad," retorted Angus, "I've seen too many snowy days not to know what I'll say. I've got cloths in my own shop six-quarters, and that is more—there, now, with your ignorance."

The following is an amusing instance of the tenacity with which the Highlanders hold to the honours and antiquity of their kindred. A dispute arose between a Campbell and a M'Lean upon the never-ending subject. The M'Lean would not allow that the Campbells had any right to rank with his clan in the matter of antiquity, who, he insisted, were in existence as a clan from the beginning of the world. Campbell had a little more Biblical lore than his antagonist, and asked him if the Clan M'Lean was before the Flood.

"Flood! what flood?" demanded the M'Lean.

"The Flood that you know drowned all the world but Noah and his family, and his flocks and herds," said Campbell.

"Pooh! you and your flood too," said the M'Lean. "My clan was before ta Flood."

"I have not read in my Bible," said Campbell, "of the name of M'Lean going into Noah's Ark."

"Noah's Ark!" snorted the M'Lean; "who ever heard of a M'Lean that had not a boat of his own?"

There was a fine exhibition of clan pride afforded during the years the late Earl of Airlie acted as Lord High Commissioner to the General Assembly of the Church of Scotland. Amongst his attendants at Holyrood were two pipers, who, at every dinner given to the clergy and other guests at the Palace, marched several times round the large dining-hall playing the wild and inspiriting music of the Highlands. One evening the Moderator of the Assembly, at some one's request, asked his Grace whether he had any objections to instruct the pipers to play "The Bonnie House o' Airlie."

"None whatever," replied the Earl, "but I doubt whether we shall get it, for the one piper is an Ogilvie and the other is a Campbell; but we shall see."

Calling the butler, he gave orders that when the pipers next came in they should play "The Bonnie House o' Airlie."

The butler went at once with the message. By and by the pipes were heard approaching, and in a little, one piper, the Ogilvie, marched in, playing the desired tune with great dignity and vigour.

"I expected this," said the Earl in a jocular way to the Moderator.

Summoning the butler again, he asked whether his message had been delivered.

"Yes, my lord."

"Then why has Campbell not come in with Ogilvie?"

"I gave him your message, my lord."

"What did he say then?"

The man hesitated.

"What did Campbell say?" again demanded the Earl.

"He said—eh—eh," still hesitating—"he said he would see your Lordship——"

The rest of the sentence was lost in a cough and the skirl of Ogilvie's pipes.

"It must be frankly admitted," says Dr. Norman Macleod, "that there is no man more easily offended, more thin-skinned, who cherishes longer the memory of an insult, or keeps up with more freshness a personal, family, or party feud than the genuine Highlander. Woe to the man who offends his pride or vanity! 'I may forgive, but I cannot forget,' is a favourite saying. He will stand by a friend to the last; but let a breach be once made, and it is most difficult ever again to repair it as it once was. The grudge is immortal." Here is a case in proof:—

A Highlander was visited on his death-bed by his clergyman, who exhorted Donald to prepare himself for another world by a sincere repentance of all the crimes he had committed on earth, and strongly urged the absolute necessity of forgiving his enemies.

Donald shrugged up his shoulders at this hard request; yet he at last agreed to forgive every person who had injured him except one, who had long been the Highlander's mortal foe, and of whom Donald hoped the parson, knowing all the circumstances of the case, would make an exception. The holy man, however, insisted so much on this point, that Donald at last said—

"Weel, weel, sir, since there be no help for it, Donald will forgive her; but," he added, turning to his two sons, "may G—d d—n you, Duncan and Rory, if you'll forgive her too!"

To be the means of causing a Highlander to emigrate from one locality to another, either by purchasing the property on which he resides, or obtaining a lease without his concurrence, is a sin not to be forgiven. A Glasgow gentleman wished to feu the patch of ground on which the Bellman's house stood at Kilmun, with the stripe of garden attached to it, at which the Highland ire of the latter could scarcely be restrained.

"Did you'll know?" queried he at an acquaintance, "a fellow—shentleman he is not; no, nor his mother before him—from your Glasgow, is going to put me away from my wee placie, where I was for all my days, an' they'll call her Macsmall—eh?"

"No," replied the Glaswegian, "I don't."

"I was thought so, nor no decent mans. Well, maybe ay, and maybe no. A stone will put up his house or a stone will put it down; I'll never did a mischiefs to no bodie, and I'll not put my hand to a murder too. But, you see, there's many friends in the glen will take a friend's part—and they'll be taking walks up the hill, an' there's many bigger stones there nor a house itself, and they'll just be in the way, so they will; a bit dunch with the foot will make them come down without any carts and wheels, they're heavy—very heavy—teet are they, and no easy to put a stop to when rinnin', poor dumb creatures; and they canna help though they were taking the house of this *trouster mosach* (dirty scoundrel) with her. I wad just like, quietly between ourselfs, to see his house, six weeks after it was biggit, and the sclates on't. Ay would I."

Donald is dour and "thrawn as the wuddie," and is consequently loath to eat his words. Yet there have been occasions when he has made the *amende honorable*. A notable case of the kind occurred not many years ago on board one of the West Highland steamers. One of the deck porters, whom we shall here call Duncan—just because his name was Donald—was much annoyed by a "pernickity" and, to say the least of it, rather troublesome lady passenger, who, without on any occasion producing the expected "tip," kept Duncan shifting her baggage here and there about the boat. Greatly irritated by these frequent interruptions, Duncan at length so far forgot himself as to tell her to "go to Jericho," or some other place in that direction. The lady, greatly shocked and insulted, complained to the captain, and insisted on an apology, failing which, she would communicate with the owners of the steamer. The captain promised to see the matter righted, and forthwith summoned Duncan to the state-room.

"Duncan," said he, "you have been charged with gross incivility to a lady passenger, who threatens that, unless you apologise, she will inform the owners of the boat as soon as she reaches Glasgow. Now, you have just until we reach Greenock to do so. Off you go and apologise to her at once."

Duncan bit his lip pretty hard, but the thing had to be done, so he went upstairs and snooved about rather sulkily until, by and by, he discovered the object of his quest, approaching whom, he said, with half-averted face, and eyes fixed on vacancy—

"Was you the old lady I was told to go to Jericho?"

"Yes," replied the lady, snappishly.

"Well, the Captain says you're not to go now!" said Duncan; and off he went, and had half a dozen passengers' trunks in confusion on deck before the lady had time to adjust her spectacles and see where he had vanished to.

Speaking of boats. Not long ago a couple of Highland farmers, recognised as folks of some importance in their own immediate neighbourhood, left Stornoway by steamer with the view of attending an important market in the South. The weather looked good at the start, and considering this in conjunction with the fact that it would be so much cheaper, and few, or none, of those on board would know them, they resolved on travelling steerage. So far so good. But they had not been long out on the billowy deep when it commenced to blow a perfect hurricane, and all on board became alarmed as to the safety of their lives, and there was running to and fro and many anxious inquiries concerning the vessel's chances of weathering the storm. Not the least perturbed in spirit were the two farmers. "Oich! Oich!" said the one to the other, "it will be awful if anything happens, and we've only got steerage tickets in oor pockets." "Indeed, and it's very true what you say, Mr. M'Donald, and that's what troubles me most of all," responded the other, looking, if possible, more doleful than his friend. "But I'll tell you what we'll do. We'll go abaft the bridge this moment, and if the worst comes, which the goodness forbid, we'll fling awa' our tickets, and *gang doon as cabin passengers anyway*."

Another example here, in evidence of the Highlander's peculiar powers of reasoning. Donald Macgregor, like his more illustrious namesake, Rob Roy, was a notorious sheep and cattle-lifter in the Highlands of Perthshire. At last he was overtaken by the grim tyrant of the human race, and was visited by the minister of the parish in which he resided. The holy man warmly exhorted the dying reiver to reflect upon the long and black catalogue of his sins before it was too late; otherwise, he would have a tremendous account to give at the great day of retribution, when all the crimes he had committed in the world would appear in dreadful array as evidence of his guilt.

"Och, sirse," cried the dying man, "and will all ta sheeps and all ta cows and all ta things that Donald has helped hersel' to, be there?"

"Undoubtedly," replied the parson.

"Och, that will pe all right then; shust let every shentlemans took her own, and Donald Macgregor will be ta honest man again."

And now, as the universal "Auld Lang Syne" has formed the parting-song of so many merry meetings at home and abroad, let the following clever set of verses, the reputed composition of a talented Perthshire divine of the "Auld Kirk," afford the finishing touch to the present sederunt of anecdotal fun:—

AULD LANG SYNE, DONE UP IN TARTAN.

Should Gaelic speech be e'er forgot,
And never brocht to min',
For she'll be spoke in Paradise
In the days o' auld lang syne.

When Eve, all fresh in beauty's charms,
First met fond Adam's view,
The first word that he'll spoke to her
Was "*Cia mar a tha thu an duidh?*"

And Adam, in his garden fair,
Whene'er the day did close,
The dish that he'll to supper teuk
Was always Athol brose.

When Adam from his leafy bower
Cam' out at break o' day,
He'll always for his morning teuk
A quaich of usquebae.

And when wi' Eve he'll had a crack,
He'll teuk his sneeshin' horn,
And on the tap ye'll weel micht mark
A braw big Cairngorm.

The sneeshin' mull is fine, my frien's,
The sneeshin' mull is grand;
We'll teuk a hearty sneesh, my frien's,
And pass't from hand to hand.

When man first fand the want o' claes,
The wind and cauld to fleg,
He twisted round about hims waist
The tartan philabeg.

And music first on earth was heard
In Gaelic accents deep,
When Jubal in his oxter squeezed
The blether o' a sheep.

The braw bagpipes is grand, my frien's,
The braw bagpipes is fine;
We'll teuk another pibroch yet,
For the days o' auld lang syne.

---

# CHAPTER X
## HUMOUR OF SCOTTISH POETS

There have been few great poets—few poets of any appreciable quality, indeed—anywhere, who have not had a lively and appreciative sense of humour, if they have not actually been positive and productive humourists. It is a faculty of the human mind without which no man can be intellectually great—without which no view of life can be comprehensive and true; a faculty without which Shakespeare could no more have sounded the gamut of human feeling as he did than a man who is colour-blind could describe the glowing iridescence of the rainbow. In Burns and Scott, the most notable among Scottish poets—and mighty influences both in the republic of letters—the faculty of original humour was revealed to an extraordinary degree. In the case of Scott the playfulness of his fancy was made manifest essentially, no doubt, in the *Waverley Novels*, and in conversations with individuals; his poetry being mainly martial and moving, and severe rather than lightsome. In Burns, the greater poet, and the more impulsive genius, there was revealed the greater humourist and the readier wit, as well as the finer sentimentalist. Alone amid the sublimities of Nature, or touched by the muse in her diviner moods, he was reverent in spirit and glowed with adoration as fervid and sincere as ever animated the breast of the royal Hebrew bard himself; but prompted to join the social circle at the festive board, and fired by the spirit of fun, he would dazzle and delight a party for hours together by the brilliance and rapidity of his flashes of ready wit and humorous satire. The most ample and effective examples of Burns's humour occur, of course, in his poems—notably in "Tam o' Shanter," and "The Jolly Beggars"; in his songs "Duncan Gray," "Tam Glen," and "Sic a Wife as Willie had"; and in some of the rhymed epistles. The impromptu epitaphs and epigrams, etc., which find a place in nearly every edition of his works, afford convincing evidence of the pungency of his electric wit, and the annihilating weight of his equally ready satire. But with all of these—particularly the poems and the songs—every adult person in Scotland is so familiar that to quote from one or other of them here would be something like superfluous labour. A few of the nimbler of the impromptu rhymes and epigrams, with descriptions of the circumstances under which they were provoked, may, however, be reproduced *en passant*. The process will freshen the reader's memory, if it does not actually enlighten his mind.

Burns, like true steel, was ever ready to give fire at the touch of the flint, and being present in a company where an ill-educated *parvenu* was boring everyone by boasting of the many great people he had lately been visiting, the poet gave vent to his feelings in the following impromptu stanza, which we may be sure effectually silenced the babbling snob before him:—

"No more of your titled acquaintances boast,

And in what lordly circles you've been;

An insect is only an insect at most,

Though it crawl on the curls of a queen."

Having been storm-sted one Sunday at Lamington, in Clydesdale, the poet went to church, but the day was so cold, the place so uncomfortable, and the sermon so poor, that he left this protest on the pew which he had occupied:—

"As cauld a wind as ever blew,

A caulder kirk, and in 't but few;

As cauld a preacher's ever spak'—

Ye'll a' be het ere I come back."

While in Edinburgh, he visited at the studio of a well-known painter, who was at that time engaged on a picture of Jacob's dream. Burns embodied his criticism of the work in the following lines, which he wrote on the back of a sketch still preserved in the painter's family:—

"Dear —, I'll gie ye some advice,

You'll tak' it no uncivil;

You shouldna paint at angels mair,

But try and paint the devil.

To paint an angel's kittle wark,

Wi' Auld Nick there's less danger;

You'll easy draw a weel-kent face,

But no sae weel a stranger."

Never perhaps was there a neater compliment paid to feminine loveliness than that paid by Burns to Miss Ainslie in an impromptu rhyme. During the poet's Border tour he went to church on Sunday, accompanied by the sister of his travelling companion, Mr. Robert Ainslie, of Berrywell, Dunse. The text for the day happened to contain a severe denunciation of obstinate sinners, and the poet, observing the young lady intently turning over the leaves of her Bible in search of the passage, took out a small piece of paper, and wrote the following lines, which he immediately passed to her:—

> "Fair maid, you need not take the hint,
>
> Nor idle texts pursue;
>
> 'Twas guilty sinners that he meant,
>
> Not angels such as you."

Ready-witted "graces before meat" were evolved by the poet on demand, time and again. Having met some friends to dine with them at the Globe Tavern, Dumfries, on one occasion, when a sheep's head happened to be the fare provided, he was asked to give something new as a grace, and instantly delivered the following, which has certainly little wit to recommend it:—

> "O Lord, when hunger pinches sore,
>
> Do Thou stand us in stead,
>
> And send us from thy bounteous store
>
> A tup, or wether's head."

After having dined, however, and greatly enjoyed the repast, he was appealed to to return thanks, and did so in four lines revealing native wit, by saying:—

> "O Lord, sine we have feasted thus,
>
> Which we so little merit,
>
> Let Meg now take away the flesh,
>
> And Jock bring in the spirit."

Than Burns's epitaph "On a Suicide," nothing more scathingly sarcastic was ever written. It is as if he could not express too much scorn of the miserable coward who would eschew the obligations of life by an act of self-destruction:—

> "Earth'd up, here lies an imp o' hell,
>
> Planted by Satan's dibble;
>
> Poor, silly wretch, he's damned himsel'
>
> To save the Lord the trouble."

Burns was standing one day on the quay at Greenock, when a wealthy merchant belonging to the town had the misfortune to fall into the harbour. He was no swimmer, and would certainly have been drowned had not a sailor, at the risk of his own life, plunged in and rescued him from his dangerous situation. The merchant, upon recovering a little from his fright, put his hand into his pocket and presented the sailor with a shilling. The crowd, who were by this time collected, loudly protested against the insignificance of the sum; but Burns, with a smile of ineffable scorn, entreated them to restrain their clamour, "For," said he, "the gentleman is, of course, the best judge of the value of his own life."

A writer who happened to be present in a company along with Burns when the conversation turned on "Tam o' Shanter," and stung, perhaps, with the sarcastic touch on the legal fraternity—

"Three lawyers' tongues turned inside out,

Wi' lees seemed like a beggar's clout,"

remarked that he thought the witches' orgies obscure.

"Obscure, sir," exclaimed the poet; "ye know not the language of the great master of your own art; the devil! If you get a witch for your client, you will not be able to manage her defence."

Burns lived five months in a house which was occupied by an old man named David Cully, or Kelly. The poet sometimes read books not usually seen in people's hands on the Sabbath. His landlord checked him for this, when the bard laughingly replied—

"You'll not think me so good a man as Nancy Kelly is a woman, I suppose?"

"Indeed, no."

"Then I'll tell you what happened this morning. When I took a walk by the banks o' the Nith, I heard Nancy Kelly praying long before I came to her. I walked on, and before I returned I saw her helping herself to an armful of my fitches." The parties kept a cow.

On one occasion Nance and the bard were sitting in the "spence," when the former turned the conversation on her favourite topic—religion. Burns sympathised with the matron, and quoted so much Scripture that she was fairly astonished. By and by she said to her husband, "Oh, Dauvit, how they have wranged that man; for I think he has mair o' the Bible on his tongue than Mr. Inglis himsel'." Mr. Inglis was the Anti-burgher minister. Burns enjoyed that compliment, and almost the first thing he communicated to his wife on her arrival was the lift he had got from old Nance.

Than "the glorious ploughman," no one was kinder to such helpless creatures as were weak in mind, and who sauntered harmlessly about. A poor half-witted creature—the Madge Wildfire, it is said, of Scott—always found a mouthful ready for her at the bard's fireside. He was equally kind, Allan Cuningham tells, to a crazy and tippling prodigal named Quin.

"Jamie," said the poet one day, as he gave this character a penny, "you should pray to be turned from the evil of your ways; you are ready now to melt that penny into whisky."

"Turn!" exclaimed Jamie, who was a wit in his way, "I wish some ane wad turn me into the worm o' Will Hyslop's whisky-still, that the drink micht dribble through me for ever."

"Weel said, Jamie," responded the poet; "you shall have a glass of whisky once a week for that if you will come sober for it."

A friend rallied Burns for indulging such creatures.

"You don't understand the matter," said he; "they are poets; they have the madness of the muse, and all they want is the inspiration—a mere trifle!"

A prophet has no honour in his own country, and few of the peasantry personally acquainted with Burns were willing to allow that his merit exceeded their own. Mrs. M'Quistan, the housekeeper at Dunlop House, where the poet was a frequent visitor, saw nothing in his writings calling for special admiration, and doubted the propriety of her mistress entertaining a mere ploughman who made rhymes. As regarded "The Cottar's Saturday Night," she declared to Mrs. Dunlop, with much shaking of the head, that "Nae doubt gentlemen and ladies think muckle o' that, but, for me, it's naething but what I saw in my ain faither's house every day, and I dinna see who he could hae tauld it ony other way." It was a splendid compliment. Yet the author once received perhaps a better—in his own hearing, too—one, at least, which he appreciated more. A little boy was asked which of the poet's works he liked best. "I like 'The Cottar's Saturday Night' far best," he exclaimed, "though it made me greet when my father made me read it to my mother."

The poet, with a sudden start, looked into the boy's face intently, and, patting him on the cheek, said, the tear glistening in his eye the while, "Well, my callant, it made me greet, too, more than once, when I was writing it at my father's fireside."

Scott, when about seventeen years of age, saw Burns in Edinburgh, and has afforded the most truthful and graphic account of his personal appearance extant. It was at a literary dinner at Professor Fergusson's that they met. The wondrous boy enlightened the party as to the authorship of the line—

"The child of misery baptized in tears,"

by telling them it was Langhorne's,[2] whereupon Burns looked towards him and exclaimed, "You will be a man yet." No prophecy received fuller fulfilment; for if Sir Walter Scott did not rise to the full stature of true manhood, no mere man ever did. Scott brought pleasure with him into every party he chose to enter. His rich, racy humour in telling stories and giving anecdotes, always on the spur of the moment, was delightful. He had an anecdote ready, a story to match, or "cap," as he used to call it, every one he heard, and with most perfect ease and hearty good humour. His first publisher, says one, Robert Millar, gave anecdotes very pleasantly, and one day, after dinner, he was telling the company that he, or some friend, had been present at an Assize Court in Jedburgh, when a farm servant had summoned his master for non-payment of wages, which he, the servant, had justly forfeited through some misconduct. After a great deal of cross-questioning—

"I'm sure, my lord," said the pursuer, "I'm seeking nowt but what I've rowt for!"

"Ay, my man," responded the judge, "but I'm thinking ye'll hae to *rowt* a wee langer afore ye get it, though;" and nonsuited him.

---

[2] The company had been admiring a print of Banbury's, representing a soldier lying dead on the snow—the dog sitting in misery on the one side—on the other, his widow with a child in her arms. These lines were written underneath:—

"Cold on Canadian hills, or Minden's plain,

Perhaps that parent wept her soldier slain;

Bent o'er her babe, her eye dissolved in dew,

The big drops mingling with the milk he drew,

Gave the sad presage of his future years—

The child of misery baptized in tears."

Burns was so much affected by the picture, or rather the ideas which it suggested to his mind, that he actually shed tears. He asked whose the lines were, and it chanced that among all who were present, and the company included the celebrated Dugald Stewart, and other men of letters, young

Scott alone remembered that they occur in a half-forgotten poem of Langhorne's, called by the unpromising title of "The Justice of the Peace."

Scott, with the others, was well pleased with this dialogue, and, in his easy unaffected manner, said—

"Well, something of a similar nature occurred when a friend of mine was present at the Justice Court at Jedburgh. Two fellows had been taken up for sheep-stealing; there was a dense crowd, and we were listening with breathless attention to the evidence, when, from what reason I have forgotten, there was a dead pause, during which the judge, observing a rosy-cheeked, chubby-faced country boy, who seemed to pay the utmost attention to what was going on, and continued to fix his eyes on his Lordship's countenance, cried out to the callant—

"'Well, my man, what do you say to the cause!'

"'Eh, gosh!' answered the boy, 'but that's a gude ane! What div I say? I whiles say, *Pui hup!* and whiles I say *Pui ho!* to the caws,' meaning, of course, the calves. But the business was quickly decided, for the whole Court, judge and jury, were thrown into such convulsions of laughter that nothing more could be said or done."

"It is interesting to observe," says Gilfillan, "how not a few of the familiar names known to Scott in his youth or boyhood have been preserved on his written pages and are now classical. Thus Meg Dods was the real name of a woman, or 'Luckie,' in Howgate, 'who brewed good ale for gentlemen.' In the account of a Galloway trial, in which Scott was counsel, occurs the name 'Mac-Guffog,' afterwards that of the famous turnkey in *Guy Mannering*. The name 'Durward' may still be seen on the signs of Arbroath and Forfar, and Scott had doubtless met it there; as well as that of 'Prudfute,' or 'Proudfoot,' in or near Perth; 'Morton,' in the lists of the Western Whigs; and 'Gilfillan,' in the catalogue of the prisoners in Dunnottar Castle. Nothing, in fact, that ever flashed on the eye or vibrated on the ear of this extraordinary man but was in some form or other reproduced in his writings." In a remarkable sense here the child was father of the man. When a lad at school, a boy in the same class was asked by the dominie what part of speech "with" was.

"A noun, sir," answered the boy.

"You young blockhead," cried the pedagogue, "what example can you give of such a thing?"

"I can tell you, sir," interrupted Scott. "You know there's a verse in the Bible which says—'They bound Samson with *withs*!'"

Mrs. Cockburn, authoress of the popular version of "The Flowers of the Forest," the one beginning "I've seen the smiling of fortune beguiling," has left a curious account of an interview which she had with Scott, when a boy not quite six years old. He was reading a poem to his mother when the lady entered, the subject of which was the description of a shipwreck. His passion rose with the storm, and he lifted up his eyes and hands—

"There's a mast gone," says he; "crash it goes; they will all perish!"

After his agitation, he turned to Mrs. Cockburn, and said—

"That is too melancholy. I had better read you something more amusing."

Mrs. Cockburn preferred a little chat, and asked his opinion of Milton and other books which he had been reading, which he gave wonderfully. One of his observations was—"How strange that Adam, just new come into the world, should know everything. That must be the poet's fancy," said he. But when told he was created perfectly by God Himself, he instantly yielded.

When he was taken to bed the same evening, he told his aunt that he liked Mrs. Cockburn, "for I think," said he, "she is a *virtuoso* like myself."

"Dear Walter, what is a *virtuoso*?" inquired his aunt.

"Don't you know?" said he. "Why, it's one that will know everything."

He was still a boy, when a lady friend remarked in company on the almost perpetual drizzle which prevails in the West of Scotland, and declared herself at a loss to account for it.

Popping his head up from below the table, "It is," said he, "only Nature weeping for the barrenness of her soil."

It was Sir Walter Scott who said that "his friends werna great book-readers, but they were maistly a' grand book-*keepers*"—a common accomplishment of the friends and acquaintances of all men, alas!

Tom Purdie, Sir Walter's favourite servant, appeared before the Sheriff first as a poacher; when Scott became so interested in his story, which he told with a mixture of pathos, simplicity, and pawky humour, that he granted him forgiveness, and ultimately engaged him as a sort of factotum at Abbotsford. Tom served him long and faithfully. Only "leeward whiles he took a bicker" towards the dram. Scott is said to have proposed for Tom's epitaph the words—"Here lies one who might have been trusted with a purse of untold gold, but *not* with a barrel of unmeasured whisky." But more pungent than this even was his remark at the funeral ceremony of the eccentric Earl of Buchan. In accordance with the Christian mode of burial, the body should have been carried into the chapel, where it was to be interred, feet first. Sir David Brewster was one of the mourners, and was the first to observe that the head of the coffin was first in. He said—"We have brought the Earl's head in the wrong way."

"Never mind," replied Scott. "His Lordship's head was turned when he was alive, and it is not worth our while to shift it now."

Long before the secret of the Waverley novels had been blown about, the Ettrick Shepherd divined it, and as the novels appeared he had them re-bound and lettered "Scott's Novels." While visiting Hogg at Altrive, the author ventured to remark in a dry humorous tone, "Jamie, your bookseller must be a stupid fellow, to spell *Scott's* with two *t's*." Hogg replied, "Ah, Watty, I am ower auld a cat to draw that strae before."

Mrs. John Ballantyne tells a story of Scott and Hogg not to be found in Lockhart.

At her dinner table in Hanover Street, she says, the Shepherd was present, and was amusing the company very much by his attempts to dissect "twa teugh auld chuckies," and was making the legs and wings and gravy fly in every direction, to the annoyance of every one in his neighbourhood. Suddenly he stopped, dipped a napkin in the finger-glass, and began to mop his face, which was "a' jappit wi' the juice."

Scott saw his friend's dilemma, and out of the goodness of his heart determined to create a diversion in his favour. Addressing Mrs. Ballantyne, he asked this question—"Mrs. John, once on a time all the letters of the alphabet were invited out to their dinner—they all came but U. Why did not U come?" On giving it up, Scott said, "Why, then, the reason why U did not come to dinner is very clear—because U never comes till after (T)."

Sometimes a very trifling joke or anecdote adds to the gaiety of a company. It was so in this case, the story passed round, but Hogg could not understand it, and he asked what they were all laughing at. "It's about U (you)," cried Mrs. Ballantyne, and this made Hogg quite indignant. He rose and brandished his knife, and inquired in a blood-thirsty sort of way what they could possibly see about him to speak and laugh about. This made the joke tell all the better, when it was explained to him.

Carlyle recites with approbation a saying of somebody to the effect that no man has written so many volumes as Scott having so few sentences that can be quoted, and Gilfillan, replying to the charge, says he is prepared to prove that in no other novelist—not even Cervantes, or Bulwer, or Goodwin—is there to be found a greater number of separate and quotable beauties than in Scott. Gilfillan's offer is not extravagant. Regarding the humorous side of the Waverley novels alone, which is all that concerns us here, one has only to think of Caleb Balderston, of Edie Ochiltree, of Cuddie Headrigg, of Andrew Fairservice; has but to utter aloud to himself the familiar "Ma conscience!" of Bailie Nicol Jarvie; the "Prodigious!" of Dominie Samson; the "Jeanie, woman!" of the Laird of Dumbiedikes—to have his mind peopled like a market-place with familiar figures, and his memory serving his tongue with passage upon passage, page upon page, and all with the freedom and rapidity of electric telegraphy. The temptation to quote now is strong; but I must resist it in order to overtake less familiar, though perhaps less delectable matter.

How humour will serve one in circumstances where sheer eloquence might pall is well illustrated by an important incident in the life of Scott. When George IV. visited Scotland in 1812, Sir Walter was largely "in evidence" in Edinburgh, eager to greet his Sovereign and afford him a royal welcome. Elaborate preparations had been made in the Capital in order that the reception might be worthy of the illustrious visitor, but when the royal yacht arrived in the Forth, the rain poured down in torrents. Sir Walter accordingly visited the King on board, and, in asking him to defer his landing on account of the inclemency of the weather, made one of the happiest speeches of his life—a speech which we may be sure delighted no one more than the King himself:—

"Impatient, Sire," said he, "as your loyal subjects are to see you plant your foot upon their soil, they hope you will consent to postpone your public entry until to-morrow. In seeing the state of the weather, I am myself forcibly reminded of a circumstance which once occurred to me. I was about to make a tour through the Western Highlands with part of my family. I wrote to the innkeeper of a certain hostelry, where I meant to halt a day or two, to have rooms prepared for me. On the day appointed it rained, as it does to-day, ceaselessly. As we drew near our quarters, we were met on the hill over his house by our Boniface, with bared head, and backing every yard as I advanced, who thus addressed me:—

"'Guid guide us, Sir Walter! This is just awfu'! Siccan a downpour! Was ever the like? I really beg your pardon! I'm sure it's nae faut o' mine; I canna think how it should happen to rain this way, just as you, o' a' men in the warld, should come to see us! It looks amaist personal! I can only say for my part, I'm just ashamed o' the weather!'

"And so, Sire, I do not know that I can improve upon the language of the honest innkeeper; I cannot think how it should rain this way, just as your Majesty, of all men in the world, should have condescended to come and see us. I can only say in the name of my countrymen, I'm just ashamed o' the weather!"

Sir Walter welcomed his Majesty not only in person, but also in song, by writing a long ballad in two parts, to the old tune of "Carle, and the King Come." Simultaneously with this loyal piece there, however, appeared in the

*London Examiner* a satirical effusion, entitled, "Sawney, now the King's Come," which caused some stir, and greatly annoyed the sensitive loyalty of the author of *Waverley*.

The writer was Alexander Rodger, of Glasgow, the well-known author of "Robin Tamson's Smiddy," "Behave yersel' before Folk," and other popular humorous songs; and the ultra-radical opinions for which he had already languished in "Bridewell," it cannot be denied, rendered the humour of this counterblast rather too broad for general circulation. Its cleverness, however, was undoubted. A poet of admitted quality, Rodger had a rich and ready humour which helped him through many a difficulty. Whilst for the treasonable character of his contributions to the *Spirit of the Union* he lay in a Glasgow prison, where he was used with reprehensible harshness, he solaced himself in his solitude by singing, at the top of his lungs, his own political song compositions, some of which were so spiced with humorous satire that they could not be very grateful to the ears of his jailors. Once, when his house was searched for seditious publications (terrible bugbears at that time to the local authorities of Glasgow), Sandy handed the Family Bible to the Sheriff's officer, with the remark that that was the only treasonable book in his possession; and for proof he referred the aghast official to the chapter on Kings, in the first Book of Samuel. Rodger's contributions to *Whistle-Binkie* form perhaps the most delightsome items of that perennial collection of Scottish lyrics, none of them being a whit less felicitous than his lyrical address to Peter M'Kay—"Ane sober advice to ane drucken souter in Perth"—of which the following forms the first verse:—

"O, Peter M'Kay! O, Peter M'Kay!

Gin ye'd do like the brutes, only drink when ye're dry,

Ye might gather cash yet, grow gaucy and gash yet,

And carry your noddle Perth-Provost pow-high;

But poor, drucken deevil, ye're wed to the evil

Sae closely, that naething can sever the tie;

Wi' boring and boosing, and snoring and snoozing,

Ye emulate *him* that inhabits—the sty."

George Outram, another Glasgow poet, claims particular attention when and wherever the humour of Scottish poets and poetry is the subject of consideration. Such of his pieces as "The Annuity," "Drinkin' Drams," and "Soumin' an' Roumin'," are amongst the most humoursome effusions in the native tongue. The temperance cause has made great progress since the bacchanalian heroic above named was penned, and it is now the teetotallers who laugh most over the ironical humour expressed in the lines. His "Annuity" is familiar to everybody, and the same may be said of "Soumin' an' Roumin'." The following illustration of his wit in the shape of an epigram, which he composed on hearing a lady praise a certain reverend Doctor's eyes, is, however, not so well known as it deserves—

"I cannot praise the Doctor's eyes,

I never saw his glance divine;

He always shuts them when he prays,

And when he preaches he shuts mine,"

and the whimsical humour contained in the subjoined little sketch will warrant its quotation:—

"My twa swine on the midden,

Wi' very fat their een are hidden;

Their wames are swell'd beyond dimension,

Their shapes!—ye hae nae comprehension.

Sic a sicht!—their tails are curly,

Their houghs sae round, their necks sae burly;

In the warld there's naething bigger

Than the tane—except the tither."

The next prominent among Scottish poet-humourists that occurs here is Professor Wilson, whose claim is made perfect by the unique and incomparable "Noctes Ambrosianæ," originally contributed to *Blackwood's Magazine* under the pen name of "Christopher North." Here there is humour to the knees, humour to the loins, humour to swim in—a great river! But we dare not enter, even though the temptation is strong. One solitary example of Wilson's genial humour, gleaned outside of the "Noctes," must serve here. It involves the name of another poet-humourist of almost equal renown—namely, Professor Aytoun, author of the celebrated *Lays of the Scottish Cavaliers* and joint-author with Sir Theodore Martin of the *Bon Gaultier Ballads*. Aytoun, as everybody knows, married Wilson's daughter, Miss Emily Jane. When, after the usual preliminaries, he made a proposal of marriage to her, the young lady, as a matter of course, referred him to her father. Aytoun was uncommonly diffident, and said, "Emily, my dear, you must speak for me. I could not summon courage to speak to the Professor on the subject."

"Papa is in the library," remarked the lady.

"Then you had better go to him," said the suitor, "and I will wait here for you."

There being apparently no help for it, the lady proceeded to the library, and, taking her father affectionately by the hand, mentioned that Aytoun had asked her in marriage, and added, "Shall I accept his offer, papa; he is so shy and diffident that he cannot speak to you himself?"

"Then we must deal tenderly with him," said the hearty old man; and writing his reply on a slip of paper, he pinned it on her back.

"Papa's answer is on the back of my dress," said Miss Wilson, as she re-entered the drawing-room. Turning her round, the delighted swain perceived these words—"With the author's compliments."

Susanna, Countess of Eglinton, Allan Ramsay's patroness, to whom he dedicated his immortal "Gentle Shepherd," once sent him a basket of fine fruit. No poet of the last century could let such a circumstance pass unsung; accordingly, honest Allan composed the following complimentary epigram, which he sent with his note of acknowledgment to the Countess:—

"Now Priam's son, ye may be mute,

For I can bauldly brag with thee;

Thou to the fairest gave the fruit—

The fairest gave the fruit to me."

Neatly turned, you say! Yes; but, not content with sending the epigram to the person for whom it was particularly intended, he enclosed a copy to his friend Budgell, who soon sent him back the subjoined comment upon it, which, we need not doubt, severely wounded the vanity of the wig-maker poet:—

"As Juno fair, as Venus kind,

She may have been who gave the fruit;

But had she had Minerva's mind,

She'd ne'er have given 't to such a brute."

The following epigram, by a living Scottish writer, is decidedly pointed and clever, and has the additional merit of being self-explanatory:—

"He was a burglar stout and strong,

Who held 'It surely can't be wrong,

To open trunks and rifle shelves,

For "God helps those who help themselves."'

But when before the court he came,

And boldly rose to plead the same,

The judge replied—'That's very true;

You've helped yourself—*now God help you!*'"


I have spoken of Professor Aytoun, and his connection with the *Bon Gaultier Ballads*. As everybody knows, "The Massacre of the Phairshon,"

"With four-and-twenty men

And five-and-thirty pipers,"

is from Aytoun's pen. In the Memoirs of the poet, written by his friend and collaborator, Sir Theodore Martin, there is this capital story of the ballad. "Being asked to get up an impromptu amusement at a friend's house in 1844, for some English visitors, who were enthusiastic about the Highlanders and the Highlands, he fished out from his wardrobe the kilt with which he had electrified the men of Thurso in his boyish days. Arraying himself in this, and a blue cloth jacket with white metal buttons, which he had got years before to act a charity boy, in a charade, he completed his costume by a scarf across his shoulders, short hose, and brogues! The brevity of the kilt produced a most ludicrous effect, and not being eked out with the usual 'sporran' left him much in the condition of the 'Cutty Sark' of Burns's poem. With hair like Katterfelto's, on end in wild disorder, Aytoun was ushered into the drawing-room. He bore himself with more than Celtic dignity, and saluted the Southrons with stately courtesy, being introduced to them as the famous Laird of Macnab. The ladies were delighted with the Chieftain, who related many highly exciting traits of Highland manners. Among other things, when his neighbours, as he told them, made a foray, which they often did, upon his cattle, he thought nothing of 'sticking a tirk into their powels,' when the ladies exclaimed, in horror, 'O, laird, you don't say so!'

"'Say so!' he replied, 'on my saul, laties, and to pe surely, I to it.'

"At supper he was asked to sing a song. 'I am fery sorry, laties,' he replied, 'that I have no voice; but I will speak to you a translation of a fery ancient

Gaelic poem,' and proceeded to chant 'The Massacre of ta Phairshon,' which came upon all present as if it were the invention of the moment, and was greeted with roars of laughter. The joke was carried on until the party broke up, and the strangers were not undeceived for some days as to the true character of the great Celtic chief."

Adam Skirving, author of the popular song of "Johnnie Cope," and the equally facetious and felicitous ballad of "Tranent Muir," was a wealthy farmer near Haddington, and a man of athletic body as well as of strong mind. Among the various persons referred to in "Tranent Muir" was a certain Lieutenant Smith, an Irishman, who displayed much cowardice in the battle. Says the poet:—

"And Major Bowle, that worthy sowl,

Was brought down to the ground, man;

His horse being shot, it was his lot,

For to get many a wound, man;


Lieutenant Smith, of Irish birth,

Frae whom he called for aid, man,

Being full of dread, lap owre his head,

And wadna be gainsaid, man.

"He made sic haste, sae spurred his beast,

'Twas little there he saw, man;

To Berwick rade, and safely said,

The Scots were rebels a', man;

But let that end—for weel 'tis kenn'd

His use and wont to lee, man,

The league is nought, he never fought

When he had room to flee, man."

Immediately on the satire and its source of emanation being communicated to the heroic (?) Lieutenant Smith, he despatched a junior officer to Skirving, with a challenge to the poet to meet him in single combat.

The bard's reply was of a piece with his attack—"Gang back," said he, "and tell Lieutenant Smith that I hae nae leisure to come to Haddington; but tell him to come here, and I'll tak' a look o' him, and if I think I'm fit to fecht, I'll fecht him; and if no, I'll do as he did—*I'll rin awa'.*"

Hard and stinging things have been uttered against poets, but the hardest and sharpest have been those hurled by one poet against another. As instance, the "Flyting" of Dunbar and Kennedy, the less remote encounter between Tennyson and Bulwer Lytton in the pages of *Punch*, and the more recent scalping scuffle which took place between Buchanan, Swinburne, and Rossetti. The wit of the poet is indispensable for affording the proper point to the sting of humorous satire. Here is a good example:—A few years ago the late William C. Cameron, of Glasgow, a shoemaker to trade, and author of a meritorious volume of verses, entitled *Light, Shade, and Toil*, contributed a little poem to the columns of the *Weekly Herald*, each succeeding stanza of which opened somewhat ostentatiously with the request—"Write me my epitaph!" one entire verse being:—

"Write me my epitaph! short let it be,

Say that here, 'neath the sod, lies one of the free,

One who has wrote and sung the lays of the poor,

One who has loved more than gold, field, wood, and moor."

Responsive to the poet's request a local bard wrote, and the *Herald* of the following week contained "His Epitaph," in these words:—

"*Toil* over, *Light* snuffed out, himself a *Shade*,

For evermore removed from pitiless chaff,

*Hic jacet!*—A judicious reader made

(Excuse his tears) this touching epitaph."

Poets there have been, too, who were their own most merciless censors. Robert Chambers tells that when the General Assembly of the Church of Scotland determined on extending their body of psalmody, they addressed a circular to the clergy, praying that those who were so inclined would compose paraphrases of scripture, and transmit them to Edinburgh for the inspection of the Assembly, that a proper selection might be made for use. A very old man, and very primitive minister in Caithness, was roused by this request from prosaic lethargy of a whole lifetime, and felt a latent spark of poetry suddenly arise in his bosom. So instantaneous was the effect of this inspiration, that on the very Sunday after he had received the Assembly's circular, he had prepared a paraphrase which he determined to read aloud to his congregation. The first verse ran as follows:—

"The Deil shall ryve them a' in rags,

That wicked are in vain;

But if they're gude and do repent,

They shall be sew'd again."

But this was quite enough, the audience burst out into such a transport of laughter on hearing it that the ingenious author saw fit to suppress the rest, and abandon his poetical attempt.

Then Zachary Boyd, of facetious memory, minister of the Barony Church, Glasgow, in the time of Charles I., and who translated the Bible into verse, the MS. of which is preserved in the library of the University of Glasgow to this day, must have been a frank fellow. He sings:—

"There was a man called Job,

Dwelt in the land of Uz;

He had a good gift of the gob,

The same thing happens us."

A fatal "gift o' the gob," alas!—for perfectly convincing proof of which see the following verses from his "History of Jonah"—a gem *per se*. Jonah—according to the poet—soliloquiseth—

"What house is this, where's neither coal nor candle,

Where I no thing but guts of fishes handle;

The like of this on earth man never saw,

A living man within a monster's maw.

Noe in his ark might goe and also come,

But I sit still in such a straitened roome,

As is most uncouth, head and feet together,

Among such grease as would a thousand smother.

In all the earth like unto me is none,

Farre from all living I heere lye alone,

Where I entombed in melancholy sink,

Choak't, suffocat, with excremental stink."

On Burns's first visit to Edinburgh he was introduced, among many others, to a Mr. Taylor, then parochial schoolmaster at Currie, and, in his own estimation, a poet of no mean order. The meeting was effected at the house of Mr. Heron, at whose table Burns was a frequent guest. Taylor brought with him his book of manuscript poems, a few of which were read to Burns for his favourable opinion previous to printing. Some of the passages were odd enough, such as this, on the title-page—

"Rin, bookie, rin, round the warld lowp,

Whilst I lie in the yird wi' a cauld dowp,"

at which Burns laughed heartily. Next morning Mr. Heron meeting Taylor, enquired of him what he thought of the Ayrshire poet.

"Hoot," quoth the self-admiring pedagogue, "the lad'll do; considering his want o' lear, he's weel eneuch."

Though not like it, the foregoing recalls a good anecdote of the poet Campbell, which recently appeared in print for the first time, in the columns of the *Christian Leader*.

The author of "The Pleasures of Hope" being on a visit to Ayrshire, happened to go into a bookseller's shop in Kilmarnock. The bookseller, as he entered, whispered something over the counter to a portly and comely old lady, who was making a small purchase of sealing-wax and notepaper. "Lord save us," she replied, in an audible whisper, "ye dinna mean it!"

"It's true, I tell ye," said the bookseller, also in a whisper.

The old lady turned towards the poet and said, not without betraying a slight embarrassment: "An' sae ye're the great Thomas Campbell; are ye? I'm vera prood to meet ye, sir, and didna think when I left hame in the mornin' that sic a great honour was to befa' me."

The poet felt much flattered by this tribute; but confusion took entire possession of him, as the worthy old soul continued: "There's no a man in Ayrshire that has the great skill ye hae, Mr. Campbell, and I wad be greatly obleeged to ye if ye wad come and see my coo before ye leave this part o' the country, an' let me ken if ye can do onything for her. She's a young beastie, and a guid beastie, and I shouldna like to lose her."

There was an eminent veterinary surgeon, or cow doctor, in the neighbouring county of Dumfries, whose name was also Thomas Campbell, and the worthy woman had mistaken the poet for this celebrated and doubtless highly respectable person.

Of Campbell and Leyden, Gilfillan tells an interesting and instructive story in his *Life of Sir Walter Scott*. The former thought the latter boastful and self-asserting; Leyton thought Campbell jealous and envious. And there was perhaps a modicum of truth in their estimates of each other. Campbell had been unfortunate and not over well conducted in his youth; had been hindered by circumstances in his path to the pulpit; and this, along with poverty, had soured him. Yet he was a fine-hearted fellow in the main, as well as a thoroughly true one. Leyden had something of the self-glorification of the wild Indian chief, fond of showing his strings of scalps, and chanting fierce war-songs over his fallen foes; but he, too, was sincere, warm-hearted and guileless. When he read Campbell's "Hohenlinden," he said to Scott, "Dash it! I hate the fellow, but he has written the best verses I have read for ever so long;" to which Campbell replied, "I detest Leyden with all my soul, but I know the value of his critical approbation."

Every Scottish reader is familiar with Burns's weird and inimitable "Address to the Deil," and some are aware that more than one of our native bards—from a desire to "give the deil his due," as we may suppose—have essayed to catch up the grim humour of the original effusion, and compose a suitable reply to it. I have myself seen three efforts of the kind, each of them more or less clever: one by Ebenezer Picken, of Paisley, who died in 1816; and two of unknown authorship. For pungency of wit and skill of versification, one of the latter—cut from a Scottish newspaper published in Burns's lifetime—indisputably "bears the gree," and forms a not unworthy companion-poem to the original "Address." It is somewhat lengthy, but its rarity, considered in conjunction with its merit, will justify its quotation in full:—

THE DEIL'S REPLY TO ROBERT BURNS.

O waes me, Rab! hae ye gane gyte;

What is't that gars ye tak' delight

To jeer at me, and ban, and flyte,

In Scottish rhyme,

And fausely gie me a' the wyte

O' ilka crime?

O' auld nicknames ye hae a fouth,

O' sharp sarcastic rhymes a routh,
And as ye're bent to gie them scouth,
'Twere just as weel
For you to tell the honest truth,
And shame the deil.


I dinna mean to note the whole
O' your confounded rigmarole,
I'd rather haud my tongue, and thole
Your clishmaclavers,
Than try to plod through sic a scrole
O' senseless havers.

O' warlocks and o' witches a',
O' spunkies, kelpies, great or sma',
There isna ony truth ava
In what you say,
For siccan frichts I never saw,
Up to this day.

The truth is, Rab, that wicked men,
When caught in crimes that are their ain,
To find a help, are unco fain,
To share the shame,
And so they shout, wi' micht and main,
The deil's to blame.

Thus, I am blamed for Adam's fa'.
You say that I maist ruined a';
I'll tell ye a' e thing, that's no twa,
It's just a lee;

I fasht na wi' the pair ava,
But loot them be.

I'd nae mair haun' in that transgression,
You deem the source o' a' oppression,
And wae, and death, and man's damnation,
Than you, yersel';
I filled a decent situation
When Adam fell.

 And, Rab, gin ye'll just read your Bible,
Instead o' blin' Jock Milton's fable,
I'll plank a croon on ony table
Against a groat,
To fin' my name you'll no' be able
In a' the plot.

Your mither, Eve, I kent her brawly;
A dainty queen she was, and wally,
But destitute o' prudence wholly,
The witless hizzie,
Aye bent on fun, and whiles on folly,
And mischief busy.

Her Father had a bonnie tree,
The apples on't allured her e'e;
He warned her no' the fruit to pree,
Nor clim' the wa',
For if she did, she'd surely dee,
And leave it a'.

As for that famous serpent story,
To lee I'd baith be shamed and sorry,

It's just a clever allegory,
And weel writ doon;
The wark o' an Egyptian Tory—
I kent the loon.

Your tale o' Job, the man o' Uz,
Wi' reekit claes, and reested guiz,
My hornie hooves, and brockit phiz,
Wi' ither clatter,
Is maistly, after a' the bizz,
A moonshine matter.

Auld Job, I kent the carl right weel;
An honest, decent, kintra chiel'
Wi' head to plan, and heart to feel,
And haun' to gie—
He wadna wrang'd the verra Deil
A broon bawbee.

The man was gay and weel to do,
Had horse, and kye, and ousen, too,
And sheep, and stots, and stirks enow
To fill a byre;
O' meat and claes, a' maistly new,
His heart's desire.

Forby he had within his dwellings
Three winsome queans and five braw callans
Ye wadna, in the hail braid Lallans,
Hae fand their marrow,
Were ye to search frae auld Tantallans
To Braes o' Yarrow.

It happened that three breekless bands
O' caterans came frae distant lands,
And took what fell amang their hands,
O' sheep and duddies.
Just like your reivin' Hielan' clans,
Or Border bodies.

I tell thee, Rab, I had nae share
In a' the tulzie, here or there,
I lookit on, I do declare,
A mere spectator,
Nor said, nor acted, less or mair,
Aboot the matter.


Job had a minstrel o' his ain,
A genius rare, and somewhat vain
Of rhyme and lear, but then again,
Just like yersel',
O' drink and lasses unco fain,
The ne'er-do-weel.

He'd sing o' lads and lasses fair,
O' love, and hope, and mirk despair,
And wond'rous tales wad whiles prepare,
And string together,
For a' he wanted was a hair
To mak' a tether.

So with intention fully bent,
My doings to misrepresent,
That Book o' Job he did invent,

And then his rhymes
Got published, in Arabic prent,
To suit the times.

You poets, Rab, are a' the same,
O' ilka kintra, age, and name,
Nae matter what may be your aim,
Or your intentions,
Maist a' your characters of fame,
Are pure inventions.

Your dogs are baith debaters, rare,
Wi' sense, galore, and some to spare,
While e'en the verra Brigs o' Ayr,
Ye gar them quarrel—
Tak' Coila ben to deck your hair
Wi' Scottish laurel.

Yet, Robin, lad, for a' your spite,
And taunts, and jeers, and wrangfu' wyte,
I find, before you end your flyte,
And wind yer pirn,
Ye're nae sae cankered in the bite
As in the girn.

For when you think I'm doomed to dwell,
The lang for-ever-mair in hell,
Ye come and bid a kind farewell—
And, guid be here,
E'en for the very Deil himsel',
Let fa' a tear.

And, Rab, I'm just as wae for thee,

As ever thou can'st be for me,

For less ye let the drink abee,

I'll tak' my aith,

Ye'll a' gang wrang, and, maybe, dee

A drunkard's death.

Sure as ye mourned the daisy's fate,

That fate is thine, nae distant date,

Stern Ruin's ploughshare drives elate,

Full on thy bloom,

And crushed beneath the furrow's weight

May be thy doom.

Much more might be written under this heading, for of the humours of living and recent poets I have scarcely dared to speak. Yea, of the humours of those about whom one may write with perfect freedom, the half has not been told; and to the bookish reader, I feel, the chapter will be interesting as much for what it suggests as for what it contains.

As a last item, the following humorous "dig" at the rigid and narrow Sabbatarianism of the early Dissenters, which has had a wonderful vitality—living as it has done for generations, more in the memory of what we may call the "long-headed" order of the community than in printed books—will be enjoyed. Its authorship—presumably a secret from the first—is still unknown; and it has no history or interesting particular other than is expressed by itself, further than this, that it is occasionally sung to a standard Psalm tune, under the old fashion of "reading the line," and, when so rendered, sounds inexpressibly droll:—

THE CAMERONIAN'S CAT.

There was an auld Seceder's cat

Gaed hunting for a prey,

And ben the house she catch'd a mouse

Upon the Sabbath day.

The Whig, he being offended

At such an act profane,

Laid by the Book, the cat he took,
And bound her in a chain.

"Thou damned, thou cursed creature,
This deed so dark with thee,
Think'st thou to bring to hell below
My holy wife and me?

"Assure thyself that for the deed
Thou blood for blood shall pay
For killing of the Lord's own mouse
Upon the Sabbath day."

The presbyter laid by the Book,
And earnestly he pray'd
That the great sin the cat had done
Might not on him be laid.

And straight to execution
Poor pussy she was drawn,
And high hang'd up upon a tree—
The preacher sang a psalm.

And when the work was ended,
They thought the cat was dead,
She gave a purr, and then a meow,
And stretched out her head.

"Thy name," said he, "shall certainly
A beacon still remain,
A terror unto evil doers
For evermore, Amen."

# CHAPTER XI
## 'TWEEN BENCH AND BAR—A CHAPTER OF LEGAL FACETIÆ

The Scottish Law Courts have been long and justly celebrated as an arena of wit and humour of the richest sort. But the facetious counsel and the witty and eccentric judge, like the humorous and quaint divine, no longer prevail; and the current collector of the native legal facetiæ who would present brilliant specimens and illustrations must riddle the records of past generations to find them, or else adopt the simpler method, which has been most frequently followed, of riddling the riddlings of those who have successfully riddled the records before them. Despising neither of the courses indicated, I shall partially here pursue both; and, first of all, will turn to the *Memorials* of the late Lord Henry Cockburn, the most extraordinary passages of which perhaps are the writer's memories of the law lords. Of Lords Braxfield, Eskgrove, Eldon, Hermand, and Meadowbank, and others, most of whom he knew personally, Cockburn tells some "unco" stories. And, surely, if we may express regret that the wit and humour of some of those are not inherited by the present occupiers of the judicial bench, we may be very thankful that the brutal severity which was practised by the first named is no longer possible. Braxfield's maxim seems to have been, "Hang a thief when he's young and he'll no steal when he's auld." It may be doubted, says Cockburn, if he was ever so much in his element as when tauntingly repelling the last despairing claim of a wretched culprit, and sending him to Botany Bay or the gallows with an insulting jest, over which he would chuckle the more from observing that correct people were shocked. To an eloquent culprit at the bar he once said—"Ye're a vera clever child, my man, but ye wad be nane the waur o' a hanging," and perhaps he got it. "Let them bring me prisoners and I'll find them law," used to be openly stated as his suggestion when an intended political prosecution was marred by anticipated difficulties. And Mr. Horner, the father of Francis, who was one of the juniors in one Mair's case, told that when he was passing the bench to get into the box, Braxfield, who knew him, whispered, "Come awa', Mr. Horner, come awa', and help us to hang ane o' thae damned scoondrels." In another political case it was pled in defence that "Christianity was an innovation, and that all great men had been reformers, even our Saviour himself." "Muckle He made o' that," chuckled Braxfield, in an under voice, "He was hangit."

Eskgrove succeeded Braxfield as the head of the Criminal Court, and a more ludicrous personage surely never existed. "His face," says Cockburn, "varied according to circumstances, from a scurfy red to a scurfy blue; the nose was prodigious; the underlip enormous, and supported by a huge, clumsy chin, which moved like the jaw of an exaggerated Dutch toy." When addressing a jury, if a name could be pronounced in more ways than one he gave them all. Syllable he invariably called sylla-*bill*, and wherever a word ended with the letter "g," the letter was pronounced, and strongly so. And he was very fond of meaningless successions of adjectives. The article "a" was generally made into *one*; and a good man he would describe as "one excellent, and worthy, and amiabill, and agreeabill, and very good man." Condemning a tailor to death for murdering a soldier by stabbing him, he addressed him thus:— "And not only did you murder him, whereby he was bereaved of his life, but you did thrust, or push, or pierce, or project, or propell the le-thal weapon through the belly-band of his regimen-tal breeches, which were his Ma-jes-ty's!"

In the trial of Glengarry, for the murder of Sir Alexander Boswell in a duel, a lady of great beauty was called as a witness. She came into court veiled. But before administering the oath, Eskgrove gave her this exposition of her duty in the situation: "Young woman, you will now consider yourself as in the presence of Almighty God, and of this High Court. Lift up your veil; throw off all modesty, and look me in the face." Having to condemn two or three persons to death who had broken into a house at Luss, and assaulted Sir James Colquhoun and others, and robbed them of a large sum of money, he first, as was his almost constant practice, explained the nature of the various crimes—assault, robbery, and hamesucken—of which last he gave them the etymology. He then reminded them that they had attacked the house and the persons within it, and robbed them, and then came to this climax—"All this you did; and God preserve us! joost when they were setten doon to their denner!"

A common arrangement of his logic, when addressing juries, was—"And so, gentlemen, having shown you that the panell's argument is utterly impossibill, I shall now proceed to shew you that it is extremely improbabill."

Brougham delighted to torment him. Retaliating, Eskgrove sneered at Brougham's eloquence by calling it, or him, *the Harangue*. In his summing up he would say—"Well, gentlemen, and what did the Harangue say next? Why, it said this———." Candidly, however, he had to declare that "that man Broom, or Broug-ham, was the torment of his life." Lord Eskgrove, of course, was an unconscious humourist. So also in great measure was Lord Hermand. When *Guy Mannering* was first published, Hermand was so much delighted with the picture of the old Scottish lawyers in the novel that he could talk of nothing else but Pleydell and Dandie Dinmont and High Jinks for many weeks. He usually carried a volume of the work about with him; and one morning on the bench his love for it so completely got the better of him that he lugged in the subject—head and shoulders—into the midst of a speech about a dry point of law. Getting warmer every moment he spoke of it, he at last plucked the volume from his pocket, and, in spite of the remonstrances of his brethren, insisted upon reading aloud the whole passage for their edification. He went through the task with his wonted vivacity, gave great effect to every speech and most appropriate expression to every joke; and, when it was done, the court had no difficulty in confessing that they had very seldom been so well entertained. During the whole scene, Mr. Walter Scott himself was present, in his official capacity as Clerk of the Court of Session, and was seated close under the Judge.

Before Hermand was elevated to the bench, and was known among men as Mr. George Fergusson, his addresses were delivered with such animation and intense earnestness that when it was known he was to speak the court was sure to be filled. His eagerness made him froth and splutter, and there is a story to the effect that, when he was pleading in the House of Lords, the Duke of Gloucester, who was about fifty feet from the bar, and always attended when "Mr. George Fergusson, the Scotch counsel," was to speak, rose and said, with pretended gravity, "I shall be much obliged to the learned gentleman if he will be so good as to refrain from spitting in my face."

Hermand was very intimate at one time with Sir John Scott, afterwards Lord Eldon. They were counsel together, says Cockburn, in Eldon's first important Scotch entail case in the House of Lords. Eldon was so much alarmed that he wrote his intended speech, and begged Hermand to dine with him at a tavern, where he read the paper and asked him if it would do.

"Do, sir? It is delightful, absolutely delightful! I could listen to it for ever! It is so beautifully written and so beautifully read! But, sir, it is the greatest nonsense! It may do very well for an English Chancellor; but it would disgrace a clerk with us."

Bacon's advice to judges is to "draw your law out of your books, not out of your brains." Hermand generally did neither. He occasionally showed great contempt for statute law, and would exclaim, "A statute! What's a statute? Words—mere words! And am *I* to be tied down by words? No, my Laards, I go by the law of *right reason*, my Laards. I *feel* my law—*here*, my Laards"—striking his heart.

Drinking, in this old fellow's estimation, was a virtue rather than a vice; and when speaking to a case where one Glasgow man was charged with stabbing another to the death in the course of a night's carousal, "They had been carousing the whole night," exclaimed Hermand, "and yet he stabbed him! After drinking a whole bottle of rum with him! Good God, my Laards, if he will do this when he's drunk, what will he not do when he's sober?"

William Maconochie (Lord Meadowbank), was an able but curious man. Before he spoke, Cockburn says, it would often have been a fair wager whether what he said would be reasonable or extravagant. All that was certain was, that even his extravagance would be vigorous and original, and he had more pleasure in inventing ingenious reasons for being wrong than in being quietly right. Sir Harry Moncrieff, who was present at his marriage, told that the knot was tied about seven in the evening, and that at a later hour the bridegroom disappeared, and on being sought for, was found absorbed in the composition of a metaphysical essay on "pains and penalties."

There has been no more famous legal notability in Scotland than John Clerk of Eldin, afterwards Lord Eldin. When Meadowbank was yet Mr. Maconochie, he one day approached his facetious professional brother, Clerk, and after telling him that he had prospects of being raised to the bench, asked him to suggest what title he should adopt.

"Lord Preserve Us!" said Clerk, and moved off.

When pleading before the same learned senator, after he had assumed the judicial title of Lord Meadowbank, it was suggested to Clerk by his Lordship that in the legal document which he had submitted to the Court he might have varied the frequently recurring expression "also," by the occasional use of "likewise."

"I beg your pardon, my Lord," said Clerk, "but the terms are not always synonymous."

"In every case," retorted Meadowbank, gruffly.

Clerk still dissented.

"Then cite an instance," demanded the Judge.

"Well," remarked Clerk, doubtless chuckling inwardly the while, "your Lordship's father was a Judge of Session. You are a Judge of Session *also*, but not *likewise*."

Clerk's ready wit helped him well on many an occasion. In pleading, he frequently dropped into broad Scotch, and once when arguing a Scotch appeal case before the House of Lords, in which his client claimed the use of a mill-stream by a prescriptive right, he contended that "the *watter* had run that way for forty years."

"Indeed," argued Clerk, "naebody kens how lang, and why should my client now be deprived of the *watter*?" etc.

The Chancellor, much amused at the pronunciation of the Scottish advocate, in a rather bantering tone, asked—"Mr. Clerk, do you spell water in Scotland with two t's?"

Nettled at this hit at his national tongue, Clerk immediately replied—"No, my Lord, we dinna spell *watter* in Scotland wi' twa t's, but we spell *manners* in Scotland wi' twa n's."

On one occasion, when he had been pleading a case before Lord Hermand, already mentioned, after he had finished and sat down to receive judgment, his Lordship took up the case rather warmly, and when in the heat of an excited harangue, the saliva from his lips was spurted in the face of the sarcastic advocate.

"I have often heard o' the dews o' Hermon," remarked Clerk, "but I never felt them before."

Mr. James Wolfe-Murray became a Judge of the Court of Session, under the title of Lord Cringletie. When he was appointed, doubts were expressed by some as to his legal acquirements, and Clerk expressed his view in the following clever epigram:—

> "Necessity and Cringletie
>
> Are fitted to a tittle;
>
> Necessity has nae law,
>
> Cringletie has as little."

When in his sixty-fifth year he was raised to the Bench, Clerk took the title of Lord Eldin, from his family estate. Some one remarked to him that his title nearly resembled that of the Lord-Chancellor Eldon.

"The difference," said he, "is all in my eye (i)."

Clerk had a halt in his gait, and when passing along on the street one day, he overheard a lady remark to a friend—"That's John Clerk, the lame lawyer."

He was about in a minute.

"No, madam," said he, "I am a lame man, but not a lame lawyer."

Quite right; *also*, but not *likewise*.

Another out-of-doors story in connection with this witty advocate refers to an occasion when he had been dining rather freely at the house of a friend in Queen Street, Edinburgh. Wending his way homewards "early in the morning, merrily, O," he failed to discover his own house in Picardy Place, and observing a housemaid busily engaged in cleaning a doorstep—"My good girl," says he, "can you tell me whaur John Clerk lives?"

"Awa' wi' yer nonsense," exclaimed the astonished girl, "you're John Clerk himsel'."

"That's true enough, lassie," said he, "but it's no John Clerk I'm seekin' for, it's John Clerk's house."

Sir James Colquhoun, Bart. of Luss, Principal Clerk of Session, was one of the odd characters of his time, and was much teased by the wags of the Parliament House. On one occasion, whilst Henry Erskine was at the Inner House Bar, during the advising of some important case he amused himself by making faces at Sir James, who was sitting at the Clerk's table, beneath the Judges. His victim was much annoyed at the strange conduct of the tormenting lawyer, and, unable to bear it, disturbed the gravity of the Court by rising, and exclaiming—"My Lord, my Lord, I wish you would speak to Harry, he's aye making faces at me!"

Harry, however, looked as grave as a judge.

Peace ensued, and the advising went on, when Sir James, casting his eyes towards the Bar, witnessed a new grimace from his tormentor, and convulsed Bench, Bar, and audience by roaring out, "There, my Lord, he's at it again!"

Erskine was remarkable for his ready wit and stinging repartee. Like the illustrious John Clerk of Eldin, he was indifferent to the rules of pronunciation, and in pleading before a learned senator he spoke of a *curator bonis*.

"Allow me to correct you," said his Lordship, "the word is *curaator*."

"Thank you, my Lord," said Erskine. "I doubt not your Lordship is right, since you are so learned a *senaator*, and so eloquent an *oraator*."

Mr. Erskine of Alva, subsequently Lord Bargaig, was a person of short stature. Having been counsel in a case in which Henry Erskine appeared on the opposite side, he was obliged on account of the crowded state of the court to have a chair brought forward on which to raise himself when addressing the judge.

"This," remarked Henry, "is one way of rising at the Bar."

To a Judge of the Commissary Court, who talked in an inflated and pompous manner, who told him that his brother in the country had fallen from a stile and sprained his foot—

"It was fortunate for your brother," remarked Henry, "that it was not from your *style* he fell, or he had certainly broken his neck."

For the foregoing anecdotes relating to this well-known witty lawyer, as well as for the one that follows, I am indebted to the late Dr. Charles Rogers'

*Illustrations of Scottish Life.* On a change of ministry, Erskine was appointed to succeed Harry Dundas (subsequently Lord Melville), as Lord-Advocate. On the morning of his appointment, he met Dundas in the Parliament House, who had resumed the ordinary gown worn by all practitioners at the Scottish Bar, excepting the Lord-Advocate and the Solicitor-General. After a little conversation, Erskine remarked that he must be off to order his silk gown.

"'Tis not worth your while," said Dundas, "for the short time you'll want it; you had better borrow mine."

"I have no doubt your gown," replied Erskine, "is made to *fit any party*; but however short may be my time in office, it shall not be said of Henry Erskine that he put on the *abandoned habits* of his predecessor."

The late Lord Rutherford was a very able lawyer, but exceedingly affected in his manner and speech, and when addressing either the Bench or a jury spoke extra-superfine English. When, however, he broke out in a passion, which was by no means an unusual occurrence, he expressed his feelings in the broad vernacular. Lord Cockburn said to him one day, "It is strange, Rutherford, that you should pray in English and swear in Scotch."

Mr. Strang and Mr. Bruce were two members of the faculty in Parliament House, Edinburgh, who were nearly equally matched in cleverness, but most unlike as to stature. Strang was quite an Anak in height, whilst Bruce was so diminutive that he was facetiously known as "Zaccheus." When Sheriff Barbour, of Inverness, was appointed a Lord of Session, under the title of Lord Skelton, he was naturally ignorant of the new members of the bar in Parliament House, from which he had been away for twenty years.

On an early day after Lord Skelton began his duties in the Court of Session he was hearing a case in which Bruce appeared for the prosecution, while Strang had been retained for the defence. Bruce, duly arrayed in wig and gown, the latter of which effectually hid his short legs, was standing behind the Advocate's table, and had got under weigh in his opening remarks for the prosecution, when his Lordship interposed, with the slightest manifestation of feeling—

"It is usual, Mr. Bruce, for an advocate to stand when he addresses the Court."

"I am standing, my Lord," replied Bruce, deferentially.

"Oh, I beg a thousand pardons!" resumed Lord Skelton, feeling bitterly his unfortunate remark, and bowing his head for a few minutes towards his papers.

Bruce continuing his opening address, his Lordship took courage and looked up, when he saw at the other end of the bar the tall figure of Strang, towering up above his fellows. Thinking he had risen to interpose some remark against the opposing counsel's speech, he hurriedly said—

"Kindly sit down, Mr. Strang; Mr. Bruce is before the Court just now. I shall gladly hear you afterwards."

"I am sitting, my Lord," explained Strang, to the utter discomfiture of the astounded judge, and amidst the roars of laughter of all the members of the bar.

It was of these two able fellows that a waggish brother-barrister made the impromptu epigram—

> "To the heights of the law, though I hope you will rise,
>
> You will never be judges, I'm sure of a(s)size."

Lawyers, like editors, have been frequently made the butt of the satirist; but illustrations of their wit and humour, such as are here deduced—and they could be multiplied almost to any extent—show how well able they have been to hold their own—yea, to rout the enemy. Jeffrey was frequently more than equal to the occasion. When addressing a jury in a certain trial, he had occasion to speak freely of a military officer who was a witness in the cause; and having frequently described him as "this soldier," the witness, who was present, could not restrain himself, but started up, and called out—

"Don't call me a soldier, sir; I am an officer!"

"Well, gentlemen of the jury," proceeded Jeffrey, "this officer who, according to his own statement, is no soldier," etc.

And what cause could the livelier of them not extract fun from? At a jury trial in the town of Jedburgh, in which Moncrieff, Jeffrey, and Cockburn were engaged as counsel, while the former was addressing the jury, Jeffrey passed a slip of paper to Cockburn, with the following case for his opinion:—

"A legacy was lately left by an old lady to the *Peer* of Aberdeen. As the will was written by the Dowager herself, and by no means distinguished for correctness of orthography or expression, a dispute has arisen as to the intent of the testator; and the following claimants have appeared for the legacy:— 1st, the Earl of Aberdeen; 2nd, the Commissioners for erecting the pier at Aberdeen; and, 3rd, the Manager of the Charity Workhouse, who grounds his right on the fact that the old lady was in the habit, *more majorum*, of pronouncing poor *peer*. To which of the parties does the money belong?"

Cockburn immediately wrote in answer—"To none of the three; but to the Horticultural Society of Scotland for the purpose of promoting the culture of a sort of fruit called, or to be called, *the Pear of Aberdeen.*"

Many humorous instances of attempts to evade the law, and successful and unsuccessful attempts to get the better of it, could be cited; but most of them, of necessity, have been wicked as well as witty, and lie somewhat outside of my subject. One or two, however, may be tolerated, and the first, which reveals a biter neatly bitten, will be enjoyed. A dealer having hired a horse to a lawyer, the latter, either through bad usage or by accident, killed the beast, upon which the hirer insisted on payment of its value; and if it was not convenient to pay costs, he expressed his willingness to accept a bill. The writer offered no objection, but said he must be allowed a long date. The hirer desired him to fix his own time, whereupon the writer drew a promissory note, making it payable at the day of judgment. An action ensued, when, in defence, the lawyer asked the judge to look at the bill.

Having done so the judge replied—

"The bill is perfectly good, sir; and, as this is the day of judgment, I decree that you pay to-morrow."

Steenie Stuart, a recently deceased and well-known inhabitant of a populous northern burgh, got "roarin' fou' ilka pay nicht," and, in consequence, had frequently to appear and answer for his sins at the bar of the Police Court. As he approached the rail with a leer of recognition and compromise in his eye one Monday morning, the magistrate hailed him with "Here again, Steenie?"

"Ou, ay, Bailie," Steenie replied.

"An' are you no ashamed o' yersel'?"

"'Deed, am I, Bailie; black ashamed."

"Then what brings ye here ilka ither week?"

"Dinna blame me, Bailie. I canna help it. There's a curse on the name."

"A curse on whatna name?"

"On my name, Bailie; on the name o' Stuart."

"What d'ye mean, sir?"

"The Stuarts, ye ken, ha'e aye been unfortunate. James the First fell by the hands o' assassins in the toun o' Perth; James the Second was killed at the siege o' Roxburgh Castle; James the Third was murdered by his rebellious subjects; James the Fourth lost his life in the Battle o' Flodden Field; James the Fifth died o' a broken heart; Mary, puir Mary, lost her head an' her croon baith thegether; Charlie had neither a head nor a croon to lose, or he wad ha'e lost the ane or the ither, or baith."

"Ay, ay, Steenie," interjected the witty Bailie, "there's nae doot the Stuarts have had a fatal habit o' losin' their heads an' their croons, but yours is a case of an especially aggravated nature. They lost nae mair than a'e croon and a'e head each, but you ha'e lost mair heads an' mair croons than a' the lave putten thegether, for you lose yer head maistly every Saturday nicht in Tam Johnstone's public house, an' yer croon afore the Court here ilka Monday mornin'. It'll no do, Steenie lad. It'll no do. *Five shillings, or seven days.*"

A Coupar-Angus man, not many years ago, was sued for debt in the Sheriff Court at Perth, and on the day of the trial was met by a friend on the High Street of the Fair City.

"By the by," said the friend, "ye've a case in the Coort the day."

"Hoch! it's owre an oor syne," was the reply.

"An' hoo cam' ye on?" inquired the friend.

"I wan."

"Ye wan!" exclaimed the surprised interrogator, who knew that the debt was a just enough one. "Hoo did ye manage to win?"

"Daugon'd!" exclaimed the erewhile defendant, "I couldna but win; the thing was left to my ain oath."

Swearers, of course, who view the oath as a thing of expediency, as evidently that man did, come in handy about Courts of Law, and not very long since, in the same Sheriff Court, a batch of witnesses "swore" a young man so clearly out of a charge of assault that a party in Court, who was subsequently to be called on a similar charge, was heard whispering to a friend—"Lord, Tam, I wad gie a pound for half an oor o' thae witnesses."

Witnesses are a widely various lot, and are often the source of much amusement 'tween Bench and Bar. Great tact is required by the lawyer who would get "the truth, the whole truth, and nothing but the truth," out of some of them; and this sometimes, not because of any desire on the witnesses' part to prevaricate, but from perfectly innocent causes. Cockburn was exceedingly happy in the management of some of those who hailed from country places, and one case in which Jeffrey and he were engaged as counsel is memorable. A vital question in the cause was the sanity of one of the parties primarily concerned.

"Is the defendant, in your opinion, perfectly sane?" said Jeffrey, interrogating one of the witnesses, a plain, stupid-looking country man.

The witness gazed in bewilderment at the questioner, and gave no answer. Jeffrey repeated the question, altering the words—

"Do you think the defendant is perfectly capable of managing his own affairs?"

Still in vain.

"I ask you," said Jeffrey, "do you consider the man is perfectly rational?"

No answer yet.

"Let *me* tackle him," said Cockburn.

Jeffrey sat down, whereupon Cockburn assumed his broadest Scottish tone and accent, and turning to the obdurate witness, began—

"Hae ye your mull wi' ye?"

"Ou, ay!" said the awkward countryman, and diving his hand into his coat pocket he drew forth his snuff-horn and handed it over to the witty counsel.

"Noo, hoo lang hae ye kent John Sampson?" inquired Cockburn, tapping the mull familiarly with his finger, and taking a pinch.

"Ever since he was that heicht," was the ready reply, the witness indicating with his hand the alleged altitude.

"An' d' ye really think noo, atween you an' me," said the advocate, in his most insinuating Scotch manner, "that there's onything ava intill the cratur'?"

"I wadna lippen him wi' a bull-stirk," was the instant and brilliant rejoinder; and Jeffrey admitted that Cockburn had fairly extracted the essence of the evidence.

Cockburn, who entered the faculty in the year 1800, was in his day the most eloquent and persuasive orator at the Scottish Bar. With his impressive oratory, writes one, his expressive face and fine eye, his mellow voice, and his pure and homely Scottish dialect, he was almost irresistible with a jury, or in the General Assembly of the Church, where he was often engaged as counsel. On the trial of the infamous Burke and his wife, in 1829, for numerous murders of unfortunate creatures whom they had lured into their den and murdered, and whose bodies they sold to the Edinburgh doctors for dissection purposes, he acted as counsel for the woman. The trial lasted till five in the morning of the second day, and after sixteen or seventeen hours' previous exertion, he addressed the jury, in one of the most impassioned, and powerful speeches he ever delivered. He spoke for an hour, and literally held the jury and the audience spell-bound. His chief aim was to break down the evidence of Hare, and his wife, who were *socii criminis*, and had been admitted by the Crown as approvers. While the miserable woman was giving her evidence, she had a child in her arms, who continued to scream almost incessantly. After drawing, in scathing and terrible words, a picture of her and Hare's atrocities, whom he represented as the real criminals, he ascribed the screaming of the child to terror, "as if it had felt the fingers of the murderous hag clutching its little innocent throat." His peroration, delivered with a glistening eye, in tones of the utmost solemnity and pathos, put it to the jury that there was no real evidence except that of the approvers, and that if they found the accused guilty upon such evidence as that of the two Hares, "these [pointing with a tremulous hand to the accused] will be murdered, and these [pointing to the jury] will be perjured." Horrified as all in Court had been at the fearful atrocities disclosed on the trial, there was, when he sat down, a universal hum of sympathy from the large audience. His speech saved the woman's life; for, while the jury found the man guilty, their verdict in the case of the woman was "not proven."

For racy wit and humour Cockburn was equally distinguished as he was for eloquence. On one occasion he was engaged in a case in which some miscreant had ill-used and maimed a farmer's cattle by cutting off their tails. At the conclusion of a consultation, at which the farmer was present, some conversation took place as to the disposal of the animals. Turning to him, Cockburn said the cattle might now be sold, but that he must be content to sell them wholesale, because he could not *retail* them. On another occasion he was counsel for a man accused of a capital crime, for which, if found guilty, the punishment was death. The evidence was quite conclusive as to the man's guilt. When the jury had retired to consider their verdict, his client roundly taxed him with not having done him justice in the defence. He bore the fellow's insolence for some time, but at last he gave him the pithy reply—"Keep your mind easy, my worthy friend, you'll get *perfect justice* about this time six weeks"—six weeks being then the period allowed to elapse between a sentence of death and its execution.

That recalls a story told by Dr. Rogers concerning Sir John Hay, Bart., at one time Sheriff-Substitute of Stirlingshire, and one of the most facetious members of his order. Sir John had a habit, even when sitting on the bench, of crooning, or whistling, in an undertone, one or other of the Scottish airs. A youthful panel was in his court, found guilty of an act of larceny, for which in those days a sentence of banishment might be pronounced. After awarding him a sentence of imprisonment for a period, Sir John added, "and take care you don't come here again, my man, or——," and he closed the interview by humming the tune "Ower the Water to Charlie," affording a gentle hint, which was no doubt well enough understood.

The Judges and Counsel engaged in our Scottish Law Courts, it has been seen, have been a peculiarly witty and entertaining set, and the same may be said of some of the witnesses who have passed through their fingers. The following examination, which took place in a question tried in 1817, in the Jury Court, between the Trustees on the Kinghorn Passage and the town of Kirkcaldy, affords a striking illustration of the cannieness of one.

The witness was called on the part of the trustees, and apparently full of their interest. The counsel having heard that the man had got the present of a coat from the clerk to the trustees before coming to attend the trial, thought proper to interrogate him on that point; as, by proving this, it would have the effect of completely setting aside his testimony. The examination was as follows:—

"Pray, where did you get that coat?"

The witness (looking obliquely down on the sleeve of his coat, and from thence to the counsel), with a mixture of effrontery and confusion, exclaimed—

"Coat, coat, sir! Whare got I that coat?"

"I wish to know where you got that coat?"

"Maybe ye ken whare I got it?"

"No; but we wish to know from whom you got it?"

"Did ye gi'e me that coat?"

"Tell the jury where you got that coat?"

"What's your business wi' that?"

"It is material that you tell the court where you got that coat?"

"I'm no obleeged to tell about my coat."

"Do you not recollect whether you bought that coat, or whether it was given to you?"

"I canna recollect everything about my coats—whan I get them, or whare I get them."

"You said you remembered perfectly well about the boats forty-two years ago, and the people that lived at Kirkcaldy then, and John More's boat; and can you not recollect where you got that coat you have on at present?"

"I'm no gaun to say onything about coats."

"Did Mr. Douglas, clerk to the trustees, give you that coat?"

"Hoo do you ken onything about that?"

"I ask you, did Mr. Douglas, clerk to the trustees, give you that coat?"

"I'm no bound to answer that question, but merely to tell the truth."

"So you won't tell where you got that coat?"

"I didna get the coat to do onything wrang for't; I didna engage to say onything that wasna true."

The Lord Chief Commissioner, when the witness was going out of the box, called him back and observed, "The Court wish to know from you something farther about this coat. It is not believed or suspected that you got it improperly or dishonestly, or that there is any reason for your concealing it. You may have been disinclined to speak about it, thinking that there was something of insult or reproach in the question put from the bar. You must be sensible that the bench can have no such intention: and it is for your credit, and the sake of your testimony, to disclose fairly where you got it. There may be discredit in concealing, but none in telling where you got it.

"Where did you get the coat?"

"I'm no obleeged to tell about my coat."

"True, you are not obliged to tell where you got it, but it is for your own credit to tell."

"I didna come here to tell about coats, but to tell about boats and pinnaces."

"If you do not tell, I must throw aside your evidence altogether."

"I'm no gaun to say onything about my coat; I'm no obleeged to say onything about it."

Witness went away, and was called back by Lord Gillies.

"How long have you had that coat?"

"I dinna ken how lang I ha'e had my coat. I ha'e plenty o' coats. I dinna mind about this coat or that coat."

"Do you remember anything near the time: have you had it a year, a month, or a week? Have you had it a week?"

"Hoot, ay, I daresay I may."

"Have you had it a month?"

"I dinna ken: I cam' here to speak about boats, and no about coats."

"Did you buy the coat?"

"I dinna mind what coat I bought, or what coat I got."

The upshot of it was, that their lordships were forced to reject the evidence of the witness.

Your city and burgh magistrates, too, by the sublime naturalness with which they "open their mouth and put their foot in it," have afforded much fun to the world. A boy being brought before a newly-installed West country bailie for stealing a turnip, he sentenced him to seven days' imprisonment, adding, in profoundly solemn tones, "And may the Lord have mercy on your soul."

A Glasgow magistrate had a young lad brought before him accused with abstracting a handkerchief from a gentleman's pocket. Without waiting for proof of the accused's guilt, the bailie addressed him, remarking, "I ha'e nae doot but ye did the deed, for I had a handkerchief ta'en oot o' my ain pouch this vera week," and passed sentence.

The same magisterial logician was on another occasion seated on the bench, when a case of serious assault was brought before him by the public prosecutor. Struck by the powerful phraseology of the indictment, the bailie proceeded to say, "For this malicious crime you are fined half a guinea." The assessor remarked that the case had not been proven. "Then," continued the magistrate, "we'll mak' it five shillings."

An unfortunate fellow, many years ago, appeared at the bar of the Glasgow Police Court for being drunk and disorderly. Both the culprit and the bailie were characters in their way. The case was conclusively proved, and the bailie fined the man in fifteen shillings.

"Fifteen shillin's!" exclaimed the man. "Bailie, you're surely no' in earnest! Bless ye! whan will I win fifteen shillin's to gie ye!"

"Well," said the bailie, "I'll make it half a guinea, and not a farthing less."

"Hauf a guinea! If ye fine me in hauf a guinea what's to come o' my puir wife an' weans? They maun starve; there's nae ither way o't!" returned the offender, in a most lugubrious tone. "Ay, we maun a' starve, or beg!"

"Well," said the bailie, relenting, "I'll make it seven and six, and not a farthing less!"

"Seeven an' six! That's just the hauf o' my week's wages—and there's no' a grain o' meal in the hoose, nor a bit coal to mak' it ready, even supposin' there was! Oh, bailie, think what an awfu' lot seven an' six is to a workin' man wi' a sma' family!"

"Well, well," returned the good-natured magistrate, "I'll make it five shillings, and I'll not make it a farthing less though you were the king on the throne!"

"Weel, weel, bailie, Mary an' me an' the weans maun just submit," said the knave, pretending to have broken into tears, at the same time saying to himself, "Blessed is he that wisely doth the poor man's case consider."

The soft-hearted bailie couldn't stand the silent appeal of tears nor the apt quotation the artful dodger had made, so, gathering together all the poor stock of savage energy he possessed, he turned on the prisoner, and said—

"Look here! I'll mak' it hauf a crown, and though you were ma ain brither I couldna mak' it less!"

---

Bailie Robertson of Edinburgh had not the advantage of an early education, nor the prudence to conceal his ignorance. A case was brought before him, in which the owner of a squirrel presented a claim of damages against a person who had it in charge, but who had allowed it to escape. The case was one of great complication, and the bailie was rather at a loss for a time. At length, collecting his faculties, he said to the defendant, "Hoo did it manage to get awa'?"

"The door o' the cage was open, and it gaed oot through the window," was the reply.

"Then, hoo did you no' clip its wings?"

"It's a quadruped, your honour," said the defendant.

"Quadruped here, or quadruped there," argued the magistrate, "if ye had clippit the brute's wings it couldna hae flown awa'. I maun decide against ye."

---

# CHAPTER XII
## HUMOURS OF SCOTTISH RURAL LIFE

Affording better opportunities for the development of individual character than are to be found in the busy town and crowded city, country life is more congenial also to the growth and exercise of the faculty of original humour. In the denser populations information on every intelligible subject is so readily accessible through the medium of books, magazines, morning and evening newspapers, and courses of lectures, etc., that it is not incumbent on any one to form his or her own idea of any particular matter. Ideas here are supplied ready-made, like everything else, and warranted free from adulteration; and thus your city and townspeople see very generally eye to eye; and from frequency of contact with each other, and the causes already indicated, are forcibly rubbed into something like a general mental, as well as physical, similitude.

In the rural districts of the country it is altogether different. Books are scarce, daily newspapers rarely appear, there are no courses of scientific or other lectures, and so the individual mind has largely to form its own idea of every particular subject; and as very much of what is most enjoyable in humorous Scottish stories and anecdotes arises from "simple and matter-of-fact references made to circumstances which are unusual," thus it is that the best as well as the most of our Scottish humour is bred of rural life. Every book of native anecdotes—every bout of story-telling—reveals this fact. And in the present chapter I shall recount, irrespective of consecutive order and design, the choicest illustrations of the humours of Scottish rural life which have not already appeared in these pages, and with which my memory shall serve me, committing them to paper simply as they rise in my mind. And, just to set the ball a-rolling, let the first story relate to the first day of the week, and be one that to some extent contrasts the town with the country notion as to the proper observance of the day of rest. It is a story which Mr. Henry Irving told, and did not tell well, some years ago, in the course of an after-dinner speech in (I think) New York, and which, with questionable propriety, he related as having happened in his own experience whilst, shortly before, he had been journeying in the vicinity of Balmoral, although it had been told in pithier form in select circles in Scotland for ten years and more. The story is to this effect:—A well-known and esteemed city Established Kirk minister, in the course of a summer vacation in the North, was prevailed upon by a brother clergyman a little distance off to occupy his pulpit for a day, during his, the local preacher's, peremptory call from home. The service consisted of a "single yokin'," which ended a little after mid-day, and the weather being fine, the D.D., for he was such, when he had "cuisten the goon" and refreshed the inner man, took his familiar staff in his hand and emerged from the manse to enjoy a stroll along the quiet country road. A few hundred yards distant from the manse gate he passed a little farm steading on the roadside, the abode of the ruling elder of the congregation, and one of the sternest Calvinists and strictest Sabbatarians in the whole parish, but had hardly done so when he heard footsteps behind him, and the next moment an arresting hand was laid on his shoulder.

"Ye'll excuse me, sir," said the farmer and elder, "but ye're the Edinborough minister that was preachin' to us the day, an' I would like to ken if ye're walkin' oot the gate for mere pleasure on the blessed day, or if ye're on a mission o' mercy?"

"Oh, it's a delightful afternoon," replied the divine, "and I am just enjoying a meditative walk amid the beauties of Nature, so rich and——"

"I just suspectit as muckle," broke in the elder; "but you that's a minister o' the Gospel sud ken that this is no a day for ony sic thing."

"Well," returned the Doctor, "we find good precedent for walking on the Sabbath. You remember that even the Master himself walked in the fields with His disciples on the Sabbath day."

"Ou, I ken a' aboot that brawly," snorted the elder; "but I dinna think ony mair o' *Him* for't either!" and immediately turning on his heel, he strode sulkily towards the steading.

But, of course, the ministers are more commonly the accusers than the accused in the matter of supposed or actual Sabbath desecration—both in town and country.

"Wherefore did you go and shoot the hare on the Sabbath day, John?" asked a reverend gentleman once of a parishioner who was "before the Session" for the misdeed in question.

"Weel, ye see," replied John, not unphilosophically, "I had a strong dreed that the beastie michtna sit till Monday, say just dressed his drodrum when I had the chance."

But a certain minister and elder in Perthshire once combined to transact dubious business, even "between the preachin's."

"Had it not been the Sabbath day, Mr. Blank," remarked the preacher, "I would have asked you how the hay was selling in Perth on Friday?"

"Weel, sir," replied the sessional *confrere*, "had it no been the day that it is, I wad just hae tell't ye it was gaun at a shillin' the stane."

"Indeed! Well, had it been Monday instead of Sabbath, I would have told you that I have some to sell."

"Imphm, ay, ou ay, sir. An' had it been Monday, as ye say, then, I wad just hae tell't ye I wad gie ye market price for't."

The significant nod which the minister gave to this last remark brought the elder with a couple of carts to the manse on Monday morning, and before mid-day the minister's hay-stack was *non est*.

These fellows were wise as serpents, though scarcely as innocent as doves.

The Dumfries old lady who was accustomed to employ the wet Sundays in arranging her wardrobe had less cunning. "Preserve me!" she would exclaim, "another gude Sabbath! I dinna ken whan I'm to get thae drawers redd up."

Dr. Guthrie says "our ancestors might have been too scrupulous. I don't say they did not fall into glaring inconsistencies" in connection with Sabbath observance, and tells a story of his going to preach for a clerical friend in Ross-shire. Before retiring to rest on Saturday night, he asked his friend if he could get warm water in the morning to shave with.

"Wheesht! wheesht!" returned his host. "Speak of shaving on the Lord's day in Ross-shire, and you need never preach here again."

And yet at the same time, in the same locality, a little warm water and whisky would have been supplied on the self-same morning without question, being regarded as a work of necessity and mercy.

Speaking of necessity and mercy. It is Dr. Guthrie also, I think, who tells of a maid-servant who refused to feed the cows on the Sabbath, although she was willing to milk them. The explanation being, "The cows canna milk themsel's, so to *milk* them is a clear work o' necessity, but let them out to the fields and they'll *feed* themsel's weel enough." And speaking of milking reminds me of a good country story. It is a native of Glenisla, in Forfarshire, and belongs to the time when Matthew Henry's famous Bible Commentary was the apple of every leal Scotsman's eye. One Geordie Scott, thereaway, was so fain to possess a copy of "Matthew Henry," as this Bible was long familiarly termed, that he suggested to his wife (the two lived alone together) that they might sell the cow and purchase one with the price she would realise. The wife demurred at first, but latterly consented, with one proviso—namely, that Geordie would be willing to take "treacle ale" to his porridge every morning. This the good man at once agreed to. So crummie departed, and "Matthew Henry" arrived. A few weeks passed, and the big ha' Bible gave great delight, but the "treacle ale" was like to turn Geordie's stamach a'thegither.

"Dod, wife," said he one morning, "I doot that treacle ale's no gaun to do wi' me, we'll need to try an' get a wee drap milk to the parritch. What do ye think?"

Janet had been missing her troke with the cow, and was rueing that she had consented to the "niffer."

"'Deed, gudeman," says she, "a bargain's a bargain. An' gin ye will hae milk, an' winna want it, ye maun just gang an' milk 'Matthew Henry.'"

Your rural Scot is reflective and argumentative to a degree.

"Dinna tell me," said a sapient Forfarshire laird of the old school, "dinna tell me that the earth's shaped like an orange, an' that it whirls roond aboot ilka twenty-four 'oors. It's a' nonsense. The Seidlaw Hills lie to the North and the Tay to the Sooth at nicht when I gang to my bed; i' the mornin' when I rise I find them the same; an' that's gude proof that the earth disna turn roond. I'll tell ye what it is—an' I speak wi' authority of ane wha's gi'en the maitter a deal o' thocht—the earth's spread oot just like a muckle barley scone, in which the Howe o' Strathmore represents a knuckle mark."

Reflective, I said. Very! And the ordinary Scotch farmer's love of gain is proverbial. Life in his eyes is valuable chiefly as a season in which to make money. Thus, not very long ago, while about half a dozen farmers were returning home by train from the Perth weekly market, they talked about how this friend and that friend was in his health; and about some others who had died recently, and how much money each of them must have left.

"Ay, but men dinna live nearly sae lang nooadays as they did in the Bible times!" remarked one, with a heavy sigh.

"Eh, man, na," broke in another, who had hitherto not spoken. "An' I was just thinkin' there to mysel' a minute syne, that Methuselah must have been worth a power o' money when he dee'd, if he was onything o' a savin' kind o' a man ava."

Waggish some of them, and wild not a few. There are many rare good fellows among the farmers of Perthshire; genuine humourists, too. Here was how one of them proposed the toast of "The Queen" at a recent Cattle Show dinner. He was Chairman, and, "Noo, gentlemen," said he, "fill a' your glasses, for I'm aboot to bring forrit 'The Queen.' (Applause.) Our Queen, gentlemen, is really a wonderfu' woman, if I may say it. She's ane o' the gude auld sort; nae whigmaleeries or falderalls aboot her, but a douce, daicent bodie. Respectable, beyond a' doot. She's brocht up a grand family o' weel-faur'd lads and lasses—her auldest son wad be a credit to ony mither; and they're a' weel married—a'e dauchter is nae less than married to the Duke o' Argyle's son and heir. (Cheers.) Gentlemen, ye'll maybe no believe it, but I ance saw the Queen. (Sensation.) I did. It was when I took my auld broon coo to the Perth Show. I mind o' her weel—sic colour! sic hair! sic——

(Interruptions, and cries of "Is it the coo or the Queen ye're proposin'?") The Queen, gentlemen. I beg your pardon, but I was talkin' aboot the coo. Hooever, as to the Queen; somebody pointed her out to me at the Perth station. And there she was, smart and tidy-like; and says I to mysel', 'Gin my auld woman at hame slips awa' ye needna remain a widow anither hour langer.' (Cheers.) Noo, gentlemen, the whisky's gude, the nicht's lang, the weather's weet, and the roads are saft and will harm naebody that comes to grief. So aff wi' ye; every gless to the boddom—'The Queen!'"

Many forces in Nature and circumstances in life conspire to disturb the peace of the farmer. Amongst them—trespassers. But, if he is a man of resource, he may summon a species of artillery that will "hold the field" against all comers. It is told of one in the South that, while some members of the Ordnance Survey were plodding here and there through growing grain and everything else on his farm, and perhaps more than was necessary, just to irritate the farmer, who, they had learned, was a crusty customer. They had not manœuvred long when the farmer approached.

"What are ye dancin' aboot there for?" he demanded.

"Oh, we have a right to go anywhere," returned one of the company. "We are surveying, and here are our Government papers."

"Papers here or papers there," returned the farmer, "oot ye gang oot o' my field."

"No, we shan't," was the reply; "and, remember, you are rendering yourself liable to prosecution for interrupting us."

The farmer said no more; but going over to a shed which opened into the field, and at the time chanced to contain a vicious bull, he gently opened the door and stood aside. The bull no sooner saw the red coats than he, of course, rushed at them in full career. The surveyors snatched up their theodolite and ran for their lives, while the old farmer held his sides with laughter, and yelled after them—"What are ye a' rinnin' for? Can ye no show him yer Government papers?"

"What are ye a' rinnin' for? Can ye no show him yer Government papers?"

Speaking of trespassing, I am reminded of a story which reveals how ready-witted the rural inhabitants can sometimes be. One day, many years ago, Willie Craig, a Perthshire village worthy, found himself in the near vicinity of Scone Palace, and by cutting through the woods there he would reach his destination much sooner than by holding to the public road. The old Earl of Mansfield could never distinguish between a trespasser and a poacher, and Willie knew this, and that if he was seen he would, at the very least, be turned back. Still the nearer road was so tempting that he ventured it, trusting his own ready wit to cope with the vigilance of the terror-striking game-preserver. All went well until about three-fourths of the forbidden ground had been traversed, when, lo and behold, the Earl appeared. Willie, alert to every sight and sound, eyed the Earl ere the Earl had time to eye him, so instantly turned on his heel and commenced to retrace his steps.

"Hi, sir!" cried the Earl, "where are you going?"

Willie snooved along and made no reply.

"Halt, sir!" cried the Earl, rushing up to where Willie was; "turn this moment, and go back the way you came."

Willie meekly and instantly obeyed. He had not gone many paces when the Earl, straining a point in favour of so pliable a culprit, again stopped him and said he might go for this time. Willie hesitated for a moment, but, mastering the situation with one bright idea, he quickened his step, and, glancing over his shoulder, retorted with energy—

"Na, na, my lord; ye've turned me ance, but ye'll never turn me twice. I'll lat ye see, noo, that I'm just as independent as ye're fit to be."

Speaking of Perthshire worthies reminds me of another characteristic story. A thrifty middle-aged crofter of that ilk, until a year or two ago, lived a life of easy bachelorhood, his only domestic companion being an antiquated maiden sister. About the period indicated, however, following the example of the majority of his sex, he took unto himself a wife, whom he brought home to reside together with his sister and himself. "Twa women is ane ower mony in ony house," says the proverb, and this instance proved no exception. The new-comer soon made the situation so hot for her sister-in-law that the crofter perceived that a reconstruction of his household was instantly necessary. He was equal to the occasion; the wife was dismissed *sans ceremonie*. On being interrogated by a neighbour on the policy of his action, Peter made reply—

"Was I gaun, think ye, to hae my sister abused by a woman that isna a drap's bluid to ony o' the twa o' us?"

Very good! And Peter's philosophic reply brings vividly before me the characteristic figure of honest Tammas Broon, a well-known denizen of a small Perthshire village. Tammas had little or no idea of things humorous; yet, as if by the inspiration of accident, he was continually passing remarks and answering questions in language and manner the most provocative of laughter. One day a Free Church minister—now of world-wide fame—was passing along while Tammas was busily engaged at the thatching of a stack in his own little barn-yard, and snatching readily at the circumstance as a means to the improvement of the moment, the divine called out—

"You are thatching, I see, Thomas. Do you think you will require to do any such work in the future existence?"

"Not at all, sir," was the instant and innocent rejoiner; "this is only to hold out *water*."

Tammas's daughter, rumour said, at one time was about to marry with a young man of the village of whose family Tammas did not approve. Village gossips are active creatures, and the spirit, if not the exact letter, of Tammas's dissent was early conveyed to the young man's mother, a bit of a randy. The result was a forced meeting on the king's highway, when the enraged matron demanded to know if Tammas had ever said that *her* son wasna a match for *his* dochter?

"I never said such a thing, lady," Tammas replied coolly, "I simply remarked that he was a hawk out of a bad nest." And the matter ended.

To be called "Fifish" is not a compliment, but there is much pawky humour in the typical Fife character. Here is a specimen:—Recently a tattered son of Orpheus attached to the end of a tin whistle penetrated the land as far as Kingsbarns, in the East Neuk. Entering at one end, he whistled himself right out at the other, without receiving a copper. As he passed the last door he turned towards an old native who sat sunning himself on a low dyke. "Man," said he, "I havena got a farden in the hale toon."

"Na, I'm no thinking ye wad," replied the ancient Fifer; "ye see, we do a' our ain whistlin' here."

"Man, I havena got a farden in the hale toon." "Na, I'm no thinking ye wad; ye see, we do a' our ain whistlin' here."

Every one who has seen much of country life has noticed with what patient skill and anxiety a ploughman builds, say, a load of hay or straw which he is afterwards to cart to the town, and the pride there is in his eye as he marches with it along the road, guiding his pair of horses with cheering words and gentle touches of the reins. Not many years ago a Perthshire ploughman was proceeding in the manner indicated when, in a narrow part of the road, he was met by a hearse and a funeral party on foot behind it. On either side of the road was a deep ditch, and it was at once evident that every inch of room would be required to effect a safe passage. The funeral party were, very naturally, most concerned about the safety of the hearse, and not less than half a dozen voices kept assailing the ploughman with "Haud t'ye! haud t'ye! haud t'ye!" The ploughman held to him, and held to him, and still being implored to yield further, he held to him just an inch too far, and heels-over-head the horses and cartload of hay went into the ditch. Jock viewed the wreck for one brief moment, then, turning to those around him, he exclaimed, "Ye see what ye've dune noo wi' yer *d—d—dawmed* burial."

There is room for the play of humour sometimes on the occasion of a "coupit cart." One day a country lad approached a man who was ploughing in a field near the highway, and said—

"Od man, I've coupit my cart."

"Coupit yer cart! That's a peety, man. Whaur is't, and what had ye on't?"

"It's doon on the road yonder, an' it was laden wi' hay. Do you think you could come an' help me to lift it?"

"Weel, I canna leave my horses in the middle o' the field, but as sune as I get doon to the end o' the furr', I'll come an' help ye."

"Man, div ye no think ye can come i' the noo?" he asked, scratching his head.

"No; ye see weel eneuch I canna come i' the noo."

"Aweel," he said, in a tone of resignation, "I maun just wait then, but it would have suited better if ye could have come i' the noo, for the hanged thing is, my—my—faither's below't!"

"Man, div ye no think ye can come i' the noo?" "No; ye see weel eneuch I canna come i' the noo." "Aweel," he said, in a tone of resignation, "I maun just wait, then, but it would have suited better if ye could have come i' the noo, for the hanged thing is, my—my—faither's below't!"

I said *burial* a minute ago, and the word recalls a little story revealing much dry humour. A country cottar lay, as was evident, on his death-bed. His wife, true and faithful, sat on a chair by his side knitting a stocking, and ready to minister to his wants. Through the half-open door of the sickroom the dying man could see into the kitchen, from the roof of which there was suspended a nice fresh stump of bacon ham. "Marg'et," he said, by and by, "there's a nice bit of ham hangin' in the kitchen roof, if ye wad fry a slice o' that, woman, I think I could tak' it."

The ham had evidently not been expected to meet John's eye, and the request disconcerted Marg'et.

"Eh, John," she replied "there's few things in the warld I cud bear to refuse ye, but I canna brak' on that bit ham. *It'll tak' it a' to ser' the fouk at the funeral.*"

A farmer not far from Coupar-Angus happened to go into the bothy and seeing all his men sitting by the fire doing nothing, he said he would bring them some books to read. On going back some weeks after he saw his books lying up on a shelf with about an inch of dust on them, and he asked if they had been reading them. One of the ploughmen said they hadn't much time, and he said he would take them back then, and did so. After he had gone one of the men said, "Does the eediot think we will wirk his wark and read his books for the same siller?"

That is humour of the unconscious type. The next illustration belongs to the other class, and is quite as fresh, being as a matter of fact only a few months old. A Glasgow dignitary, with a very fine handle to his name, was recently rusticating in Western Perthshire; and expressing the desire to his host to know at first hand the feeling of the rural mind on the subject of Disestablishment, he was taken to the nearest roadside smithy and introduced to the smith. On being interrogated on the matter, the smith's reply was, "O'd, sir, I dinna ken verra weel what to say aboot it. This Kirk affair seems to me a'thegither just like a bee's skep that's cuisten twa or three times. First there was the Anti-Burgher, or auld Licht, hive that cam aff. Syne there was the Seceders, or U.P.'s, as ye ca' them. Then there was the Free hive. An' noo, because it's no like to cast ony mair, they wad fain hae us to start an' smeek the auld skep—a gey ungratefu' like piece o' wark."

There is an old proverb which says—"Fules shudna use chappin'-sticks, nor weavers guns." Drawing an inference therefrom, townspeople should be careful how they express themselves on country affairs to a country-bred person.

After the late Lord Cockburn had become proprietor of Bonaly, at the foot of the Pentland Hills, he was sitting on the hillside with his shepherd one day, and observing the sheep reposing in the coldest situation, he remarked—

"John, if I were a sheep, I would lie on the other side of the hill."

"Ah, my Lord," said the shepherd, "but if ye was a sheep, ye wad hae mair sense."

"John, if I were a sheep, I would lie on the other side of the hill." "Ah," said the shepherd, "but if ye was a sheep, ye wad hae mair sense."

Lord Rutherford, having entered into conversation with a shepherd on the Pentland Hills one day, complained bitterly of the weather, which prevented him enjoying his visit to the country. In specially forcible language he denounced the mist, and expressed his wonder how, or for what purpose, an East wind was created.

The shepherd, a tall, grim figure, turned round sharply upon him, and—

"What ails ye at the mist, sir?" he said. "It wats the sod, it slockens the yowes, and," adding with much solemnity, "*it's God's wull*," he turned away with lofty indignation.

Lord Rutherford used to repeat this with much candour as a fine specimen of rebuke from a sincere and simple mind.

Fine-spun theories and a high-falutin form of address may be wasted energy when applied to your ordinary rural inhabitant; but, even when his ignorance comes out, it is frequently seen in the garb of humour.

When Dr. Johnson was travelling in Scotland, he came up one day to a peasant who was busily engaged cutting turf, *i.e.—casting divots*.

"Pray, sir," inquired the lexicographer, "can you point out the way to the most contiguous village, for we are dreadfully fatigued, having deviated from our road these two hours?"

"Tired wi' *divoting* twa hours!" exclaimed the rustic, with scornful surprise. "I have been *divoting* here since four o'clock this morning, and maun do sae as lang as I can see, tired or no."

A burly Clydesdale farmer visiting Glasgow a number of years since, entered a chemist's shop to purchase a quantity of salts and senna for domestic purposes, and found the man of drugs—a bit of a wag—busily engaged with a galvanic battery. The farmer looked on for some time at the operations of the chemist, and, his curiosity becoming aroused—

"What kind o' a machine do ye ca' that, maister?" said he.

"Oh, man, that's the new patent machine for sawin' turnips," was the reply.

"For sawin' neeps!" cried the astonished son of the soil. "Hoo dis't work?"

"Take hold of the handles," said the chemist, "and I'll show you."

No sooner had he taken hold of the handles than the chemist set the thing in motion. In less than a minute the farmer was dancing and howling in the most dreadful manner.

"Throw the handles on the counter, man," cried the chemist.

This the farmer was, of course, unable to do.

At length he cried, "Woa! woa! man! Dod, it's perfect murder haudin' that thing."

The chemist then stopped the current of electricity; and as soon as he was released the farmer rushed from the shop, shouting, "By the Lord Harry, I'll stick to the auld-fashioned barrow yet!"

At a sale of an antiquarian gentleman's effects in Roxburghshire, which Sir Walter Scott happened to attend, there was one little article—a Roman patera—which occasioned a good deal of competition, and was eventually knocked down to the author of *Waverley* at a high price. Sir Walter was excessively amused during the time of the bidding to observe how much the price being realized was exciting the astonishment of an old woman who had evidently come there to buy culinary utensils on a more economical principle. When the sale of the article was affected—"Lord, bless me," she exclaimed, "if the *parritch pan* gangs at that, what will the *kail pat* gang for?"

When, some years ago, an old woman in Perthshire had occasion for the first time in her life to make a journey by rail, she hied to the nearest station and demanded a ticket.

"*First* or *third?*" inquired the clerk.

"Oh, a first ane," said she, "for I'm in an awfu' hurry, an' wad like to be hame again afore it's dark."

Burns prayed that the deil might "tak a thocht an' mend." "Janet, 'oman," said a Perthshire cottager to his wife, "d'ye ken, I was prayin' last nicht that the deil micht dee."

"Dinna fash doin' onything o' the kind again, then," replied Janet. "I'm thinking we micht get a waur ane."

"Hoo's yer mither the day?" was once asked of a country laddie.

"She's nae better," was the reply; "but there's waur than that, the coo's turned ill this mornin'."

"I'm thinkin', Nanny," said an aged country cottager to his faithful spouse, one day, while he lay in bed contemplating his end, "I'm thinkin' it canna be lang noo. I feel as if this very nicht the end wad come."

"Indeed, gudeman," said Nanny, in the most pensive tones. "If it were the Lord's will it wad be rale convenient, for the coo's gaun to calve, and I dinna weel see hoo I'm to be able to attend to you baith."

Dr. Alexander Fraser, of Aberdeen, was a homely and somewhat gruff but skilful physician. Among his patients was a sturdy country wife of the working class order, who had, upon very slight pretence, as Fraser felt satisfied, taken into her head that she was unwell—indeed, "was just dwynin' awa," as she herself phrased it. "And fat could he do for her?"

The doctor did not feel called upon to search the pharmacopœia very deeply, and asked if she thought she could eat a herring.

"Ay," she said, "I rather like them."

"Weel," said he, "ye canna do better than haud tichtly at them."

On his next visit the patient was asked if she had felt herself equal to carrying out the prescription.

"Ou ay."

"An' how many herrin' did you contrive to eat?"

"Weel, sir, I managed eleven."

"Eleven! indeed; that is quite as many as I expected. How did you manage them?"

"Weel, they were rather strong, sir," replied the patient, "but I just conquered them wi' bread."

I have heard of another country wife in the North who was "sairly fashed wi' her stamach." "Eh," said she, "the time was when I could hae ta'en a harl o' onything that was gaun, but noo, gin I sud eat a bittie o' bawcon to my dinner twice the buik o' yer steekit neive, sorra's in me, but I'll hae the ruft o't the hale aifternoon."

Mr. Inglis, in his book, *Our Ain Folk*, tells a story of a grand dinner that was given inside the ruins of Edzell Castle in honour of Fox Maule, who had succeeded his father, Lord Panmure. Sandie Eggo, a small landowner from Glenesk, had got seated between two burly farmers, who were too much taken up cracking their own jokes to heed the meek, shrinking Sandie, who, starving with hunger, could not attract the attention of any of the busy waiters. Dish after dish was whipped away from the table without his tasting it; and though he had paid a guinea for his ticket, he sat unnoticed and unattended to. At length, in desperation he seized a spoon and attacked a dish in front of him, which turned out to be mashed turnips, on which he gorged himself. By and by Mr. Inglis, the minister, met Sandie in the grounds, and asked how he enjoyed the grand dinner.

"Graund denner!" growled Sandie; "ye can ca't graund if ye like; but I can only say the fodder's michty dear at ane an' twenty guid shillin's for a wheen chappit neeps no fit to set doon to a stirk."

The same banquet gave rise to another story concerning a sheep farmer from Lethnot. He was a hard-headed man, and could stand any amount of whisky at a market fair without "turning a hair," but a banquet fairly bambaized him.

He had got among some lawyers, who were drinking champagne, and looking with the utmost contempt on the potency of the "thin fizzin' stuff," he quaffed bumpers of it at every toast. Some time after Mr. Inglis came upon him at another table covered with toddy tumblers and whisky bottles, and arrived at that state of intoxication known as "greetin' fou." On the minister inquiring what was the matter with the poor man, he replied, weeping copious tears—

"Ah, Maister Inglis, I'm failin'; I'm failin' fast. I'm no lang for this warl'!"

"Oh, nonsense," said the minister, "don't be foolish! You look hale and hearty yet. You just try to get away home."

"I'm clean dune, sir! I'm clean failed," persisted the lachrymose farmer, with intense pathos. "As fac's death, sir, I've only haen aucht tumblers, and I'm fou, sir—I'm fou!"

The Carlyles were a country-bred family, and the country roadman's criticism of them would have made "Teufelsdröckh" laugh as only readers of *Sartor* know how. "I ken them a'," said he. "Jock's a doctor aboot London. Tam's a harem-scarem kind o' chiel', an' wreats books, an' that. But Jamie—yon's his farm you see ower yonder—Jamie's the man o' that family, an' I'm proud to say I ken him. Jamie Carlyle, sir, feeds the best swine that come into Dumfries market."

"I ken them a'. Jock's a doctor aboot London. Tam's a harem-scarem kind o' chiel', an' wreats books, an' that. But Jamie—yon's his farm ye see ower yonder—Jamie's the man o' that family, an' I'm proud to say I ken him. Jamie Carlyle, sir, feeds the best swine that come into Dumfries market."

He was a country boy—the son of the village blacksmith—who, when he joined the evening singing class at the schoolhouse, and the precentor asked him if he had an ear for music, replied, "I dinna ken, but ye can tak' a cawnil an' look."

Love has been described in rural phraseology as "a yeukieness o' the heart that the hand canna claw."

It was a country lass who defined it as "just an unco fykieness i' the mind." It is very often, alas! nothing more. Another declared that unsalted porridge—"wersh parritch"—"just tasted like a kiss frae a body ye dinna like." It was a country wife who said to Dr. Chalmers, in answer to the question if she knew what was meant by *believing*, "Ou, ay; it's just to *lippen*, sir."

Any apt illustrations and choice examples of the humours of Scottish rural life might be multiplied to almost any extent. Only one or two more here, however, and first, one of Sir Walter Scott's, which should convey a lesson to those who cater for cheap compliments. A jolly dame, says Scott, who, not "sixty years since," kept the principal caravansary at Greenlaw, in Berwickshire, had the honour to receive under her roof a very worthy clergyman, with three sons of the same profession, each having a cure of souls. Be it said, in passing, none of this reverend party were reckoned very powerful in the pulpit. After dinner was over, the worthy senior, in the pride of his heart, asked Mrs. Buchan, the landlady, whether she ever had had such a party in her house before.

"Here sit I," said he, "a placed minister in the Kirk of Scotland, and here sit my three sons, each a placed minister of the same Kirk. Confess, Lucky Buchan, you never had such a party in your house before."

"Indeed, sir," replied Lucky Buchan, "I canna just say that I ever had such a party in my house before, except ance in the forty-five, when I had a Highland piper here and his three sons, a' Highland pipers, and the deil a spring could they play amang them!"

The simplicity of rural love-making, to unsuccessful as well as successful issues, has found illustration in many a humorous tale of Scottish life and character, but seldom with truer naivete than in the subjoined narrative of Betty's courtship and marriage, from the pen of an unknown author. It first appeared in an Edinburgh newspaper many years ago, and afforded the ground plan of the late Alexander M'Laggan's popular and really clever song, "Tibby and the Laird."

"Come noo, Betty," said an acquaintance, "an' gie me a sketch, an' tell me a' about your courtship an' marriage, for we dinna ken what's afore us, an' I may have a chance mysel' yet."

"Deed," says Betty, "there's was little about it ava'. Our maister was awa' at the fair a'e day, sellin' the lambs, an' it was gey late afore he cam' hame. Our maister very seldom stays late, ony place, for he's a douce man as can be. Weel, ye see, he was mair hearty than I had seen him for a lang time, but I opine he had a gude market for his lambs, and there's room for excuse when ane drives a gude bargain. Indeed, to tell ye the even-doun truth, he had rather better that a wee drap in his e'e. It was my usual to sit up till he cam' hame, when he was awa'. When he cam' in that nicht an' gied up stairs he fand his supper ready for him. An' 'Betty,' says he, 'what's been gaun on the day?—A's richt, I houp?' 'Ou, ay, sir!' says I. 'Very weel, very weel,' says he, in his ain canny way, an' gae me a clap on the shouther an' said I was a gude lassie. When I had telt him a' that had been dune through the day, just as I aye did, he gae me anither clap on the shouther, an' said he was a fortunate man to hae sic a carefu' person about the house. I never had heard him say sae muckle to my face afore, though he had aften said mair ahent my back. I really thocht he was fey. When he had got his supper finished, he began to be very jokey ways, an' said that I wasna only a gude but I was a bonnie lassie. I ken that fouks arena themsel's when they have a dram, an' say rather mair than they wad do if they were sober, sae I cam' awa' doun into the kitchen— Na, the maister never offered to kiss me; he was ower modest a man for that.

"Twa or three days after, our maister cam' into the kitchen. 'Betty,' says he. 'Sir,' says I. 'Betty,' says he, 'come upstairs; I want to speak to ye,' says he. 'Very weel, sir,' says I. Sae I went upstairs after him, thinking a' the road that he was gaun to tell me something aboot the feedin' o' the swine, or something like that. But when he tellt me to sit doun, I saw there was something serious, for he never bid me sit doun afore but ance, an' that was whan he was gaun to Glasgow Fair. 'Betty,' says he, 'ye ha'e been lang a servant to me,' says he, 'an' a gude an' an honest servant. Since ye're sae gude a servant, I aften think ye'll mak' a better wife. Ha'e ye ony objections to be a wife, Betty?' says he. 'I dinna ken, sir,' says I; 'a body canna just say hoo they wad like a bargain until they see the article.' 'Weel, Betty,' says he, 'ye're very richt there again. I ha'e had ye for a servant these fifteen years, an' I never knew that I could find faut wi' ye for onything. Ye're carefu', honest, an' attentive. And——' 'Oh, sir,' says I, 'ye aye paid me for't, an' it was only my duty.' 'Weel, weel,' says he, 'Betty, that's true; but then I mean to mak' amends to ye for the evil speculation that Tibby Langtongue raised about you an' me, an' forby—the world are taking the same liberty; sae, to stop a' their mouths you an' I sall be married.' 'Very weel, sir,' says I; for what could I say?

"Our maister looks into the kitchen anither day, an' says, 'Betty,' says he. 'Sir,' says I. 'Betty,' says he, 'I'm gaun to gie in our names to be cried in the kirk, this and next Sabbath.' 'Very weel, sir,' says I.

"About anither eight days after this, our maister says to me, 'Betty,' says he. 'Sir,' says I. 'Betty,' says he, I think we'll ha'e the waddin' put owre neist Friday, if ye ha'e nae objections.' 'Very weel, sir,' says I. 'An' ye'll tak' the grey yad, an' gang to the toun on Monday, an' get your bits o' waddin' braws. I ha'e spoken to Mr. Cheap, the draper, an' ye can tak' aff onything ye want, an' please yoursel', for I canna get awa' that day.' 'Very weel, sir,' says I.

"Sae I gaed awa' to the toun on Monday, an' bought some wee bits o' things; but I had plenty o' claes, an' I couldna think o' bein' extravagant. I took them to the manty-maker to get made.

"On Thursday nicht our maister says to me—'Betty,' says he. 'Sir,' says I. 'The morn is our waddin'-day,' says he; 'an' ye maun see that a' thing's prepared for the denner,' says he, 'an' see everything dune yoursel',' says he; 'for I expect some company, an' wad like to see a'thing feat an' tidy, an' in your ain way,' says he. 'Very weel, sir,' says I. Sae I got everything in readiness.

"On Friday mornin' our maister says to me, 'Betty,' says he. 'Sir,' says I. 'Betty,' says he, 'gang awa' an' get yoursel' dressed,' says he. 'For the company will sune be here, an' ye maun be decent. An' ye maun stay in the room upstairs,' says he, 'until ye're sent for,' says he. 'Very weel, sir,' says I. But there was sic a great deal to do, an' sae many grand dishes to prepare for the denner, to the company, that I couldna get awa', an' the hale fouk were come afore I got mysel' dressed.

"Our maister cam' dounstairs an' tell't me to go up that instant an' dress mysel', for the minister was just comin' doun the loan. Sae I was obleeged to leave everything to the rest o' the servants, an' gang upstairs an' put on my claes.

"When I was wanted, Mr. Brown o' the Hazelybrae cam' an' took me into the room amang a' the grand fouk an' the minister. I was maist like to fent, for I never saw sae mony grand fouk thegether a' my born days afore, an' I didna ken whaur to look. At last our maister took me by the hand, an' I was greatly relieved. The minister said a great deal to us, but I canna mind muckle o't; an' then he said a prayer. After this I thocht I should hae been worried wi' fouk kissin' me; mony ane shook hands wi' me I had never seen afore, an' wished me much joy.

"After the ceremony was owre, I slippit awa' doun into the kitchen again amang the lave o' the servants, to see if the denner was a' richt. But in a maument's time, our maister cam' into the kitchen, an' says—'Betty,' says he. 'Sir,' says I. 'Betty,' says he, 'ye maun consider that ye're nae langer my servant, but my wife,' says he, 'an' therefore ye must come upstairs an' sit amang the rest o' the company,' says he. 'Very weel, sir,' says I. Sae what could I do but gang upstairs to the lave o' the company, an' sit doun amang them? Sae, Jean, that was a' that was about my courtship an' marriage."

---

# CHAPTER XIII
## HUMOURS OF SCOTTISH SUPERSTITION

It is consistent with the earnestness of the Scottish character that, so long as the light of intelligence was but feebly diffused in the land, there should be a strong tendency towards superstitious imagining in the minds of the people. For superstitious notions, be it noted, have not been wont to spring so much out of *listless* as out of *restless* ignorance. Each notion and theory they embrace, however wild and wide of the mark, has been a guess at the truth. In the dim days of the Middle Ages, ere yet the sunshine of science had lit the hilltops of our country, whatsoever came within the living experience of the people, and was not palpable to sense, was readily attributed to supernatural agency, good or bad—generally the latter. Thus it was that the heavens above, and the earth beneath, and even the waters under the earth, became peopled with fairies, brownies, hobgoblins, waterkelpies, warlocks, ghosts, and witches. The powers attributed to these—each monster and spirit in its place—afforded to the popular mind an explanation of what, in the circumstances, was otherwise inexplainable, and thus, so long as ignorance abounded, superstition did much more abound. As the world has grown older the people have, happily, grown wiser. The grosser superstitions of Scotland have entirely disappeared. No living mortal outside of Bedlam, nowadays, believes in witches' cantrips—that ghosts walk the earth—or that fairies dance beneath the dim light of the moon. No; and the stories of faerie machinations, and of warlocks and witches, which our great-grandmothers related, in the light of the "oilie cruizie," to the wide-mouthed horror and bewilderment of our youthful grandfathers and grandmothers, would excite the youth of the present generation only to laughter. While saying that the grosser superstitions are gone, however, it must be admitted that some of the milder forms of superstitious belief—such as "freits" and omens—still find acceptance among us. "Marry in May, an' ye'll rue't for aye," says an old "freit"; and an examination of the Registrar's books, in town and country, will reveal that, comparatively, very few have the temerity yet to defy the ill-favoured prediction. It is an old "freit" that when children are brought to church for baptism, if the females receive sprinkling before the males, the latter will grow up effeminate, and the former will develop beards; and not very long ago I witnessed myself in a city church a rather unseemly scramble by a parent to have his boy brought to the front in preference to a neighbour's girl. It is not half a dozen years since a friend of mine in the West of Scotland was advised to pass her children through below a donkey's belly to cure them of whooping-cough. The night howling of a dog is still believed by many to betoken the early demise of some person in the near neighbourhood of that in which it occurs. "Dream o' the dead and you'll get news o' the livin'," is a prediction one may hear vented almost any day yet.

The practice of "first-footing" at New Year time is a remnant of superstition; as is also the practice, still adhered to in country districts, of throwing a "bauchle" at the heels of a bride as she is quitting her father's and mother's house. An old rhyme has come down embracing a number of omens, thus—

"West wind to the bairn when gaun for its name,

Rain to the corpse carried to its lang hame;

A bonnie blue sky to welcome the bride

As she gangs to the kirk wi' the sun on her side."

And better confidence is inspired in many when the conditions of each case are favourably meted out.

But to get at the broader humours of superstition, we have to go back a hundred years or more, when the broader superstitions were in vogue; when fortune-tellers and dealers in incantations plied a roaring trade—when the devil—not figuratively, but really—went about like a roaring lion seeking whom he might devour; and when—

"——guidly folks gat many a fricht

When the mune was set an' the stars ga'e nae licht,

At the roarin' linn in the howe o' the nicht,

Wi' soughs like Aiken Drum."

One's journey through life was fairly beset with supernatural agents, excitements, and influences. Much, indeed, depended on what day in the week one made his or her "first appearance on any stage," for, as that day was lucky or unlucky, so would their life be. Thus it was rhymed and written:—

"Monday's bairn is fair o' face,

Tuesday's bairn is fu' o' grace,

Wednesday's bairn's the child of woe,

Thursday's bairn has far to go,

Friday's bairn is loving and giving,

Saturday's bairn maun work for its living,

But the bairn that's born on the Sabbath day

Is lucky, and bonnie, and wise, and gay."

During the period of infancy—particularly, prior to receiving the sacrament of baptism—the utmost watchfulness had to be maintained lest the fairies should steal away a healthy child and leave a weakly infant of their own in its stead. A fairy child, it seemed, when it fell ill could be restored to health only by human milk. When there was a suspicion that a substitution of the kind had been effected—and this was jaloused if a child became extra fractious—a common and effectual test was to hold the youngster over the fire. If it was a changeling it would disappear up the lum with a "puff." If not, it would remain, perhaps to be burned, and be more fractious than before. Still there was satisfaction if it stood the test. Various superstitious rites were practised by the skilly wives to prevent catastrophe. The child immediately after birth might be turned three times contrary to the course of the sun. The bed containing the mother and child might be drawn to the centre of the floor, where the nurse would wave an open Bible over them three times—once for each person in the Holy Trinity—and adjure the evil spirits, by the name of all that was sacred, to depart to whatever place they came from. The sign of the cross made on the floor in front of the bed, or on the husband's nether garments laid at the foot of it, might suffice also to keep the elves aloof.

After a birth the mother was not permitted to cross the threshold of the door after the hour of sunset till she was "kirkit," lest the fairies should carry her off to nurse their children.

Baptismal customs were more ceremonious then than now. A young unmarried woman invariably carried the child to church. In her hand she took with her a slice of bread and cheese, wrapped up, and fastened with a pin taken from the child's dress, and this she presented to the first male passer she met. This person constituted the child's "first-foot"—it had not previously been allowed to cross the doorstep; and if he was a dark-haired man, there was good luck for the child; if fair, the reverse would happen to it.

Connected with this practice, Dr. Classon tells an amusing story. An English Duke had arrived in Glasgow on a Sunday, and was wandering in the streets during the time of afternoon service, when a young woman came up to him with a child in her arms, and offered him a piece of bread and cheese. In vain he protested that he did not know what she meant—that he had nothing to do with her or her child—that he was an entire stranger—that he had never been in Scotland before—that he knew nothing of the usages of the Presbyterian Kirk, being of the Church of England, and that she should give the "piece" to somebody else. The young woman was deaf to all his arguments, and held out authoritatively the bread and cheese. Thinking, probably, that the lass had not given him credit for what he had said, he told her in perfect simplicity that he was the Duke of —, and that he had just arrived at a hotel in the city, which he named. Her answer shut his mouth—

"Though ye were the king on the throne, sir, ye maun tak' that bread an' cheese."

Marriage was set about with rites and usages, some of which were peculiarly funny. First of all, in respect to date, the fateful month of May had to be avoided. If the "send," or bridal party, in going to or from the manse, met a funeral procession or a hearse on the way, it was a bad omen. When the bride entered her house for the first time, she had to be careful to step over the threshold, if she would be lucky. An oaten cake, or a cake of shortbread, was broken over her head, usually by the mother of the bridegroom, as she entered. In some instances the bread was placed on a plate and thrown over her head. If the plate was broken, so much the better luck. Then the links of the crook were put round her neck, and she was led to the meal girnal and compelled to take up a handful of meal. On the morning after marriage, in some parts of the country, the youth of both sexes, or perhaps females, would assemble out of doors, along with the newly-married couple. A basket would be transmitted among them, and gradually filled with stones until it reached the bridegroom, when it would be suspended from his neck. On receiving some more additional load, his affectionate helpmate, to testify her sense of the caresses he had lavished on her, would cut the cord and relieve him of the oppressive burden. The person who declined to comply with the latter ceremony would have come under a certain degree of discredit.

Liable at all times to the malevolent influences of the "Evil Eye," in addition to the many other ills already indicated, human life in the olden time was a serious matter. If a person died suddenly, or was laid aside by any sickness or disease, which the doctor might not readily comprehend the nature of, he was declared to have fallen the victim to an evil eye. When a death occurred the corpse was dressed and laid out in the manner still in practice, but with this addition—the friends laid on the breast of the deceased a wooden platter containing a small quantity of salt and earth, separate and unmixed—the earth an emblem of the corruptible body; the salt an emblem of the immortal spirit. No fire was allowed to be lit in a room where a corpse was kept; and it was reckoned so ominous for a dog or a cat to pass over it, that the poor animal was at once laid by the heels and killed without mercy. If a mourner's tear falls on the shroud, the spirit of the deceased might in consequence be so disturbed that it could not rest in the grave. During the several nights that intervened betwixt death and interment, the friends and neighbours took their turn at "sittin' up wi' the corpse," and were provided with a candle, a Bible, and a bottle of whisky. This practice was known as the "Lykewake," and its main purpose was to protect the body of the deceased person from supernatural interference. If a funeral *cortege* proceeded to the kirkyard in an irregular and straggling manner, it was accepted as a portent that there would ere long be another funeral in the same family.

In a village in Aberdeenshire, we read in the *Statistical Account*, where it was believed that the ghost of the person last buried kept the gate of the churchyard till relieved by the next victim of death, a singular scene frequently occurred when two burials were to take place in one churchyard on the same day. Both parties hurried forward as fast as possible to consign their respective friend in the first place to the dust. If they met at the gate, the dead were thrown down till the living decided by blows whose ghost should be condemned to porter it. Suicides were denied the right of Christian burial, and were interred either within the crossing of two public roads, with a stake driven through the body to hold it down, or were deposited in the march or ditch dividing two lairds' lands—as in the case of "Jenny Nettles," the heroine of the old song—and had a huge cairn of stones raised over the spot for the same purpose of protection.

Ghosts, of course, were numerous enough, and there was little need to make reckless additions to their number. The floating ballads were studded with them, and each district had its tales of ghostly horror. Among the ghosts of national celebrity there was "Pearlin' Jean," of whom the traditional catch runs—

"O Pearlin' Jean! O Pearlin' Jean!

She haunts the house, she haunts the green,

And glowers on us a' wi' her wul'-cat een."

"In my youth," says Mr. Charles Kirkpatrick Sharpe, "Pearlin' Jean was the most remarkable ghost in Scotland, and my terror when a child. Our old nurse, Jenny Blackadder, had been a servant at Allanbank, and often heard her rustling in silks up and down stairs and along the passages. She never saw her, but her husband did. She was a French woman, whom the first Baronet of Allanbank, then Mr. Stuart, met with at Paris during his tour to finish his education as a gentleman. Some people said she was a nun; in which case she must have been a Sister of Charity, as she appears not to have been confined to a cloister. After some time young Stuart either became faithless to the lady, or was suddenly recalled to Scotland by his parents, and had got into his carriage, at the door of his hotel, when his Dido unexpectedly made her appearance, and, stepping on the fore-wheel of the coach to address her lover, he ordered the postillion to drive on, the consequence of which was that the lady fell, and one of the wheels going over her forehead, killed her.

"In a dusky autumnal evening, when Mr. Stuart drove under the arched gateway of Allanbank, he perceived Pearlin' Jean sitting on the top, her head and shoulders covered with blood. After this, for many years, the house was haunted—doors shut and opened with great noise at midnight; the rustling of silks and pattering of high-heeled shoes were heard in bedrooms and passages. Nurse Jenny said there were seven ministers called in together at one time to lay the spirit; 'but they didna muckle good, my dear.' The picture of the ghost was hung up between those of the lover and his lady, and kept her comparatively quiet; but when taken away she became worse-natured than ever."

Another was "Thrummy Cap," a kindly ghost, celebrated in popular verse by John Burness, the cousin-german of the national poet. Then there were "Lady Greensleeves," who haunted the castle of Huntingtower, in Perthshire; the "Ghost o' Mause," a Blairgowrie spectre, who revisited the glimpses of the moon in the shape of a fox; but such a fox as had the power of speech, and to which no farmer's dog in the parish would be induced to give chase—and many besides. One of "Lady Greensleeves'" appearances was mercifully opportune. In a lone house on the estate of Huntingtower there lived an old man, the sole occupant of the building, and reputed to have hidden riches in some secret place in his dwelling. One night a number of masked villains broke in upon him and demanded, on pain of death, that he should show them where his money was concealed. In vain did he protest that he had no money in the house, save a few shillings, to which he made them welcome. Laying hands on him, dragging him to the floor, and brandishing their drawn knives over his hoary head, they swore that he must die for the lie which he had told them. As the oath was on their lips their intended victim uttered a wild shriek, and stretched out his hands imploringly towards a small two-paned window in the wall of the house. To that window the ruffians turned their eyes keenly, when lo! through the under pane a female face, pale as death, but with eyes sparkling like diamonds, stared in on them. "Oh, Lady Greensleeves," cried the old man, "winna ye come an' help me?" The name was as terror-striking as was the weird face at the window, and throwing down their knives, the robbers rushed from the house, and fled through the darkness, as if all the rogue-catchers of the shire had been at their heels.

Belief in the supernatural, it is worth noting, has not been confined exclusively to the ignorant classes. Lord Byron was sensitively superstitious. Sir David Brewster admitted it to have a certain power over him. James Thomson, the author of the "Seasons," had a great horror of the supernatural; and his fear of ghosts and goblins afforded much amusement to his fellow-collegians at Edinburgh. His bedfellow, knowing that he was afraid to remain alone in the dark, quietly slipped away from him one night when he was asleep. On waking, he rushed out of the room like a frightened child, and called loudly on his landlady for assistance. Dr. Somerville, who relates this anecdote upon the authority of Mr. Cranston, late minister of

Ancrum, who lodged in the same room with the poet at Edinburgh, attributes his weakness on this subject to the following circumstance:—

"The belief in ghosts, witches, fairies, etc., was so exceedingly prevalent at the beginning of this century that it would have been deemed heretical in any clergyman to have called in question their existence, or even their palpable interposition. One of the last appearances of these tremendous agents happened (I am speaking in the language of the vulgar) at Woolie, in the parish of Southdean, where Mr. Thomson was minister. Ever since I entered into life, it was necessary to speak guardedly upon the subject of the Woolie Ghost, as I myself have more than once given offence by my silence on the subject. The sequel of the story I heard, not at second-hand, but from the lips of a person, and that of rank and education, above the vulgar. Mr. Thomson, the father of the poet, in a fatal hour, was prevailed upon to attempt laying the evil spirit. He appointed his diet of catechising at Woolie, the scene of the ghost's exploits, and behold, when he had just begun to pray, a ball of fire strikes him on the head. Overwhelmed with consternation, he could not utter another word, or make a second attempt to pray. He was carried home to his house, where he languished under the oppression of diabolic malignity, and at length expired. Only think what an impression this story—I do not say fact, I say this story, for of it there can be no doubt—must necessarily have made upon the vigorous imagination of the young poet."

The ghost stories of Scotland would fill a large volume. Pennant tells of a poor visionary in Breadalbane who had been working in his cabbage garden, and imagined that he was suddenly raised into the air and conveyed over the fence into a corn field, where he found himself surrounded by a crowd of men and women, many of whom he knew to be dead. On his uttering the name of God they all vanished, except a female sprite, who obliged him to promise an assignation at the very same hour of the same day next week. Being left, he found his hair tied in double knots, and that he had almost lost the use of speech. However, he kept his appointment with the spectre, whom he soon saw coming floating through the air towards him; but she pretended to be in a hurry, bade him go on his way, and no harm should befall him. Such was the dreamer's account of the matter. But it is incredible, adds the narrator, what mischief this story did in the neighbourhood. The friends and relatives of the deceased, whom the old dotard had named, were in the utmost distress in finding them in such bad company in the other world; and the almost extinct belief in ghosts and apparitions seemed for a time to be revived.

Next to ghosts, witches ranked as objects of preternatural dread; and "for ways that were dark, and tricks that were vain," the witches, no doubt, were peculiar. And yet, surely most of the poor wretches who suffered and died at the stake because of the suspicion that they practised the forms of diablerie popularly attributed to warlocks and witches, were more sinned against than sinning.

The burning of witches—based, no doubt, on the command given in the twenty-second chapter of Exodus, namely—"Thou shall not suffer a witch to live"—forms a black chapter in the history of Scotland, and one in which we look in vain for the discovery of much humour. In the powers popularly assigned to these "withered beldams, auld and droll," there was, however, a world of humour. They were accused of having intercourse with Satan, and making bargains with the Evil One to serve him—of attending meetings of witches—of raising storms at sea—of taking away milk—of blasting the corn—of spoiling the success of the fishing—of curing diseases, and of inflicting diseases, and of receiving money in payment for the one and the other. Among the warlocks and witches who danced to satanic strains in "Alloway's auld haunted kirk," the poet was careful to note—

"There was ae winsome wench and walie,

That night enlisted in the core,

Lang after kenn'd on Carrick shore:

For mony a beast to dead she shot,

And perish'd mony a bonnie boat,

And shook baith meikle corn and bear,

And kept the country-side in fear."

"It is astonishing," says one, "that the *Reformed* clergy could have believed that his sable majesty, to whom they ascribed so much cunning, should have employed only ignorant, old, and decrepit women as his instruments in carrying out his war against mankind." It is equally matter for astonishment, surely, that many of these ignorant, old, and decrepit women themselves believed that they possessed the powers of diablerie popularly attributed to them. Isobel Gowdie, who was burned as a witch in 1662, gives the following as the charm which had to be repeated when she resolved to change into a hare—

"I sall go intill a hare,

With sorrow, sigh, and muckle care;

And I sall go in the devil's name,

Ay while I come back again."

This from her Confessions, as reported in the Appendix to Pitcairn's *Criminal Trials*, is of interest:—"He (the devil) would send me now and then to Auldern on some errands to my neighbours, in the shape of a hare, and Patrick Papley's servants, in Kilhill, being going to their labouring, his hounds being with them, ran after me, being in the shape of a hare. I ran very long, but was forced, being weary, at last to take to my own house. The door being left open I ran in behind a chest, and the hounds followed in; but they went to the other side of the chest, and I was forced to run forth again, and ran into another house, and there took leisure to say—

'Hare, hare, God send thee care;

I am in a hare's likeness now,

But I sall be a woman e'en now;

Hare, hare, God send thee care,'

and so I returned to my own shape, as I am at this instant, again. The dogs will sometimes get some bites of us when we are in hares, but will not get us killed. When we turn out of a hare's likeness to our own shape we will have the bites and rives and scratches on our bodies. When we would be in the shape of cats we did nothing but cry and wraw, and riving, and, as it were, worrying one another; and when we come to our shapes again we will find the scratches and rives on our skin very sore. When one of us, or more, are in the shape of cats, and meet with any others, our neighbours, we will say—

'Devil speed thee,

Go thou with me!'

and immediately they will turn into the shape of a cat and go with us. When we will be in the shape of crows we will be larger than ordinary crows, and will sit upon branches of trees."

The spells, incantations, and cantrips, employed by witches when working out their diableries were quaint and curious enough. Students of Shakespeare are familiar with the

"Toil and trouble, toil and trouble,

Fire burn, and cauldron bubble,"

of the witches in the play of *Macbeth*, as well as the request of the first witch, to

"Pour in sow's blood, that hath eaten

Her nine farrow; grease that's sweaten

From the murderer's gibbet throw

Into the flame,"

making an uncouth mixture. But think of the following—one of two snatches of cantrip rhymes quoted by M'Taggart in the *Scottish Gallovidian Encyclopedia*—

"In the pingle or the pan,

Or the haurnpan o' man,

Boil the heart's blude o' the tade,

Wi' the tallow o' the gled;

Hawcket kail, and hen dirt,

Chow'd cheese, and chicken-wort;

Yellow paddocks champit sma',

Spiders ten, and gelloch's twa;

Sclaters twall, frae foggy dyke,

Bumbees twenty, frae their byke;

Asks frae stinkin' lochens blue,

Aye will mak' a better stew;

Bachelors maun hae a charm,

Hearts hae they a' fu' o' harm,

Aye the aulder, aye the caulder,

Aye the caulder, aye the baulder.

Taps snaw white, and tails green,

Snappin' maiden's o' fifteen,

Mingle, mingle, in the pingle,

Join the cantrip wi' the jingle;

Now we see, and now we see,

Plots o' poachin' ane, twa, three."

By tugging at a hair-rope, in the usual manner of milking a cow—said rope being made up of tufts of hair drawn from cows' tails, and having on it a knot for each cow—and chanting the following, or a similar charm—

"Cow's milk, and mare's milk,

And every beast that bears milk,

Between St. Johnstone's and Dundee,

Come a' to me, come a' to me,"

it was vulgarly believed, as late as the beginning of the century, that a witch could draw away every drop of milk from the cattle in her neighbourhood. Only a horse-shoe nailed to the byre door, and sprigs of rowan-tree tied with red thread to the cow's tail, was a certain protection here; for

"Rowan-tree and red thread

Gar the witches tyne their speed."

Where such protection was neglected, to discover the witch, the gudeman's breeks might be put upon the horns of the cow—a leg upon each horn—when, for certain, crummie being let loose, would run straight to the door of the guilty party.

When the late Reverend Dr. Andrew A. Bonar as a young man laboured in the position of assistant minister in Collace parish, less than half a century ago, I have been told, he found the practice of wearing horse-shoes on byre doors so prevalent there that he tried to reason the people out of the absurdity. He so far succeeded, but no further than this, that they took them off the *outsides* of the door and fastened them upon the insides—where, I believe, some are to be seen even to this day and hour.

"Scoring abune the breath" (executing with a rusty nail, to the effusion of blood, the sign of the Cross, on the upper parts of the face of a suspected witch) was another means of protection. Whoso performed this ceremony was henceforth secure against personal attack from the particular witch, or witches, he may have "scored." An old joiner, or "wricht," in a Perthshire village, with whom I was well acquainted in my boyhood, had a belief in witches which no human argument could dissolve. He suspected a neighbour's wife of witchcraft, and lived in terror of her until, one day, finding a favourable opportunity of performing the operation, he "scored" her "abune the breath" with a rusty nail, which he carried with him concealed for the purpose; and, this done, he started back, and shaking his clenched fist in her face, bragged her to "do her warst noo."

In Hogg's tale of "The Witch of Fife," is to be found the pleasantest stories of witches' "ongauns" to be met with anywhere. Hogg had no peer in the delineation of the mysterious and uncanny, and the students of fairy mythology will ever esteem his picture of "Kilmeny," as one of the most beautiful and perfect of its kind.

"Bonnie Kilmeny gaed up the glen,

But it wasna to meet Duneira's men."

Like many another, before and since, she was taken possession of by the fairies, and led to a land where

"The emerald fields were of dazzling glow,

And the flowers of everlasting blow."

Fairies were popularly believed to inhabit certain round grassy eminences, where they celebrated their nocturnal festivities by the light of the moon. It was believed that if, on Hallowe'en, any person should go round one of these hillocks nine times, contrary to the course of the sun, a door would open, by which he would be admitted into the realms of fairyland. Many, it has been said, of mortal race have been entertained in their secret recesses, there to have been received into the most splendid apartments, and regaled with the most sumptuous banquets and delicious wines. Their females surpassed the daughters of men in beauty, and fairy life was one eternal round of festivity and dancing. Unhappy was the mortal, however, who dared to join in the joys, or ventured to partake of their dainties, as, by this indulgence, he forfeited for ever the society of men, and was bound down irrevocably to the conditions of a *Shi ich*, or "man of peace."

There is a Highland tradition to the effect that a woman, in days of yore, was conveyed into the secret recesses of the *Daoine Shi*, or men of peace. There she was recognised by one who had formerly been an ordinary mortal, but who had, by some fatality, became associated with the fairies. This acquaintance, still retaining some portion of human benevolence, warned her of her danger, and counselled her, as she valued her liberty, to abstain from eating and drinking with them for a certain space of time. She complied with the counsel of her friend; and when the period assigned was elapsed, she found herself again upon earth, restored to the society of mortals. It is added, that when she examined the viands which had been presented to her, and which had appeared so tempting to the eye, they were found, now that the enchantment was removed, to consist only of the refuse of the earth.

"It is the common opinion," says Sir Walter Scott, "that persons falling under the power of the fairies, were only allowed to revisit the haunts of men after seven years had expired. At the end of seven years more, they again disappeared, after which they were seldom seen among mortals. The accounts they gave of their situation differ in some particulars. Sometimes they were represented as leading a life of constant restlessness, and wandering by moonlight. According to others, they inhabited a pleasant region, where, however, their situation was rendered horrible by the sacrifice of one or more individuals to the devil every seventh year. This circumstance is mentioned in Alison Pearson's indictment, and in the 'Tale of the Young Tamlane,' where it is termed 'The paying the kane to hell'; or, according to some recitations, 'the teind,' or tenth. This is the popular reason assigned for the desire of the fairies to abstract young children as substitutes for themselves in this dreadful tribute. Concerning the mode of winning or recovering persons abstracted by the fairies, tradition differs; but the popular opinion supposes that the recovery must be effected within a year and a day, to be held legal in the Fairy Court. This feat, which was reckoned an enterprise of equal difficulty and danger, could only be accomplished at Hallowe'en at the great annual procession of the Fairy Court." Burns refers to this fairy pageant in the opening lines of his "Hallowe'en," thus—

"Upon that night, when fairies light,

On Cassilis Downan's dance,

Or ower the lays, in splendid blaze,

On sprightly coursers prance."

It was at Miles Cross, on Hallowe'en, that fair Janet succeeded in the rescue of her lover, "The Young Tamlane":—

"She pu'd him frae the milk-white steed,

And loot the bridle fa';

And up there raise an eldritch cry,

'He's won among us a'!'


"They shaped him in fair Janet's arms

An ask, but and an adder:

She held him fast in every shape—
To be her bairn's father.

"They shaped him in her arms at last
A mother-naked man;
She wrapped him in her green mantle,
And sae her true love wan."

Hallowe'en as it is popularly observed in Scotland nowadays, is a "merry meeting," and nothing more; but in the times from which Burns drew his inimitable picture of it, it was a festival pregnant with superstitious significance and prophetic awe, and some of the olden time customs are worth recounting:—The first ceremony of Hallowe'en was, pulling each a stock or plant of kail. The parties went out hand in hand with eyes shut, and pulled the first they met with. Its being big or little, straight or crooked, was prophetic of the size and shape of the grand object of all their spells—the husband or wife. If any yird or earth stuck to the root, that meant tocher or fortune, and the taste of the custock—that is the heart of the stem—indicated the temper or disposition. The "runts" were placed over the doorway; and the christian names of the people whom chance brought into the house, were, according to priority of placing the "runts," the names in question. When burning the nuts, they named the lad and lass to each particular nut, as they laid them in the fire, and, according as they burned quietly together, or started from beside one another, the course and issue of the courtship would be. Among various other charms to be practised were those:—To take a candle and go alone to the looking-glass, and eat an apple before it—combing your hair all the time—when the face of your conjugal companion would be seen in the glass as if peering over your shoulder. To steal out, unobserved, and sow a handful of hemp seed, harrowing it with anything you could conveniently draw after you—a grape or a rake or the like—repeating now and again—

"Hemp seed I saw thee, hemp seed I saw thee,
Whaever's to be my true-love, come after me and maw thee,"

and, on looking over your shoulder, you would see the appearance of the person invoked, in the attitude of reaping hemp. To take the opportunity of going unnoticed to a bean-stack, and in fathoming it three times round with both arms, in the last fathom of the last round you would embrace the appearance of your future yoke-fellow. To go to a south-running spring or rivulet, where "three lairds' lands meet," and dip your left shirt-sleeve. Go to bed in sight of a fire, before which you had previously hung the wet sleeve to dry. Lie awake, and about midnight an apparition having the exact figure of the grand object in question, would come and turn the sleeve, as if to dry the other side of it. Take three dishes: put clean water into one, foul water into another; leave the third empty. Blindfold a person (say a male) and lead him to the hearth where the dishes are ranged. If he dips the left hand by chance into clean water, his future wife will come to the bar of matrimony a maid; if into the empty dish, he will have no marriage at all; if into the foul, he will marry a widow. This charm had to be repeated three times, and every time the arrangement of the dishes had to be altered.

There are other decayed and rapidly decaying forms of popular superstition—such as those relating to animals and places, the characteristics of the Brownies, and the various, vast, and extravagant ideas which have been entertained concerning the personality and behaviour of that much abused party known as "Auld Hornie, Satan, Nick, or Clootie"—but these must suffice here.

# CHAPTER XIV
## HUMOUR OF SCOTCH NATURALS

Humour, I have already asserted, is part and parcel of a Scotsman's being, and is common to all classes of the Scottish people; and the remark receives point from the fact that even the daft folk in our land are touched with a rough-and-ready sense of it. Idiocy, unhappily, has obtained in all countries, and among all peoples, and "Naturals," and persons of sadly inferior intellect, have not been uncommon in Scotland. Like many another familiar figure in recent Scottish life, the village or parish idiot, however, is no longer apparent in the native highways and byways. He has been legislated on, and from his listless and perilous wanderings hither and thither in the earth, has mercifully been placed within the confines of some private or charitable institution. When he roamed "at lairge" he was a striking individual, and claimed no little attention. The children laughed and ran at his heels, attracted thereto by the eccentricities of his speech and behaviour. Adult men and women, sound of head and heart, indulged his idiotic fancies, and treated him kindly for pity's sake; while the thoughtless and cruel-minded among the robust order of the community too often teased his silly soul into a frenzy, and made him the butt of their cruel and wanton jokes. That he might be secure from the torment of the latter class is partly the reason why he has been deprived of his liberty. Every parish has its daft Jamie, daft Willie, or daft Davie, as the case might be; and being all touched, less or more, with a sense of humour, as we have said, and daring to give audible speech to unpleasant truths, which sane persons dared not more than think, many good stories are told of them. Not unfrequently they exhibited a degree of cunning and readiness of wit quite unlooked for in members of their class. Thus, whilst lounging listlessly along the roadside one day, a North country natural was accosted by a late Professor in one of our Universities.

"Pray, sir," inquired the learned servant, "how long may a man live without brains?"

"I dinna ken," responded the natural, scratching his head, and eyeing the Professor critically from top to toe; "how auld are you yersel'?"

Remonstrated with for his do-nothing kind of life, one was told he might at least herd cows.

"Me herd kye!" said he; "I wonder to hear ye. I'm far ower daft. Man, I dinna ken grass frae corn."

Previous to the amelioration in the Poor Law, men of the imbecile class were found constantly as "hangers-on" about hotels and coach offices, as well as churchyards on occasions of funerals. About seventy years ago there lived one of this class in Dunbar, who regularly frequented the kitchen of the "White Swan," where he received all his meals. His appetite was of no common order, and when remonstrated with for eating all food that came in his way, he was wont to exclaim, "Better belly burst than gude meat spoil;" and the saying has become a proverb.

Daft Willie Law was the descendant of an ancient family nearly related to the famous John Law of Laurieston, the celebrated financier of France. Willie, on that account, was often spoken to and taken notice of by gentlemen of distinction. Posting one day through Kirkcaldy with more than ordinary speed, he was met by Mr. Oswald of Dunnikier, who asked him where he was bound for in such a hurry.

"Gaun!" says Willie, with apparent surprise at the question. "I'm gaun to my cousin, Lord Elgin's burial."

"Your cousin, Lord Elgin's burial, you fool! Lord Elgin's not dead," responded Mr. Oswald.

"Ah! deil ma care," quoth Willie, "there's sax doctors out o' Embro' at him, an' they'll hae him dead afore I win forrit," and off he posted at an increased rate.

These poor creatures, as Dean Ramsay observes, had invariably a great delight in attending funerals. In most country places hardly a funeral ever took place without the attendance of the parochial idiot. And habit has such a powerful influence that it seemed almost a necessary association. Funeral scenes of this description had been familiar to the experience of Sir Walter Scott, who thus portrays a funeral incident in *Guy Mannering*:—

"The funeral pomp set forth," says he, "saulies with their batons and gamphions of tarnished white crape. Six starved horses, themselves the very emblems of mortality, well cloaked and plumed, lugging along the hearse, with its dismal emblazonry, crept in slow pace towards the place of interment, preceded by Jamie Duff, an idiot, who, with weepers and gravat made of white paper, attended on every funeral, and followed by six mourning coaches filled with the company."

It was the free and ample feast of fat things, of course, that generally proved the attraction; and it serves as a commentary on the social life of Scotland, in the days of our grandfathers, to find a "natural" declaring that a certain funeral, which he had attended, "was a puir affair; there wasna a drunk man at it."

Asked why he never went to church, a Fife "natural"—at least a Fifer more *Fifish* than his fellows—struck a dramatic attitude and exclaimed—"I love the lark that rises from the green sod with the dew sparkling from his breast, and soars far up in the blue heavens—*that's my* religion." Many perfectly sane persons have not so much. And your "natural" could admonish a stinging reproof when the occasion seemed to demand it. About the year 1820, at the time of the trial of Queen Caroline, Dr. Wightman was the popular and esteemed minister of Kirkmahoe, in the County of Dumfries, and he, like all the old Established clergymen, had been ordered to omit the Queen's name from his public prayers. In those days the Doctor was often seen in the streets of the County town on market days, and on one of those occasions he happened to meet with daft Jock Gordon, and as usual stopped to have a little chat with him.

"Good morning, Jock, and how are you to-day?" said the kindly divine.

"Oh, gaily weel, gaily weel, Doctor," replied Jock; "but, man, they tell me ye dinna pray for the Queen noo."

"Quite true, Jock, for I'm afraid she is not a good woman," replied Dr. Wightman.

"God bless me, Doctor, ye ken I'm a puir daft creature, and maybe kens nae better," said Jock, "but I aye thocht, the waur a body was they aye wanted the prayin' for the mair."

Dr. Wightman felt he had been justly rebuked, and quietly slipped away.

It has become a proverb that "everybody has his bubblyjock," and the well-known aphorism rose from the remark of a Scottish half-wit. The circumstances which produced it occurred in the experience of Sir Walter Scott, and deserves to be told.

A gentleman conversing with the illustrious author, remarked that he believed it possible that perfect happiness might be enjoyed, even in this world.

Sir Walter dissented.

"Well," said the gentleman, "there is an idiot whom I am certain will confirm my opinion, he seems the very beau-ideal of animal contentment."

The daft individual was moving along humming to himself, when Sir Walter addressed him.

"Weel, Jamie, hoo are ye the day?"

"Brawly, ou brawly," answered he.

"Have you plenty to eat and drink, Jamie?"

"Ou ay."

"There," said the poet's antagonist, crowing, "is a perfectly happy creature."

"Not so fast," continued Sir Walter. Then to Jamie—

"Is there nathing that bothers ye ava, Jamie?"

"Ou ay," said the idiot, changing his merry look, "I'm sair hadden doon by the muckle bubblyjock; he follows me whaurever I gang."

"Now," said Sir Walter, "you see from this that the simplest and most stupid of mankind are haunted by evil of some kind or another—in short, sir, everybody has his bubblyjock."

Dour and self-willed, your Natural is frequently moved by the strongest prejudices either for or against persons and things. I knew of one in Perthshire who could never be induced to go into a boat, and this although he was born and lived all his lifetime within a few hundred yards of the river Tay. "Gang into a boat! Na, na," he would say, "just a wee thin dealie atween ye and eternitie!" Of this same individual a good story is told, which happened in this way. Jock was a frequent visitor at the "big hoose," and being neither lame nor lazy, was always ready to perform a needed turn for a small gratuity. Some years ago, on the occasion of a shooting battue over the estate, when each sportsman was appointed a separate bag-carrier, Jock got apportioned to one who occasioned more deaths among the birds than the majority of the sportsmen, and consequently he soon made a bag which was not easily lugged o'er field and fence. Still, on the party hurried, each short interval adding to Jock's burden. The sweat oozed from every pore of his sonsy face, and trickled from his chubby chin; still he complained not. However, 'tis the last straw that breaks the camel's back, and a crisis was imminent. One of the "beaters," a boy, who had been several times found fault with by the sportsmen, was sternly rebuked, and was told by Jock's man that if he did not steer clear of the guns he would blow his brains out. Jock saw in the threat an impending big addition to his already too heavy load, and throwing the bag at the sportsman's feet, he wiped his steaming temples, and exclaimed in his own peculiar stuttering manner—

"Ye can sh-sh-shoot him gin ye like, but I'll be h-h-hanged if I'm to c-c-carry him," and in the highest dudgeon he quitted the field.

Another, who was employed about a farm town, showed, at least on one occasion, a "sma' glimmerin' o' common sense." Some one had given him a penny, and this he went and hid in a crevice in the barn wall. The farmer, observing what had been done, watched the opportunity, and, extracting the penny, placed in the crevice a two-shilling piece.

"Strange," said Jock, when he went to look at his treasure; "turned white in the face—maun hae catched the cauld," so rolled the florin in a rag and put it back.

Next day the farmer changed the coin to a shilling.

"Getting to be a case o' consumption, I doot," said Jock on his next visit.

Next day the rag contained a sixpenny piece.

"Gallopin' consumption!" exclaimed the natural, and replaced the coin with a dowie shake of his head.

The farmer next day substituted a half-sovereign.

"Noo ye've ta'en the jaundice," exclaimed Jock on a subsequent visit. "Ye'll need to be keepit warm," and so saying, he placed the coin in his breek-pooch and *kept it there.*

A minister of the North of Scotland, who was not too ready at paying his debts, but very fond of a joke, meeting a fool he was in the habit of teasing, asked him how the potatoes were selling in the moon just now. "Oh, very cheap, and plenty of them," said the fool.

"But don't you think," said the minister, "that there might be a difficulty in getting them down?"

"Nae fear o' that," answered the fool. "Send up the money, and they'll soon send them down."

A Perthshire tradesman, recently deceased, who was not naturally weak-minded, but whose intellect had been partially ruined by dissipation, was confined for several months, a number of years ago, to Murthly Asylum. On his liberation, he received, in accordance with the custom of such institutions, the written assurance of two doctors that he was a person perfectly sane, and safe to be at large. Some time subsequently, when he was engaged on a "job" along with a number of his fellow craftsmen at a country farm, a wordy war arose which waxed so hot and furious that one of the combatants turned savagely on our hero and told him he was "daft."

"Daft!" echoed he, plunging his hands into the oxter pocket of his jacket. "Daft! blast ye! Look here, I can show twa certificates that I'm wise, and there's not anither man on the job that can produce ane!"

He was right.

About the middle of the last century there lived in the neighbourhood of Denholm a natural named Daft Jamie, who was occasionally employed by the Laird of Cavers and his brother, Captain Douglas, who resided at Midshields, to transport them on his back across the water which flowed between their places of abode. One day Captain Douglas resolved to have a little fun at the expense of his brother, and bribed Jamie to drop the Laird in the middle of the river.

Accordingly, having taken Cavers on his back, and proceeded to the middle of the stream, "Oh! Laird," exclaimed Jamie, standing stock-still, "my kuit's yeukie!"

"Well, well; never mind that," exclaimed Cavers.

"Ay, but I maun mind it;" and, notwithstanding orders, entreaties, and threats, Jamie plumped the Laird down into the water and began scratching his ankle to the infinite amusement of the Captain, who stood on the bank laughing like to split his sides. Jamie soon returned for the Captain, who, thinking of no other trick than his own, was speedily mounted and carried to the middle of the stream. At exactly the same spot where he had dropped the Laird, Jamie again stood still.

"Noo, Captain," said he, "gin ye dinna gie me twa shillin's mair, I'll lat you doon too."

It is almost needless to say the Captain had to "purchase his discharge" from the threatened immersion, besides suffering the retributive ridicule of his brother.

Jock Scott, a half-witted lad, who had been employed by the minister to cart some firewood, finding he had got the worst of the bargain, the reverend gentleman remarked severely, "Jock, when I came here they told me you were a fool." "Ay, sir," replied Jock; "and they told me ye wis a grand preacher; but," he added in a lower tone, "it's never safe to believe a' that ye hear!"

In Perthshire, not long ago, a gang of workmen were digging a trial pit previous to some excavations being done. While they were at work throwing up the earth a half-wit named Jock Howe, belonging to the district, appeared on the scene, and addressing the foreman, said, "What are ye howking doon there for?" The foreman, taking in at a glance the character of his questioner, answered, "O, we're diggin' doon to Australia. Would you like to come?" Jock, after thinking for a minute, answered, "Ay man! Howkin' doon to Australia, are ye? Lo'd! ye maun be far dafter than me yet. Can ye no' sail to Australia an' *howk up*, an' ye wad be saved a' the bother o' liftin' the earth oot, for a' yer stuff wad then fa' awa' frae ye?"

Of our native half-wits, four at least have enjoyed a national reputation. These are Jamie Fleeman, the Laird of Udny's fool, who will have a chapter here all to himself; Daft Rab Hamilton, Daft Jock Amos, and Daft Will Speir.

Of the latter three—as well as of Fleeman—there are many good and interesting stories extant.

Rab Hamilton, like others of his class, was an example to some sane folks from the fact that he was a frequent, if not regular, attender of the church. In Ayr he was well known as a staunch Seceder. One day, however, he went to hear a sermon in a church belonging to the Establishment, and produced a sensation which was not soon forgotten by those who witnessed it. He took his seat on an inside stair, which had what is known as a "wooden rail," and having put his head through the railing, in attempting to pull it back he found himself caught by the ears. He shouted at the utmost pitch of his stentorian voice—

"Murder!—my head'll be cuttit aff! Holy minister! congregation!—oh, my head maun be cuttit aff! It's a judgment for leaving my ain godlie Mr. Peebles at the Newton, an' comin' to hear a paper minister."

After being extricated, and asked why he put his head there, he said, "It was to look on wi' *anither woman*!"

Rab was one day offered the choice of a sixpence or a penny.

"I'll no be greedy," said he, "I'll jist tak' the wee white ane."

Receiving a gratuitous dinner at a favourite inn in Kilmarnock one day, and dining to his heart's content, the waiter remarked, as he was preparing to leave the table—

"I'm sure ye've gotten a guid dinner the day, Rab!"

"Ou, ay," replied Rab; "atweel have I; but if the folk o' Ayr speir if I got a dram after't, what will I say?"

Rab's dream is well known. Dr. Auld often showed him kindness, but being once addressed by him when in a hurry, and out of humour, he said—

"Get away, Rab—I've nothing for you to-day."

"Whaw! whew!" cried Rab, in a half howl, half whining tone, "I dinna want onything the day, Mister Auld. I wanted just to tell you aboot an awsome dream I had; I dreamed I was dead."

"Well, what then?" asked Dr. Auld.

"Ou, I was carried far, far, far, and up, up, up, till I cam' to heaven's yett, whaur I chappit, an' chappit, till at last an angel keeked out an' said, 'Wha are ye?'

"'I'm puir Rab Hamilton,' says I.

"'Whaur are ye frae?' says he.

"'Frae the wicked toun o' Ayr,' says I.

"'Hech, man,' says the angel, 'I'm glad to see ye here. I ken the place, but there's naebody come this gate frae the toun o' Ayr sin' the year'" so and so (mentioning the year when Dr. Auld was inducted into the parish).

Finding Jock Amos busily engaged with a knife on a piece of wood one Sabbath day, Mr. Boston, the minister, approached him, and said, "John, can you tell me which is the Fourth Commandment?"

"I daresay, Mr. Boston, it'll be the ane after the third," was the reply.

"Can you repeat it?" asked the divine.

"I'm no sure aboot it," answered Jock. "I ken it has some wheeram by the rest."

Mr. Boston repeated it, and tried thereby to show Jock his error, but—

"Ay, that's it, sir," said Jock, and kept whittling away.

"Why, what is the reason you never come to church, John?" inquired the minister.

"Oh, because you never preach on the text I want you to preach on."

"What text would you have me to preach on, John?"

"On the nine-and-twenty knives that cam' back frae Babylon."

"I never heard of them before."

"Ha! ha! the mair fool ye! Gang hame an' read yer Bible, Mr. Boston! Sic fool; sic minister."

Subsequently Mr. Boston found the text sure enough in Ezra i. 9th, and wondered greatly at the 'cuteness of the fool, considering the subject on which he had been reproving him. And now, "The mair fool ye, as Jock Amos said to the minister," is a well-worn proverb.

It was to this same Jock Amos that a female acquaintance, following a common Scotch idiom, said one day, "Jock, how auld will you be?" They had been talking of ages.

"Humph! It wad tak' a wiser head than mine to tell ye that," was Jock's reply.

"It's unco queer that ye dinna ken how auld ye are?" returned she.

"I ken weel enough how auld I *am*," said Jock, "but dinna ken how auld I'll *be*." Jock had to be addressed by the book.

Will Speir was the eldest son of the Laird of Camphill, Dalry, Ayrshire, and many witty stories are put to his credit. Report had it that the cause of his mental aberration arose in this simple way. When a boy, some of his companions, in mere frolic, caught him, and suspended him by the heels over the parapet of a bridge of very considerable height, and from that hour the hitherto lively boy became dull, absent, and unsociable in his habits. Will, when he chanced to visit the village of Dalry, lodged with two personages—Souple Sandy, and Rab Paik, or Pollock—whose intellects were at a greater discount than even his own. Robert Speir, the brother of the witty natural, was precentor in the Parish Church of Dalry, and, when present, Will usually threw in the whole strength of his lungs to assist his brother, so that no voice but his own sometimes could be heard within the range of a dozen pews. Rab Paik, his fellow-lodger, tried to keep up with him, but could not muster such volume of voice as his associate. This annoyed Will rather than otherwise, and one day he glared over in the direction of his confederate, and shouted—

"Sing, man, Rab, sing, for the hail burden o' the Psalm lies on you and me an' our Rab."

Will was accustomed to assist the beadle of the church, whereof he was an unworthy member, in some of the less important functions of his office. On one occasion, during service, a fight took place between two sturdy collies, in one of the aisles of the church, which interrupted the service for a time. Will rushed to the scene of the riot, and belabouring the belligerents with a stick, he exclaimed, "If you would pay mair attention to what the minister's sayin' to you, it would be muckle better for you than tearing your tousie jackets at that gate. Tak' better care o' your claes, you blockheads, for there's no a tailor in Beith can either mend thae, or mak' new anes to you when they're dune," and having delivered such stinging reproof, the censor gravely returned and resumed his seat.

Seated on the bench below the pulpit, Will one Sabbath joined in the psalmody with such noisy zeal that Mr. Fullerton, the minister, tapped him on the head, saying, "Not so loud, Will."

"What, sir," retorted the natural, "will I no praise the Lord *with a' my micht?*"

Mr. Fullerton had advertised from the pulpit that he was to hold a diet of examination in a certain district of the parish, and meeting Will on his way thither, he inquired of the half-wit why he never appeared on such occasions.

"Because ye dinna gi'e fair play," was the reply.

"Why," said the minister, "what do you mean Will?"

"Ye should aloo question aboot," returned Will.

This point was conceded by the minister, and Will, accordingly, appeared at the next diet.

"How many Gods are there, William?" the catechiser asked.

"There is but one only, the living and true God," replied Will.

Mr. F. was proceeding with the next question, "How many persons," etc., when he was interrupted with, "Na na, minister, a bargain's a bargain; it's my turn noo. How many deevils are there?"

"I really cannot tell," replied the divine.

"Is that the gate o' ye already?" exclaimed Will, and made off with himself as quickly as possible.

Will was a sort of half-privileged haunter of Eglinton Castle and grounds, and knew the Earl very well. Discovering him crossing a fence one day preparatory to making a "short cut" towards some point in the demesne, the Earl called out, "Come back, sir; that is not the road."

"Do you ken," asked Will, "whaur I'm gaun?"

"No," replied his Lordship.

"Weel, hoo the deil do you ken whether this be the road or no?" and having said so, away he went.

The Earl called out, "Come back, sir: that is not the road." "Do you ken," asked Will, "whaur I'm gaun?" "No," replied his Lordship. "Weel, hoo the deil do ye ken whether this be the road or no?"

Entering the house of a clergyman in Beith, famed as a skilful performer on the violin, and hearing the minister playing on the fiddle, Will began to dance, and continued in his own unmeasured style till the clergyman was fairly tired. The practical commentator on catgut then handed Will a shilling. "Hech," said Will, "this world's uncoly changed, for in my young days it was the dancers that aye pay'd the fiddler."

Passing along the road by the side of the minister's glebe one morning, whilst haymaking was in progress, the minister asked Will if he thought the weather would keep up, as it looked rather like rain.

"Weel," says Will, "I canna be sure sae early in the day, but I'll be passin' this way the nicht again, an' I'll ca' in and tell ye."

On making his way to a farmhouse one day where he was usually quite at home, Will accidentally lighted on a young cow of his host's, which had got swamped in a bog.

The poor creature was sunk so deep that no more than the ridge of the back, the head, and half the neck was to be seen. Will ran to the house at his utmost speed, and threw open the kitchen door flat against the wall, which rebounded back again with a noise like the discharge of a piece of artillery. The whole family, who were engaged at morning prayers, started from their knees. "Ye're losin' mair than ye're winnin'," exclaimed Will, almost out of breath. "There's ane o' yer stirks doun in the bog there. Rin an' tak' her out, or she'll sune be o' nae mair value to you than the hide an' horns. Prayers are a' richt, an' ye're no sae aften at them maybe as ye should; but dinna be prayin' when ye should be puttin' to hands." Will's gospel was thoroughly orthodox.

Surely, my reader, these anecdotes and illustrations, besides revealing the strong and ready sense of humour which obtains in the mind and manifests itself in the speech of the ordinary Scottish natural, serve to corroborate the witty saying of the Rev. Walter Dunlop of Dumfries, namely, that "Ye'll often see a bricht licht shinin' through a *crack*."

# CHAPTER XV
## JAMIE FLEEMAN, THE LAIRD OF UDNY'S FOOL

Jamie Fleeman, the Laird of Udny's Fool, the most illustrious, was probably the very last of his order in Scotland. A real "natural," Jamie had, notwithstanding, rare "glimmerings of common-sense," as Bailie Nicol Jarvie avowed concerning the Dugal Craitur, and possessed a pungency of ready wit and humour and withering sarcasm which caused him to be dreaded as a foe and trusted as a friend. Without troubling to follow the details of Jamie's career, interesting as these are, we will simply glance *en passant* at his strange personality, and proceed to account some well-authenticated stories in which he was a prime actor.

Biographically, suffice it to say that, according to one writer, he was a native of Longside, in Aberdeenshire, and was born on the 7th April, 1713, whilst an earlier chronicler asserts that the place of the great man's birth is so uncertain that the eighty-and-one parishes of Aberdeenshire might, if they pleased, contend for that honour in like manner as the seven cities of Greece contended for the glory of having been the birthplace of Homer. Jamie spent the days of his boyhood about the house of Sir Alexander Guthrie of Ludquharn, and at a very early period of life began, by his bluntness of manner and shrewdness of remark, to attract the notice of his superiors. By and by he gravitated to Udny, which remained his "head-quarters" during many pleasant years. He had a strange appearance. "His countenance—indescribably, and even painfully, striking—wore that expression which at once betrays the absence of sound judgment; his head large and round—his hair perhaps naturally brown, but rendered, by constant exposure to the weather, of a dingy fox-colour, and not sleek, but standing on end—as if Jamie had been frightened out of his wits—indicated that his foolishness was not assumed but real." A person of strong and reliable affection, Jamie had equally strong and confirmed prejudices. The latter had respect to places, persons, and animals. No red-haired woman, for example, could gain his respect. "Whaur saw ye ever a lady wi' scarlet hair?" he would growl. He had a prejudice in favour of dogs, and a hatred of cats, and this, he said, was "gentlemanny." All the curs in the country knew him, and were glad to see him. Wherever he stayed, the dog was generally permitted to share his bed and board. At Waterton he taught a large house-dog to observe a line drawn across the porridge pot. On one side of the line the porridge belonged to Jamie, on the other the dog was permitted to feed, Jamie's spoon making the boundary line to be duly respected. One morning the dog being from home, the cook insisted that the cat should be permitted to take Curry's place. Fleeman's countenance fell at the suggestion, but he did not venture to remonstrate and run the risk of losing the cook's favour. Pussy was accordingly placed at the opposite side of the pot from Jamie, but ignorant of the law of the pot, she speedily transgressed by putting her nose across the marshes. Fleeman suspended operations, and viewed her for a moment with an eye of sovereign contempt. A like transgression on the part of the dog would have been adequately punished by a slap over the head with the back of his spoon; but less mercy must be shown to the cat, so, quietly slipping his hand down on the enemy's head, he, with a sudden jerk, plunged her over the ears into the scalding mess, gravely remarking the while, "Desperate diseases require desperate cures, ye curst wretch!"

Factors were no favourites with Jamie either, and it was a trait in his character that he employed every opportunity that presented itself to annoy those whom he held in aversion. One day a proprietor, at whose house he was on a visit, was walking out with his factor, and showing him a field of hill-land which he had cultivated at considerable expense, but which had proved very unproductive. "I have tried many things," said the gentleman; "what do you think, if planted, would be likely to thrive in it?"

The factor, a very corpulent man, put on an air of great consequence, and stood musing for a time, during which Jamie was overheard saying—

"O'd, I could tell ye what would thrive in't."

"Well, Fleeman," said the Laird, "and what would that be?"

"Plant it wi' factors, Laird," said the fool, "they thrive in every place; but for a' that," added he, "deil curse the crap, it's no a very profitable ane."

The proprietor of an estate near by Udny was held in special aversion by Jamie, and one day when the fool was lolling on the bank of the Ythan, basking himself in the sun, he was hailed from the other side of the water by this laird, who asked him where was the best ford. The malicious knave directed the laird to the deepest pool in the river, and the laird attempting to cross narrowly escaped drowning. When he arrived, sorely drenched and "forfouchen," on the other side, he made up to Fleeman, and in a voice hoarse with passion, accused the poor fool of a design to drown him. "Gosh be here, Laird!" said Jamie, "I've seen the geese and the deucks crossin' there hunders o' times, and I'm sure your horse has far langer legs than they ha'e."

To try if Jamie was proof against the allurements of pelf, some one about the place scattered a few copper coins on the way between the house and the well, and kept watch at the time when he would be sent out for water. Fleeman, carrying his buckets, came to the place where the coins lay, and, eyeing them for a moment, he muttered to himself—just loud enough to be heard by those who watched his conduct—"When I carry water, I carry water; and when I gather bawbees, I gather bawbees," and passed on. This shows that if Jamie was a fool, he possessed a virtue which many who are not accounted so cannot lay claim to.

Another story illustrates his extraordinary sagacity. On one occasion he was sent all the way to Edinburgh with a letter to the Laird, who had gone thither some short time previously. Jamie arrived in Edinburgh safely, but he was quite ignorant of the Laird's address; and this he set about to discover. And thus—as he wandered about in the streets, he narrowly inspected every dog he met, and was at last sufficiently lucky to recognise one of his old bed-fellows. Seizing him in his arms, he ran into a shop, and, asking a coil of rope, measured off five or six yards, and fastening the end of this round the dog's neck, he set him down, and giving him a few hearty kicks, cried, "Hame wi' you, ye scoonging tyke! hame wi' ye!" and, following at the heels of the half-frightened-to-death dog, he discovered the Laird's temporary dwelling-place.

Fleeman's wit was sometimes of a playful cast, sometimes of a grave and didactic nature; but grave or gay, it rarely failed to effect the object for which it was called forth. Passing along the road one day, he was accosted by a foppishly-dressed individual, who eyed him from head to foot, and exclaimed in a rather impertinent manner, "You are Udny's fool, are you not?"

"Ay," replied Jamie, with an odd stare, peculiar to himself, "I'm Udny's feel. Fa's feel are ye?"

Being at Peterhead, Fleeman was one day on the shore near the "Wine Well," where several gentlemen belonging to the town were assembled, and looking very earnestly through a telescope at some distant object. Always of an enquiring nature, Jamie asked one of the gentlemen what it was they were so intently surveying. "Oh, Jamie," said he, bantering the fool, "we are looking at a couple of limpets that are trying a race on the Skerry! D'ye no see them?"

"I canna just say that I do," replied Jamie, as grave as a judge. Then, turning up one side of his head as if listening intently, he all of a sudden assumed an animated expression of countenance, and exclaimed with ludicrous gravity, "Lo'd bless me, sir, I hear the sound o' their feet as they scamper up the face o' the rock!" and passed on.

Jamie's practice was never to call any person a liar, but when any one told him what he considered was a deliberate falsehood, he just capped the initial lie with a bigger one.

"Man, Jamie," exclaimed an individual whom he met on the road one day, "have ye heard the news?" (Jamie had a well-known *penchant* for news).

"Na, faith I," said Jamie, all expectation. "What news, man?"

"O'd man," said he, "there's seven miles o' the sea burned at Newburgh this morning."

"Ay, man," replied Jamie, apparently very much in earnest. "Weel, I little ferlie, for I saw a flock o' skate that darkened the very air fleein' ower this way about breakfast-time. They gaed ower by Waterton to the woods o' Tolquhon, and they'll likely be biggin' their nests there."

As is often the case with naturals, Jamie was possessed of extraordinary strength, particularly in his arms; and in this connection there is a good story told of him. There happened to be in Aberdeen an English regiment, the commander of which was a gasconading fellow, who constantly bragged of the extraordinary strength of his men. One day the Laird of Udny and this officer were of the same party at dinner. When the glass began to circulate, the officer began to boast, and, as was his wont, got louder and louder in praise of his men, as he became more and more heated with wine. At length, Udny, believing that the insult was levelled at his countrymen, by the pertinacity of the officer's boast, said rather smartly—

"From all accounts, these famous grenadiers of yours are the best wrestlers that England can produce. I'll take you a wager of twenty guineas that the lad who herds my cows, and carries peats and water to the kitchen, will throw the best man in your regiment."

The officer was in a paroxysm of rage, but confident that his men were as good as he had represented them to be, he readily took the bet, clenching it with an oath, and added that the pride of the Scotch would soon be laid as low as it was on Drummossie Moor.

Time and place for the trial of strength being appointed, Udny, after ordering his servant to purchase half a pound of fine twist tobacco, set off to his residence. Fearing that Jamie might not relish the job he had prepared for him, Udny thought it the wisest course to coax him a little, and knowing his passionate fondness for tobacco, he presented the half-pound, at the same time remarking—

"I have got myself into a scrape, Fleeman, and no man but you can take me out of it."

Jamie eyed the tobacco with a look of great satisfaction, clapped a couple of inches from the end of it in his cheek, and looking Udny in the face, with an air of great seriousness, said—

"What is't Laird?"

"You must shak'-a-fa' for me, Fleeman," said Udny.

"Is that a'?" cried Jamie.

"But it is with soldiers, Jamie; and if ye throw them, ye shall get another half-pound of tobacco."

Jamie began to gambol and cut capers, as was his custom when in good humour, and Udny saw his point was gained.

On the appointed day Jamie appeared at the Cross of Aberdeen bareheaded, his hair standing on end as on ordinary occasions, and dressed in the sackcloth coat which he usually wore. The soldiers, not deeming that they jested with their antagonist, were playing on him all sorts of tricks. When the hour approached the Colonel appeared, and had his men drawn up in order. Seeing no person with Udny, he demanded him, with an air of triumph, to produce the cowherd who was to throw the best man that England could produce. Udny beckoned to Jamie, who came capering forward. The officer looked with an air of contempt on Udny and his cow-boy, whilst a loud laugh burst from the soldiers when they saw the poor idiot whom they had lately been jeering brought forward as a match for any man in the company. As the soldiers were really fine men, and expert wrestlers, their commander, instead of selecting the strongest of his party, ordered out one of the weakest, determined, as he thought, to turn the laugh, as well as the bet, against Udny.

"Do you take the first shake?" inquired the soldier, approaching Jamie not without some evidence of aversion.

"Na, na," replied Jamie; "tak' ye the first shake, for fear ye getna anither," and he threw the soldier from him as he would have done a child.

Another and more powerful man shared the same fate. The Colonel now began to suspect that Udny's man was better than he looked. He was likewise irritated by the smiles on the faces of the bystanders, and ordered out the best man in his regiment.

Jamie, too, was beginning to be in earnest, and the champion was seized and dashed to the ground in an instant, which done, Jamie ran up to the Laird and inquired—

"Lo'd! have I a' that dyke o' men to throw, Laird? If sae, tell their maister to ca' oot twa or three o' them at ance, for I maun be hame in time to tak' in the kye."

The Castlegate rang with shouts of laughter, and the bet was declared off.

Jamie liked to accompany the Laird whithersoever he went, and, mounted on a huge "rung," he could keep pace with his master's pony, if the journey was not a very long one. One year the Laird set out for Perth Races, and, as the sequel indicates, without—purposely or forgetfully—making Fleeman aware of his intention. Udny had not proceeded far on his journey, however, until the scene of his sojourn was being talked about the house. Jamie's ears, always on the cock, caught the word, and, taking to his rung, he cut across the country, and reached St. Johnstone before his master. Jamie had a friend in the kitchen of every house at which Udny was in the habit of visiting, and, calling on one or other of his Perthshire benefactors, he had got served with the larger half of a leg of mutton. With this he repaired to the Brig of Perth to make a meal, and wait the Laird's arrival. It was not long until the Laird of Udny made his appearance.

"Hilloa, Fleeman," said he, reining up his nag, "are you here already?"

"Ca' awa', Laird," said Jamie, smacking his lips, and not deigning to look his interrogator in the face—"ca' awa'! Ye ken a body when they hae something."

It is recorded of him that one day when travelling along the road he found a horse shoe. Shortly after Mr. Craigie, the minister of St. Fergus, came up to him. Jamie knew the minister well, and, holding up the shoe and examining it carefully all round the while—

"Od, minister," he said, "can ye tell me what that is?"

"That!" said the minister, "you fool, that's a horse shoe!"

"Ah!" said Fleeman, with a sigh, "sic a blessin' it is to hae book lear! I couldna tell whether it was a horse's shoe or a mare's!"

The following is about the only anecdote recorded of Fleeman which exhibits a mingling of the rogue with the fool:—He had been sent to Haddo House to fetch some geese thence to Udny Castle. Finding the task of driving them before him a very arduous one, by reason of their many perverse digressions from the public road, Jamie, when his patience was fairly exhausted, procured a straw rope, and twisting this about their necks, he took the double of it over his shoulder and walked swiftly on, dragging the geese after him, and never casting "one longing, lingering look behind." On his arrival at Udny, he discovered to his horror, that the geese were all strangled and stone-dead. The breed was a peculiar one, and strict injunctions had been given to him to be careful in conducting the geese safely home. So his ingenuity, which never failed him, had to be drawn upon to devise a plan that would free him from disgrace. Accordingly, dragging his victims into the poultry yard, he stuffed their bills and throats with food, then boldly entered the castle.

"Well, Jamie, have you brought the geese?"

"Ay have I."

"And are they safe?"

"*Safe!* I put them into the poultry yard, an' they're goble, goblin' an' eatin' yonder as if they hadna seen meat this twalmonth. I only hope they haena chokit themsel's afore noo!"

If Jamie Fleeman's wits were "ravelled," his heart was generally found sound and in the right place. His sympathies invariably went with the weak, the suffering, the poor, and the oppressed; and many anecdotes, not a few of them quite pathetic in their character, are on record, in illustration of this delightful side of his nature. Just one here:—There was a young fellow, a servant about a farmhouse where Fleeman sometimes stayed for a day or two at a time, who had seduced a poor girl in the neighbourhood, and added to his first fault by resolutely denying that he was the father of the child, and strenuously endeavouring to make it be believed that the girl's reputation had always been of a very doubtful nature. Before the Kirk-Session he appeared again and again, where he declared his own innocence, and denounced the poor girl as a liar and worse, although, up to that time, she had really borne an unimpeachable character. With all these facts Jamie was, along with everybody else in the district, perfectly familiar, and he formed his own opinion regarding them. One evening at the farmhouse aforesaid, when the servants were gathered round the kitchen fire, and, with the fool in their midst, were playing off little jokes upon Jamie, in order to get amusement by his quick repartee, no one teased him more than he who had lately figured so conspicuously before the Kirk-Session.

"Man, Jamie," said he, "ye're sic a fool that I'll wager ye that ye canna tell whether ye be your father's son or your mither's? Fat answer ha'e ye got to that? Just tell me?" And he burst into a loud fit of laughter, as if he had got the better of Jamie.

"Tell ye me first, then," said Fleeman, gravely, "fat answer ye have to gie your Maker at the last day, when He asks you if ye didna break the lass's character, and then swear that ye did nae sic thing. It will maybe then be asked of you if you can tell whether her boy be not your son as well as his mither's; and, faith, I'm thinking it will puzzle you to mak' it out that his being the son o' the ane hinders him from being the son o' the ither."

Some of those present laughed, others looked as if they did not know what to do. But the upshot of the matter was that, in the course of a few days after, the man waited on the minister, declared himself mis-sworn, confessed he had purposely endeavoured to injure the girl's character, and begged to be absolved from Church censure.

To an accident which befell him when following his avocation of cowherd, is to be ascribed the origin of a proverb very current in Buchan—"The truth aye tells best." Fleeman had, in repelling the invasion of a corn-field by the cattle under his charge, had recourse to the unwarrantable and *unherd-like* expedient of throwing stones. One of his missiles, on an evil day and an hour of woe, broke the leg of a thriving two-year-old. Towards sunset, when the hour of driving the cattle home had arrived, Jamie was lingering by a dykeside, planning an excuse for the fractured limb of the unfortunate *stot*. "I'll say," he soliloquised, "that he was loupin' a stank an' fell an' broke his leg. Na! that winna tell! I'll say that the brown stallion gied him a kick and did it. That winna tell either! I'll say that the park yett fell upon't. Na! that winna tell! I'll say—I'll say—what will I say? Od, I'll say that I flung a stane and did it! That'll tell!"

"Ay, Jamie," cried the Laird, who had been an unseen listener, "ay, ay, Jamie, the truth aye tells best."

In course of time Jamie was waited on to pay the debt of Nature, and, while standing round his death-bed, one said to another—

"I wonder if he has any sense of another world or a future reckoning?"

"Oh, no, he is a fool!" replied the other. "What can *he* know of such things?"

Jamie opened his eyes, and looking this man in the face said, "I never heard that God seeks where He did not give."

After this he lay quiet for a short time, when he again opened his eyes, and looking up into the face of one standing near, whom he respected, he said in a firm tone, "I'm of the gentle persuasion, dinna bury me like a beast!"

His remains lie in the churchyard of Longside, in close proximity to the grave of the Rev. John Skinner, the author of "Tullochgorum"; and in kindly recognition of the humanity in poor Jamie, a handsome polished granite obelisk has been erected as near as is known to his grave, which bears the following inscription:—

Erected
in 1861
to indicate the grave
of
JAMIE FLEEMAN,
in answer to his prayer,
"Dinna Bury Me like a Beast."

# CHAPTER XVI
## "HAWKIE"—A GLASGOW STREET CHARACTER

The streets and lanes, highways and byeways, of our large cities form platforms on which many a quaint and curious character appears and cuts capers to draw forth the surplus coppers of the impressionable portion of the lieges. Here it is a fiddler—there it is a ballad singer—here a clog-dancer—there a spouter—now a mute, hungry-looking soul, whose rags appeal to the crowd with a thousand tongues—anon one who rends the air with a manufactured tale of woe. But amongst all the tatterdemalion class of public entertainers, street beggars, etc.—and their name is legion—there has not perhaps appeared within the memory of living men one who was better known whilst he lived, and whose memory is likely to remain longer green, than the animated bundle of rags and bones known amongst men by the self-created pseudonym which stands at the head of this paper. Verily, who has not heard of Hawkie; and where in broad Scotland have not his jibes and jests, his flashes of wit and humour, not been told and retold? Every book of Scottish humorous anecdotes of any account, from *The Laird o' Logan* downwards, contains specimens of his smart *repartee*, biting sarcasm, and reckless wit, as its choicest bits; and a brief biographical sketch, interspersed with the most telling of the *tellable* witticisms of this king of Scottish beggars, will be read with interest, if not with profit. His real name was William Cameron, and he was born at a place called Plean, in the parish of St. Ninians, in Stirlingshire, where his maternal forbears had been residenters for generations unknown. His mother's name was Paterson. His father, Donald Cameron, was a native of Braemar, and claimed distant relationship to the Camerons of Lochiel. At the time of our subject's birth, he (the father) was engaged as a mashman at a distillery in the neighbourhood of Plean. His parents were very poor, and during the harvest season his mother went forth to the shearing, leaving William in charge of a girl about six years of age. Whilst thus imperfectly nursed and attended he caught damage to his right leg, so serious that it left him a cripple for life. At the age of four he was sent to school. His teacher, he said, was an old, decrepit man, who had tried to be a nailer, but at that employment he could not earn his bread. He then attempted to teach a few children, for which undertaking he was quite unfit. Writing and arithmetic were to him secrets dark as death, and as for English, he was short-sighted, and a word of more than two or three syllables was either passed over, or it got a term of his own making. At this school he continued four years, but was not four months advanced in learning, although, he said, he was as far advanced as his teacher. He next went to a school at a place called Milton, about a mile distant, where he racked his memory learning psalms, chapters of the Bible, and the catechisms, till he could begin at the Song of Solomon, and by heart go on to the end of

Malachi. At the age of twelve he was bound apprentice to a tailor in Stirling, and in the course of his Autobiography, which, at the request of the late David Robertson, of *Whistle Binkie* fame, Hawkie wrote whilst he was a winter inmate of the Glasgow Hospital, between the years 1840-1850, he gives the following graphic account of this engagement:—

"The first glisk that I got o' this slubberdegullion o' a maister gied me the heartscad at him. Quo' I to mysel', bin' me as ye like, I'll no rowt lang in your tether, I'se warrant ye. We're no likely, for a' that I can see, to rot twa door-cheeks thegither, and if a' reports were to be believed, better at padding the inside o' the pouch-lids than handlin' the goose. The first job that he gied me was to mak' a holder (needle-cushion) to mysel', and to it I set. I threaded the best blunt, and waxed the twist till it was like to stick in the passage. I stour'd awa', throwing my needle-arm weel out, so that my next neighbour was obliged to hirsel' awa' frae me to keep out o' harm's way. I stitch'd it, back-stitch'd it, cross-stitch'd it, and then fell'd and plaed it wi' black, blue, and red, grey, green, and yellow, till the ae colour fairly kill'd the ither. My answer to every advice was, I kent what I was doin', did I never see my mither makin' a hussey? By the time I had gi'en my holder the last stitch, my maister hinted that it wasna likely that I wad e'er mak' saut to my kail sowthering claith thegither, and that though the shears were run through every stitch o' the indenture it wadna break his heart. Thinks I to mysel', there's a pair o' us, as the coo said to the cuddie, and my crutch can do the job as weel as your clippers, so I laid the whip to my stilt, and took the road hame."

William was again sent to school, his anxious parents still thinking that his habits would settle down, and that he might be fitted for acting as a dominie in some country district. There was, however, no "settlement" in his nature, and he broke away from the dominie as abruptly as he had previously done from the tailor. Wandering to Glasgow he joined a journeyman tailor's house-of-call, then in the Pipe Close, High Street, and soon found employment. At this time, walking in Glasgow Green in company with a brother tradesman one Sabbath morning, they came across a field preacher holding forth to a large audience, "while the lining of his hat spoke more for the feelings of his hearers than himself."

"I could beat him myself," said Cameron.

The remark was carried to the workshop by his companion, and next day—

"You think you could beat the preacher," said one of the tailors, addressing our subject.

"And so I could," retorted Cameron, not expecting the thing would be continued further.

On Saturday night, however, he fell in with some tailors, and the "preaching" was again the subject of remark. Cameron still maintained that he could beat him, and it was agreed that he should be put to the test on the following day. About forty or fifty of the principal journeymen in the city accordingly assembled next day in the house-of-call, when the unfledged orator was dressed in a borrowed suit of "blacks," in order to try his mettle in the preaching art. At about twelve o'clock they set out, and Westmuir, on the road leading to Airdrie, was selected as the scene of action.

"My father and mother," writes Hawkie, "were Burghers, and possessing the works of Ralph Erskine of Dunfermline, whose sermons my mother took great pleasure in reading and hearing read. I had often to read them aloud to her, which, although to her a pleasure, was to me a punishment; and having a good memory, which was much improved at school, I preached one of Ralph Erskine's sermons. I had got a number of lessons in elocution, for which I had a peculiar liking, and my voice at that time not being broken, I made a favourable impression on the people. We had an elder chosen to go round with the hat, but the money came in so quick that there was no need for that." Such was Hawkie's first public appearance as an orator.

For the following Sabbath another sermon was planned, but in the interim the budding preacher vacated the city. He is next found keeping a school at Bloack, in Ayrshire, behaving exemplary, and carefully studying the nature of his scholars. Soon again he is in Glasgow, working at the tailor trade, and anon keeping a school at a coal work at Plean Muir, in the vicinity of his birthplace. Next move, the tawse are thrown once more aside. He attaches himself to a band of strolling players, and "stars" it through part of the county of Fife. The stage turns out an unprofitable speculation, and the scene again changes. He is now a toy manufacturer. This proves too laborious an occupation, and he next becomes a china-mender. No cement will, however, bind the unsettled changeling. At the end of nine months he abandons the china trade, starts for Newcastle, and embarks in field-preaching among the collier population, who were nearly all Methodists. This he found to be a lucrative job.

"I got so dexterous at that craft," he writes, "that I might have had a church, and was approved to be admitted into the brotherhood, but was afraid that the *holes of my robe would not hold a button, and a small breeze of wind would expose the inside work.*"

He abandons preaching, quits Newcastle, sets out for Carlisle, and remains there until his money is done. He then starts for Scotland, coming through Annandale, and asks charity for the first time in his life in the village of Ecclefechan, Dumfriesshire. In his brief career he has already acted many and varied parts, and each one has left him a little lower down than it found him. At the age of thirty he lets slip the spirit of independence that had hitherto struggled against his natural inclination towards utter depravity, and becomes a common beggar. Attempts to rescue him had been put forth time and again, but all to no purpose; his nature was predisposed gutterwards, and down he went.

"Oh, man," he was once heard to say, when remonstrated with about his dissolute life, "if I hadna the heart o' a hyena, my mither's tears would hae saftened it lang afore now. My conscience yet gies me sair stangs when I think aboot her, and I hae just to huzzh't asleep wi' whisky."

Begging from door to door, and occasionally selling chap books in the streets, he wandered over the most of Scotland, as well as over a large part of England, and had many strange experiences, which, in course of time, were faithfully recorded in his "Autobiography" already referred to. These records, I may state in passing, edited by John Strathesk, the well-known author of *Bits from Blinkbonny*, were recently published by David Robertson & Co., of Glasgow. The book is a revelation of beggar-life well calculated to do good, as its perusal will convince any unbiased mind that ninety-nine per cent. of your door-to-door beggars are arrant rogues and vagabonds. Read alongside of Hawkie's Autobiography, Burns's "Jolly Beggars" is found to be no fancy picture. In his description of Beggars' Dens of any consequence all over the land there are found life-like portraits of the various "randie gangrel bodies," who, "in Poosie Nansie's held the splore to drink their orra duddies." Andrew Gemmells, the original of Scott's "Edie Ochiltree," averred, in his remoter time, that begging had become scarcely the profession of a gentleman. As a trade it was forty pounds in the year worse than when he practised it, and, if he had twenty sons, he would not be easily induced to breed one of them up in his own line. Even in Hawkie's time the profession, however, was not quite played out. The Canonmills Road in Edinburgh, when he first started, was, he says, worth on an average five shillings and a few pence daily. The King's Park was not worth anything except on Sunday, but the first Sunday he begged in it, standing hat in hand from three in the afternoon until nine at night, he lifted over seventeen shillings. Paisley and a number of villages in the neighbourhood are admitted to be excellent ground for the "cadger." A beggar may remain in Paisley, Hawkie avers, and live on the best of the land. Gangrel bodies will therefore do well to take Hawkie's experience along with Lord Beaconsfields hint and "keep" their "eye on Paisley."

But we must return to what is more particularly our present subject—Hawkie and his witticisms. Glasgow was the scene of his triumph as a street orator and wit. Whilst he wandered to and fro in the earth, he was a nameless, unknown gangrel, drifting towards a "cadger pownie's death at some dykeside." But settling down in the mercantile capital, the keen struggle for existence which obtains there roused his dormant energies into full play, and he soon became a "man of mark." Diogenes with his tub was not better known in the streets of Athens than was Hawkie with his crutch for many years in the streets of St. Mungo. He first made his presence felt there some time subsequent to 1818. About this time an impostor of the name of Ross had been gulling the gaping mob with a prediction that the Bridgegate of Glasgow, with its swarm of motley inhabitants, was doomed to sudden and complete destruction. Cameron possessed a ready turn for satirical burlesque; so, envying Ross his following, he set up a claim for prophetic vision also, and made his Seer "Hawkie, a twa-year-auld quey frae Aberdour, in the County of Fife, and sister-german to Ross." She also foretold the destruction of the Bridgegate, but from a different cause than that given by Ross. "It is to be destroyed," said the Aberdour stirk, "by a flood o' whisky, and the wives will be ferrying in washing tubs frae ae door to anither, and money o' their lives will be lost, that itherwise micht hae been saved, by louting ower their tubs to try the flood, whether it was Sky-blue or the real Ferintosh." This production was a profitable speculation for some time, and Cameron continued to cry it so frequently that the name of the "stirk" took the place of his own.

Hawkie was ever ready to enter into a religious discussion, and frequently showed great skill in the management of an argument. One day he fell into a discussion on the doctrine of Baptism with a spirit-dealer in the city, who maintained that the mere observance of the external ceremony was all that was required.

"Do you," says the gangrel, "insist that sprinkling wi' water constitutes baptism?"

"Yes, I do," replied the bar-master.

"Weel, then, gin that be a' that's necessary, your whisky casks may dispute Christianity wi' ony Protestant Bishop in the hale country." This clinched the argument.

Hawkie's besetting sin was an inveterate love of ardent spirits. "I am surprised, Hawkie," said a person remonstrating with him one day on his dissolute life, "that a person of your knowledge and intellect can degrade himself by drinking whisky until you are deprived of reason, and with whom the brute could justly dispute pre-eminence. I would allow you two glasses per day, if you can't want it, but not more."

"Now, that's fair," replied the wit; "but will ye lodge't in a public-house? Man, ye dinna ken what I hae to do. My forefathers, and foremithers, too, were a' sober folk, and I hae had to drink for them a'. Ye see, they ran in debt to the British Government, and left me to pay't; and when I cudna do't I got an easy settlement wi' the folks o' the Exchequer, on condition that I was to pay't up by instalments, and wherever I saw a house wi' reading abune the door-head, 'British spirits sold here,' to pay in my dividend; and there was nae fear o' it comin' to them."

Hawkie once had a watch, and the only one, moreover, that ever beat in his fob. "It didna cost me muckle," he said. "I bocht it at a sale ae nicht, and the match o't against time was never in onybody's pouch, for it gaed a' the four-and-twenty hours in the first ane after I row'd it up."

"You are well acquainted with the but and ben end of the 'Land of Cakes,' Hawkie," said a gentleman to him.

"Ay, man," replied the wit; "I micht throw the halter ower the neck o' my stilt, and it would turn in o' its ain accord to its quarters for the nicht, without happin' or windin' in ony corner o't."

"It's a wonder, Hawkie, that ye can live," said another. "A man o' your intellect, trampin' up and down among a' the riff-raff that beg the country."

"Oh, but man, is that a' ye ken," replied the indomitable one; "I hae a profession to support—I'm a collector o' poor's rates."

"You must have a surplus of funds," continued the gentleman; "for I think you are a talented and industrious collector."

"Weel, man," returned Hawkie, "I admit baith; but for a' that I ne'er got what paid the collector decently."

"I have myself something to do with collecting accounts, Hawkie, but if your rates are as difficult to call in as my accounts are, you must have battle enough in your profession?"

"Oh, man, you're no up to your business. Ye're but a green hand. I could learn you to get your accounts! I ca' in accounts regularly whaur there's naething awin' to me."

"Hae, Hawkie," said one of his almoners, "there's a penny to you, and gae awa', man, and get your beard ta'en aff; ye micht draw lint through't for a heckle, I'm perfectly ashamed to see you gaun about like a Jew."

"Oh!" replied Hawkie, "but you forget, freend, that it disna suit a beggar to be bare-faced."

"I shall endeavour to provoke Hawkie into retort," said a gentleman who was well known to the wit, to a friend. And passing the beggar, with head turned away to avoid recognition, he remarked, in a voice sufficiently audible,

"He's a perfect blackguard and impostor, that Hawkie. He should be sent to Bridewell!"

"Hech, man," retorted Hawkie, "you're the only neebour-like person I hae seen the day."

"What will you charge to teach me the profession of begging, Hawkie?" inquired one.

"Man, ye couldna come to a better hand for your education," replied Hawkie; "and I'll just tak' ye on the terms the poor weavers used to tak' their apprentices; I'll gie you the half o' your winning."

"That's a shocking-like hat you have got on your head, Hawkie," said one. "You never had anything like a decent one, but that is certainly the worst I ever saw you have."

"I got it in Paddy's Market," said the wit, "and it's made on the sliding scale," said he, taking it off, and lifting off the upper portion. "Man!—I kent the sliding scale afore Peel."

"Did you ever hear an ass, bray, Hawkie?" queried a young whiskered puppy.

"Never till the noo," was the instant reply.

The street orator entered a shop one day where there happened to be a gentleman from Perth standing at the counter.

"Were you ever in Perth, Willie?" said he.

"Yes, I hae been there," said Hawkie; "and I hae gude reason to mind Perth. I gaed in at a street ill-lichted, and I thocht, nae fear o' the police here; so I commenced my story. But I hadna weel begun when a voice frae a window cries out, 'Get you gone, sir, or the police will find quarters for ye.' I ne'er loot on that I heard the threat, but cried awa' till I got to the end o' the street, and then took the road to my lodgings. I hadna been there mony minutes when in comes ane o' the police, and lugs me aff to jail, whaur they keepit me till Monday—this was Friday—and just let me out then wi' as much daylicht as would let me see across the brig. That's a' that I ken about the Fair City." Standing for a few minutes, he held out his left hand, and, gathering the fingers of his right to a point, he dipped them into the hollow of his left, saying, "Weel, sir, what are ye gaun to gie to redeem the character o' your town?"

Hawkie entered the shop of one of his almoners one day whilst a process of painting was going on. "Take care of your clothes!" shouted an attendant at the counter.

"Tak' ye care o' your paint," retorted the ragged wit. "It's mair likely to be damaged by me than I am by it."

The orator was addressing an audience in the street one day when he was interrupted by a passer-by—"I see you are preaching, as usual, Hawkie."

"Yes, I am," said he, holding out his open hand, "and there's the plate for the collection."

A little carpenter, with a shaving tied round as a hat-band, observing Hawkie standing at a corner, accosted the orator with, "Man, Hawkie, do you see, I'm gaun in mournings for you?"

"Is't no," replied Hawkie, appealing to the crowd, "a puir account o' Presbyterian Glasgow, when a brat like that is permitted to gang about in mournings for a man before he's dead?"

Our *orateur du pavè*, by reason of his calling and behaviour together, got into frequent conflict with the police.

"Take the road, sir, and not obstruct the street," was the imperative demand of a batonman to him one day.

"I hae nae richt till't," replied the wit; "I pay nae road money."

On another occasion he was told to be off and not disturb the street by collecting mobs.

"Dinna blame me," was the reply, "but the congregation."

"Don't stand there, sir, and collect a crowd," exclaimed a gentleman in blue to him one day.

"Man," responded Hawkie, "there's a power o' hearers, but few believers."

Calling on a shopkeeper somewhat late one evening soliciting a trifle to help to pay his lodgings, the merchant remarked that he had surely come little speed during the day when he had not made so much as would defray that small matter.

"That's a' ye ken," replied Hawkie; "my lodging costs mair than yours does."

"How do you make that out?" was asked.

"I'll tell ye," said the vagrant. "In the first place, it tak's fifteenpence to mak' me drunk—boards and banes mak' up the bed and contents, and unless I were drunk I couldna sleep a wink—the bed that I hae to lie doon on wad mak' a dog yowl to look at; and then the landlady maun be paid, though a week's lodgings wad buy a' the boards an' bowls that's in the house. I hae made but little the day. I was up at the Cowcaddens, whar they hae little to themsel's, an' less disposition to spare; an', wearied oot, I lay doon on the roadside to rest me. The laddies as they passed were sayin, 'Hawkie's drunk! Hawkie's drunk!' An', man, my very heart was like to brak', I was sae vex'd to think it wasna true."

Some forty years ago, when the Very Rev. Bishop Murdoch was Bishop in Glasgow, Hawkie, in his rambles often made his way to the Bishop's residence in Great Clyde Street, and as the Bishop was well acquainted with Hawkie and his pawky sayings, he often rewarded him with a plate of soup or a glass of spirits, whichever he appeared to be most in need of. On one occasion a clergyman from the Highlands was paying a visit to the Bishop, and as they both chanced to be standing at the window conversing, they saw Hawkie slowly making his way in their direction. The Bishop, turning to the clergyman, told him that that was one of Glasgow's characters, famous for his witty sayings, etc., and that he would call him in, when he would probably hear for himself. Accordingly, Hawkie was brought in and shown into the room beside the reverend gentlemen. The Bishop spoke a few words to him, and then, as he saw Hawkie looking at the pictures on the walls, he asked him if he knew any of them.

"Maybe," was the answer.

The Bishop, pointing to a likeness of himself which was hanging on the wall, asked him if he knew it, and if it was a good likeness.

"Ou, ay," said Hawkie, "it's no bad."

He was then shown an engraving of the Pope, and, being told who it was, he said, "I dinna ken, I never saw him."

"Well," said the Bishop, pointing to a picture of the Crucifixion, which was hanging between the two likenesses, "you surely know that?"

Hawkie gazed intently at it for a minute, and then said, "I aye heard that Christ was crucified between twa thieves, but I ne'er kent wha they were afore."

It is needless to say Hawkie was rewarded with his glass of spirits, and both the gentlemen enjoyed a good laugh at the witty answer.

On one of the Glasgow half-yearly Fasts (now an unknown institution) Hawkie took his beat on the Dumbarton Road, between Glasgow and Partick. As the day happened to be fine, the "collector of poor's rates" justly calculated that this district would be well frequented. "I am sent out here this afternoon," said the ever fertile "collector" to the objects of his assessment,

"I am sent out here this afternoon by the clergy of Glasgow to put a tax on a' you gentry that hae mista'en the country for the kirk the day."

He cherished an inveterate hatred of the Irish, and the lash of his satirical tongue never wagged with more delight than when it was flaying the back of poor Paddy. "Gae hame to your bogs and ditches!" he would shout. "Blast ye! the Glasgow folk canna get the honest use o' their ain gallows for ye!"

"I'm neither," said our public lecturer, "a Tory nor a Radical. I like middle courses—gang ayont that, either up or doon, it disna matter—it's a wreck ony way ye like to tak' it."

A few gentlemen going home from a supper party, amongst whom was the amiable John Imlah, the writer of many popular Scottish songs, were accosted by Hawkie for the beggar's impost.

"There's a bawbee," said Mr. Imlah, "will that do?"

"No," says the collector, "it winna pay for ye a'."

"How much, then, are we owing to you?"

"I was looking ower my books last nicht, and I think you are owing me tippence."

"How much will you let us off for—present, past, and to come?"

"Pope Leo X.," said Hawkie, "in the sixteenth century, commenced the sale of indulgences, for the purpose of aggrandising his Church, and the harlot kirk never fairly damned hersel' till then. I'm no gaun to follow such an example."

This ingenious argument, we may be sure, brought forth more than the stipulated amount.

Our "collector of poor's rates" frequently took his stand at the north end of Glasgow Bridge. On the occasion of a special public rejoicing, a grand floral arch had been thrown over there, bearing in its very appearance the evidence of a lavish expenditure of the public funds.

"What height do you think that arch will be?" asked some one of Hawkie.

"The heicht o' hanged nonsense," was the instant reply.

During the latter years of his life the poor waif had to take winter shelter in the Town's Hospital, leaving which, in the spring, Dr. Auchincloss, surgeon, who was very attentive to him, gave him some money, remarking, "Weel, Hawkie, I'll tak' a bet that the first place ye land in is a spirit-cellar."

"I'll tak' odds on your side, doctor," replied Hawkie.

On his first appearance in the street to follow his wonted calling, he thus addressed his hearers,—"Weel, ye'll hae been thinkin' I was dead, but I needna tell ye that that's no true, for I'm a living evidence to the contrary. I have been down in the Town's Hospital this while taking care o' mysel', for I hae nae notion o' puttin' on a fir jackit as lang as I can help it. But I'm nae better otherwise than when I gaed in, and, if I may believe my ain een, there's as little improvement on you."

The "fir jacket" so much dreaded encircled the poor gangrel in 1851, and the streets and lanes which once knew him so well, will know him no more for ever.

The following genuine illustration of Hawkie's street oratory, contributed by William Finlay, a Paisley poet, to the pages of *Whistle Binkie*, will fitly conclude the present paper.

"A-hey! bide a wee, bodies, and dinna hurry awa' hame, till ye hear what I hae gotten to tell ye; do you think that I cam' out at this time o' nicht to cry to the stane wa's o' the Brig-gate for naething, or for onything else than the public guid?—wearing my constitution down to rags, like the claes on my carcase, without even seeking a pension frae Her Majesty; though mony a poor beggar wi' a star o'er his breast has gotten ane for far less."

(*Voice from the crowd*)—"Hawkie, ye should hae been sent to Parliament, to croak there like some ither Parliamentary puddocks till yer throat were cleared."

(*Reply*)—"Tak' aff yer hat when ye speak to a gentleman—it's no the fashion in this country to put hats on cabbage stocks—a haggis would loup its lane for fricht afore ye—ye'll be a king where a hornspoon is the emblem of authority!" (*Resumes*)—"Here ye hae the history of a notorious beggar, the full and particular account of his birth and parentage—at least on his mither's side. This heir to the wallets was born in the byre o' a kintra farmer, an' just in the crib afore the kye, an' was welcomed to the world by the nose of honest Hawkie."

(*From the crowd*)—"Was this a sister o' yours, Hawkie?"

(*Answer*)—"Whatna kail yard cam' ye out o'? That's yer brither aside ye, is't? You're a seemly pair, as the cow said to her cloots." (*Continues*)—"It ne'er could be precisely ascertained the hour of this beggar's birth, though the parish records hae been riddled to get at the fact. I maun also tell ye, for I dinna like to impose on my customers, that there is a great doubt about the day o' the month, an' even about the month itsel'; but that he was born hasna been disputed, though it might hae been, if we hadna an account o' his life and death to convince the gainsayers. He arrived sooner at the years o' discretion than usual; an' if ye dinna ken the period when a beggar's bairn comes to his estate duly qualified, I'll tell you—it's when he ceases to distinguish between ither folk's property and his ain."

(*From the crowd*)—"What a poor stock ye maun hae; ye hae been yelling about that beggar, till the story is as bare as your ain elbows."

(*Retort*)—"Hech, man, but you're witty—when ye set out on the tramp, dinna come to me for a certificate, for I really couldna recommend ye; ye havena brains for a beggar, and our funds are no in a condition to gi'e ony pensions the now." (*Continues*)—"Ye hae an account o' the education which he received riding across the meal pock; and the lair that he learnt aff the loofs o' his mither, which was a' the school craft he e'er received; but sic a proficient did he himsel' grow in loof lair, that, like a' weel trained bairns, he tried his hands on the haffits of his auld mither in turn, and gied her sic thunderin' lessons, that she gied up her breath and business in begging at the same time to her hopeful son and successor."

(*Voice from the crowd*)—"Ye should hae keepit a school amang beggars, and micht hae taen your stilt for the taws."

(*Retort*)—"Oh, man, I would like ither materials to work wi' than the like of you! it's ill to bring out what's no in; a leech would as soon tak' blood out o' my stilt as bring ony mair out o' you than the spoon put in." (*Resumes*)—"Ye hae an account of his progress in life after he began business on his ain account, and what a skilful tradesman he turn'd out—he could 'lay on the cadge'[3] better than ony walleteer that e'er coost a pock o'er his shouther.

[3] Skilful address in begging—*Dict. of Buckish Slang.*

"Ye hae an account o' his last illness and death—for beggars dee as weel as ither folk, though seldom through a surfeit; ye hae also a copy o' his last Will and Testament, bequeathing his fortune to be drunk at his dredgy—the best action he ever did in his life, and which mak's his memory a standing toast at a' beggars' carousals—when they hae onything to drink it wi'; and really, you'll allow me to remark, if we had twa or three mae public-spirited beggars in our day that would do the like, the trade might yet be preserved in the country—for it has been threatening to leave us in baith Scotland and England, in consequence of the opening up of the trade wi' Ireland, and the prices hae been broken ever since; we hae a' this to contend wi' to preserve the pocks frae perishing, for the sake o' our children."

(*Voice from the crowd*)—"Och, Willie, is it your own self that I'm hearing this morning? and how did ye get home last night, after drinking till the daylight wakened ye? troth, ye did not know your own crutch from a cow's tail."

(*Retort*)—"Oh, man, Paddy, it's naething new to me to be drunk, but it's a great rarity to you—no for want o' will, but the bawbees. What way cam' ye here, Paddy? for ye hae naething to pay for your passage; and your claes are no worth the thread and buttons that haud them thegither; gin I had a crown for every road that your trotters could get into your trowsers by, it would be a fortune to me. 'Take me over,' said you, to your ould croak-in-the-bog; 'I wish I had my body across agin, out of this starvation could country, for there's nothing but earth and stones for a poor man to feed on; and in my own country I'll have the potato for the lifting.' Hech, man—but the police keeps ye in order—and ye thought when ye cam' o'er to live by lifting? man! aff wi' ye to your bogs—there's nae place like hame for ye, as the Deil said when he found himsel' in the Court o' Session.

"Ye hae an account o' this beggar's burial, and his dredgy."

(*Boy's voice from the crowd*)—"Was ye there, Hawkie? surely, if the stilt could haud ye up!"

"Och, sirs, are ye out already—you're afore your time—you should hae staid a wee langer in the nest till ye had gotten the feathers on ye, and then ye would hae been a goose worth the looking at."

(*Continues*)—"Sic a dredgy as this beggar had wad mak' our Lords o' Session lick their lips to hear tell o'—thae gentry come down among us like as mony pouther-monkeys—with their heads dipped in flower-pocks, to gie them the appearance o' what neither the school nor experience in the world could teach them—gin hangie would gie them a dip through his trap-door, and ding the dust aff their wigs, there's no a beggar frae John o' Groats to the Mull o' Galloway that wadna gie his stilts to help to mak' a bonfire on the occasion.

"Ye hae the order o' the procession at the burial—it's the rank in the profession that entitles to tak' precedence at a beggar's burial—ye never hear tell o' blood relations claiming their right to be nearest the beggar's banes. We'll be thinking the warld is on its last legs, and like to throw aff its wallets too, when sic an event occurs."

(*Interrupted*)—"Your stilt would, nae doubt, be stumpin' at the head o' them a'."

(*Reply*)—"Stan' aside, lads, I'm just wantin' to see if he has cloots on his trotters, for horns are sae common, nowadays, amang the gentry o' the blood, whar we should look for an example, that they hae ceased to distinguish the class that nature intended them for." (*Goes on*)—"First in order was Tinklers, the beggars' cavalry, wha being in constant consultation with the gentry of the lang lugs, hae some pretensions to wisdom; next Swindlers, wha mak' the best bargains they can wi' their customers, without pretendin' to hae ony authority for doin't—no like our black coats, wha can only get authority on ae side, to gang to a scene of mair extensive usefulness, whar the preaching pays better—our brethren of the pock a' follow this example; they never stay lang whar there's naething either to get or to tak'—but I'm forgetting mysel'; at their heels were Pickpockets, wha just tak' the hangman's helter wi' them, and gang the length o' their tether—for hangie aye keeps the hank in his ain hand.

"Next, Chain-drappers—the jewellers in the camp, wha are ready to sell cheap, or half the profits wi' everybody they meet, and wha are like mony o' our public instructors—aye get mair than they gie—then Prick-the-loops, wha are sae familiar wi' the hangman's loop that they've turned the idea into business, and set up wi' their garter—which they can easily spare, as they hae seldom ony stockings to tie on wi't; by this simple expedient they mak' large profits on sma' capital. Next, Chartered-beggars, or Blue-gowns—wha get a licence frae the authorities to cheat and lie over the whole country.

"Next, the hale clanjamfrey o' Vagrants—for they're a' but beggars' bairns the best o' them—Randies, Thieves, Big-beggars, and Wee-beggars, Bane-gatherers and Rowley-powleys. Criers o' Hanging-speeches—wha, generally, should hae been the subject o' their ain story—some wi' weans, but a' wi' wallets, broken backs, half arms, and nae arms; some only wi' half an e'e—ithers, wi' mair een than nature gied them—and that is an e'e after everything that they can mak' their ain; snub-noses, cock-noses, and half-noses; Roman-noses, lang-noses—some o' them like a chuckie-stane, ithers like a jarganell pear; hawk-noses, and goose-noses; and mind ye I dinna find fault wi' the last kind, for nature does naething in vain, and put it there to suit the head; but whatever the size and description o' the neb, they could a' tak' their pick, for the hale concern, man and mither's son, had mouths, and whar teeth were wanting, the defect was mair than made up by desperate willin' gums.

"Some were lame, though their limbs were like ither folks. There are mae stilts made than lame folk, for I maun tell you some gang a-begging and forget their stilts, and hae to gang back for them afore they can come ony speed; ithers hae nae legs to be lame wi'; a few, like mysel', had only ae guid ane, like the goose in a frosty morning, but made up the loss by the beggars' locomotive—a stilt—which a poor goose canna handle wi' advantage.

"The rear o' this pock procession was closed by bands o' sweeps, wha are ready for a' handlings, whar there's onything to do for the teeth; an' they hae the advantage o' us, for they're aye in Court-dress, and, like honest Collie, dinna need to change their claes.

"In the hame-coming there was a scramble, wha should be soonest at the feast, and a quarrel, an' you'll maybe be surprised that there was but ae quarrel, but I maun tell you that they were a' engaged in't, an' maist o' them kentna what they were gettin' their croons cloored for, but just to be neighbour-like. The cracking o' stilts, the yelly-hooings o' wives and weans, and the clatter o' tinklers' wives, wad hae ca'm'd the sea in the Bay of Biscay—do ye ken the distance at which a beggar fights his duel?—it's just stilt length, or nearer, if his enemy is no sae weel armed as himsel'.

"Ye hae a return o' the killed and wounded—four Blind Fiddlers wi' their noses broken—four Tinklers' wives wi' their tongues split, and if they had keepit them within their teeth, as a' wives' tongues should be, they would have been safe—there's nae souder or salve that can cure an ill tongue—five Croons crackit on the outside—sixteen torn Lugs—four-and-twenty Noses laid down—four Left Hands with the thumb bitten aff—ten Mouths made mill doors o'—four dozen Stilts wanting the shouther-piece—twenty made down for the use of the family—in ither words, broken in twa! an' they are usefu', for we have a' sizes o' beggars. After a' this, the grand dredgy; but I havena time to tell you about it the night; but ye see what handlings beggars would hae if the public would be liberal.

"Buy this book; if ye hae nae bawbees I'll len' ye, for I'm no carin' about siller. I hae perish'd the pack already, an' I am gaun to tak' my Stilt, the morn's morning, and let the Creditors tak' what they can get."

Closing the extraordinary scene, the poet adds, as a sort of epilogue—

> "This is the end of all,
>
> High and low, great and small;
>
> This finishes the poor vain show,
>
> And the King, with all his pride,
>
> In his lifetime deified—
>
> With the beggar is at last laid low."

# CHAPTER XVII
## THE LAIRD O' MACNAB

No collection of the national humours could be regarded as representative or complete that did not contain more than a passing reference to the Laird of Macnab, who was the hero of many a ludicrously funny story, and who, like Sir John Falstaff, was not only witty himself, but frequently the cause of wit in others. The Macnabs were originally the proprietors of extensive estates in the Highlands of Perthshire, and were sometimes styled "The Macnabs of Auchlyne," at other times "The Macnabs of Bovain," "The Macnabs of Kinnell," and "The Macnabs of Glendochart." Francis—our hero—was the last relic of the ancient, stern, feudal system. His obtrusive peculiarities were pride of family antiquity and rank, and a withering scorn of the trousered Sassenach. He was extremely poor, but was extremely proud, and, having no money to boast of, he boasted all the more of his "lang pedigree." On this latter, indeed, he could scarcely ever speak dispassionately. As compared with the Macnabs, the Campbells and the M'Leans and such like were creatures of yesterday. These might trace their ancestral line even to the Flood, but that afforded them next to nothing in the comparison, for the Macnab, bless you—the chief of all the Macnabs—why, he had a boat of his own, and would never condescend to be beholden to Noah, or any such plebeian individual. No, no, the Macnab recognised no superior, and there were doubtless many Maister Macnabs, "but the auld black lad may hae my saul," he would say, "if I ken but o' *ae Macnab*." How it would have roused the Laird's ire had he lived to see the Highlands overrun with Cockney tourists—and not only so, but to see many ancient family seats passing into the hands of wealthy brewers and manufacturers—we can from his own words form some idea.

"Macnab, are you acquainted with Macloran of Dronascandlich, who has lately purchased so many acres in Inverness-shire?" asked a fellow-guest of the Laird one day at a dinner party.

"Ken wha?" burst in the Macnab, thus easily sent off on his genealogical steed. "The puddock-stool o' a creature they ca' Dronascandlich, wha no far bygane daured, curse him! to offer siller, sir, for an auld ancient estate, sir? An estate as auld as the Flood, sir; a hantle deal aulder, sir. Siller, sir, scrapit thegether by the miserable sinner in India, sir, not in an officer or gentleman-like way, sir; but, hang him, sir, by makin' cart wheels and trams, sir, and barrows, and the like o' that wretched handicraft. Ken him, sir? I ken the creature weel, and whaur he comes frae, sir; and so I ken that dumb tyke, sir, a better brute by half than a score o' him."

"Mercy on us, Macnab! you surprise me," interjected the querist; "I thought from the sublime sound of his name and title, that, like yourself, he had been a chief of fifteen centuries' standing, at least."

"By the saul o' the Macnabs, sir," rejoined the Laird, snorting like a mountain whirlwind with rage at the daring comparison, "naething but yer diabolical Lowland ignorance can excuse ye for siccan profanation! Hear me, sir! It's fifty years and mair bygane, a'e time I was at Glasgow, wanting some tyking, or Osnaburgs, or what the fiend ca' ye them, what ye mak' pillows and bowsters, o'? Weel, sir, I was recommended to an auld decent creature o' a wabster, wha pickit up a miserable subsistence in the Gallowgate. I gaed east a bit past the Spoutmouth, then up a'e pair o' stairs—twa—three—four pair o' stairs—a perfect Tower o' Babel in meeniature, sir. At last I quat the regions o' stane an' lime an' cam' to timmer, sir—about twenty or thirty rotten boards, that were a perfect temptation o' Providence to venture the fit o' a five-year-auld bairn on. I gaed in at a hole—door it was nane—and there I found a miserable anatomy—the picture o' famine, sir; wi' a face as white as a clout, an auld red Kilmarnock night-cap on his poor grey pow, an' treddle, treddling awa' wi' his pitifu' wizened trotters. Wha think ye, sir, was this abortion o' a creatur—this threadbare, penniless, and parritchless scrap o' an antediluvian wabster? This was Macloran's grandfather, sir! This was the origin o' Dronascandlich, sir!! And a bonnie origin for a Highland chief, by the saul o' the Macnabs!!!"

Recognising no superior, the Laird was consequently a law unto himself, or rather claimed the right to be so. He rarely, however—never in fact—was known to concede another's title to exception from the strictures of law and order. "Like the Laird o' Macnab's Volunteers," has become a Scotch proverb, and thereby hangs the following tale, which shows that the Laird's ideas of volunteering were as original as any Irishman's could possibly be. When the French war broke out the Laird organised a corps of infantry, which he styled "Macnab's Volunteers." A kenspeckle lot they were, we may be sure; but to our tale.

One day while Lord Breadalbane was driving down Strathyre on his way from Taymouth Castle to Stirling, he encountered a horse and cart, the latter containing the living carcasses of six brawny Highlanders tied neck and heel, and the whole in charge of a cordon of armed gillies. On his lordship inquiring as to the meaning of the strange spectacle, he was informed by the kilted driver that—

"Tem are six tam scoundrels, my Lort, that refuse to pe the Laird o' Macnab's Volunteers, and we're just takin' tem doon to Stirling, ta curst hallions tat ta are, to see if ta cauld steel will mak' tem do their duty."

This is quite as good as the wife's request to her husband to "gang awa quietly and be hangit, and no anger the Laird."

Speaking of the Laird and his volunteers calls to memory an episode which exhibits our hero in the character of a strategist of the first water. Macnab was proceeding from the West, on one occasion, towards Dunfermline, in charge of a company of the Breadalbane Fencibles. In those days, the Highlanders were notorious for their smuggling propensities, and an excursion to the Lowlands, whatever might be its cause or import, was an opportunity by no means to be neglected. The Breadalbane men, accordingly, contrived to store a considerable quantity of the genuine "peat reek" into the baggage carts. On the party reaching Alloa, the excisemen located therein got a hint as to the contents of the carts, so hurried out and intercepted them. Meanwhile, Macnab, accompanied by a gillie, in true feudal style, was proceeding slowly at the head of his men, and the intelligence reaching him that the baggage had been seized by a posse of excisemen, at once roused the lion within his breast.

"Did the lousy villains dare to obstruct the march of the Breadalbane Fencibles?" he exclaimed, inspired with the wrath of a thousand heroes, as away he rushed to the scene of contention.

"Who the devil are you?" he demanded as soon as he reached the excisemen.

"Gentlemen of the Excise," was the answer.

"Robbers, thieves, you mean!" shrieked the Macnab. "How dare you lay hands on His Majesty's stores? If you be gaugers, show me your commissions."

Unfortunately for the excisemen, they had not deemed it necessary to bring such documents with them.

"Ay! just what I took you for; a parcel of highway robbers and scoundrels. Come, my good fellows" (addressing the soldiers in charge of the baggage, and extending his voice with the lungs of a Stentor) "prime! load!"

The excisemen did not wait the completion of the order, but fled at full speed.

"Now, my lads," said the Laird, "proceed—the whisky's safe."

Another anecdote illustrates how equal he was to a delicate occasion. The Laird was a regular attender at Leith races. He rode a most wretched-looking steed, which gave occasion for many jibes at his expense, and one year, while rushing in to see the result of a heat, his horse fell and was seriously injured.

The year following, a puppy, who thought he might raise a laugh at Macnab's expense, looked up to him as he passed by, and enquired—

"Is that the same horse ye had here last year, Laird?"

"No," retorted Macnab, bringing his whip-shaft down on his interrogator's head with a force that made him bite the dust, "but it's the same *whup!*"

But the Laird's grand escapade—his *coup d'état*—remains yet to be related. It happened to be the last in his life, and it forms a fitting climacteric to a truly wonderful career. It is narrated at great length in a MS. scrap book of his adventures still preserved at Breadalbane Castle, and is briefly as follows:—

The pressure of a declining revenue began to tell heavily on the Laird, and he had occasionally to grant bills for his purchases. For many years these bills were regularly discounted at the Perth Bank, the Directors of which, knowing their money to be sure, though perhaps not soon, humoured his idiosyncracies, and took his acceptances although signed "The Macnab." Unluckily for the Laird, one of these "cursed bits o' paper," as he termed them, found its way to the Stirling Bank, an establishment with which he had no direct connection, and, having no personal friend to protect his credit at Stirling, it was duly noted and protested, and notice was sent to him. These formalities the Laird treated, of course, with the most lofty indifference. He was effectually roused, however, when the alarming information reached his ear that a "caption and horning" had been issued against him, and that a clerk, accompanied by two messengers, would proceed to Auchlyne House on the following Friday for the purpose of taking him into custody. The Laird called a council of war. Janet, his faithful old housekeeper, and other two trusty retainers, were made familiar with the disgrace that was threatening to fall on the Chief of all the Macnabs. Janet was a diplomatist of the true Caleb Balderstone type, and the Laird trusted chiefly to her wit and ingenuity in the emergency. "To clap me within four bare stane wa's," said he, addressing his female major-general, "and for what, think ye? A peetifu' scart o' a goose's feather—deil cripple their souple shanks. It would ill become me to hae ony hobble-show wi' siccan vermin, so I'll awa' doun to my Lord's at Taymouth, and leave you, Janet, my bonnie woman, to gie them *their kail through the reek.*" And off he went, leaving Janet to master the situation as best she could. This was on Friday morning. In the course of the day the officers made their appearance at Auchlyne House.

"O, sirs," quoth Janet, receiving them blandly, "ye maun be sair forfouchten wi' your langsome travel. Sit down, and get some meat. The Laird's awa' to see a friend, and will be back momently. What gars ye gloom that gate? There's a' ye want, and muckle mair, locked up in that kist there, in bonnie yellow gowd, fairly counted by his honour this very mornin'," and, so saying, she spread before the wayworn travellers a plentiful store of Highland cheer—including kippered salmon and braxtie ham, and a "good williewaucht" of the "rale peat reek." The gloaming came, but brought no signs of the Laird's returning. "Nae doot," said Janet, "his honour will be down at the Earl's, so ye'll just e'en mak' yer beds here for the nicht, and the first thing ye'll get for your handsel in the mornin' will be a sonsie breakfast and weel-counted siller."

The terms were sufficiently tempting, and were accordingly closed with. The two limbs of the law were quartered in a room the window of which faced the East, while the clerk was, in deference to his social status, bestowed in a room the window of which looked towards the setting sun.

Now, opposite the window of the room in which the officers slept there grew a huge tree, the great spreading branches of which creaked and moaned beneath the blast during the entire night, and now and again made a crash which caused the drowsy beagles to start in their sleep, and shiver when they had fairly awakened. Being utterly ignorant of the cause of these disturbances, and anxious to ascertain, the first glimmer of daylight brought one of the officers to the window, when, horror! there, before his eyes, swinging backwards and forwards, suspended from one of the main branches of the tree, was the body of the clerk, coated, booted, and fully attired, as if he had been taken and lynched just when ready for the road. The poor man gave a howl which nearly lifted the roof off the house. Five minutes later the domestics were alarmed by the officers rushing headlong down the stairs, and making in the direction of the door, and by Janet demanding of them in fierce tones—"What the foul fiend d'ye mak' sic a din for?"

"W—what's that on the t—t—tree!" gasped out the officers, simultaneously.

"Oh," said Janet, with an eldritch laugh, "it's a bit clerk bodie frae the Bank o' Stirling that cam' here last nicht to deave the Laird for siller. We've ta'en and hangit the silly elf."

Not another word was needed. The limbs of the law disappeared like water poured on quick-sand, and were beyond the reach of Janet's voice ere she had well finished her sentence. During this brief parley Janet's confederates slipped out and cut down the man of straw, which, for the occasion, had been filling the clerk's clothes; and, quickly divesting it of the latter, they had these deftly replaced on the chair beside the bed where lay their still soundly sleeping owner.

By and by the all-unconscious clerk came tripping leisurely downstairs.

"Are my companions not astir yet?" said he to Janet.

"Yer companions?" queried Janet, with a grim leer in her eyes; "the Laird's gillies have ta'en them awa' to the Holy Loch at Crianlarich and droon'd them—and they'll be here for you directly."

"I hear them comin'!" cried Janet, as the clerk's heels disappeared out at the doorway.

Whether the money was ever paid history deponeth not. One thing however, is certain, and it is this, that not all the estates of all the Macnabs that ever existed would have tempted another embassy of the same three to Auchlyne.

The Laird o' Macnab paid the debt of Nature (there was no shirking this creditor!) in the early part of the present century. His portrait—full length, and in Highland costume—painted by Raeburn, is still in the possession of the Breadalbane family.

# CHAPTER XVIII
## KIRKYARD HUMOUR

"God's acre" should be about the last place in the world to which any mind blessed with an average sense of consistency, not to employ a stronger term, would turn with deliberate purpose in search of entertainment of a frivolous and amusing character. And yet, paradoxical as it may appear, the most serious of all events, solemn of all ordinances, and weird of all situations—death, burial, and the grave—have been the subjects of the most mirth-provoking puns and jokes; whilst some of the wittiest and most audaciously sarcastic of epigrammatic compositions are among those which have been discovered among the tombs in the silent cities of the dead. Like the dry and caustic humour of the Scottish beadles, to which, in essence and order they are nearly related, humorous and curious epitaphs no longer prevail amongst us. This is not to be regretted, for they have yielded to a more decorous, if perhaps less truthful and enlivening order of things. The wonder is that they ever obtained favour at all, here or elsewhere. I say elsewhere, because eccentricities of the kind under notice have not been peculiar to the kirkyards of the North. In England the punning and eccentric epitaph has prevailed to a greater extent even than in Scotland. Every representative collection of tombstone literature reveals this fact. Scotland alone, however, has produced an abundant crop. So much, indeed, as to form quite a distinct and interesting department of the humour of the country. The utter unpreparedness of the mind for the reception of humour in such a place as a kirkyard has occasionally, no doubt, helped what was incongruous to pass for humorous, as from the sublime to the ridiculous there is but one step; but the following, which is still "to the fore," though more than two hundred years old, and may be seen and read of all men in the Reid kirkyard, in the parish of Gairtney, in Annandale, is sufficiently ludicrous in itself to tickle the risible sensibilities of any rightly organized person independently of circumstance or association:—

"I, Jocky Bell o' Brakenbrow, lyes under this stane,

Five of my awn sons laid it on my wame;

I liv'd aw my deyes, but sturt or strife

Was man o' my meat, and master o' my wife;

If you've done better in your time than I did in mine,

Take the stane aff my wame, and lay it on thine."

The same may be said of the next.

Many years ago a strolling musician, of remarkable appearance, of the name of Abercromby, or "Crummy," as he was usually called, was well known throughout the north of Scotland. He supported himself and his partner by his penny whistle, with which he had no difficulty in charming the musical of any village. He was buried in the churchyard of Cruden, in Aberdeenshire. He composed his own epitaph in these words:—

> "Here Crummy lies, enclosed in wood,
>
> Full six feet one and better,
>
> When tyrant Death grim o'er him stood,
>
> He faced him like a hatter.
>
> Now lies he low without a boot,
>
> Free from a world of bustle,
>
> And silent now is Crummy's flute,
>
> And awful dry his whustle."

The following is copied from a tombstone in the East Neuk o' Fife—Crail, I think:—

> "Here lies my good and gracious Auntie,
>
> Wham Death has packed in his portmanty,
>
> Threescore and ten years God did gift her,
>
> And here she lies, wha de'il daurs lift her?"

On a tombstone in the old churchyard of Peterhead there was wont to appear this interrogatory inscription:—

> "Wha lies here?
> John Sim, ye needna' spier.
> Hullo, John, is that you?
> Ay, ay, but I'm deed noo."

This is from Haddington kirkyard:—

> "Underneath this stone doth lie
>
> As much beauty as could die,

> Which while it lived did vigour give
> To as much virtue as could live."

The next is from the same place:—

> "Hout, Atropos, hard-hearted Hag,
> To cut the sheugh of Jamie Craig;
> For had he lived a wheen mae years,
> He had been owre tough for all your sheirs;
> Now Jamie's deed, sua man we a',
> And for his sake I'll say this sa,
> In Heiven Jamie be thy saul!"

Mr. Pryse Gordon relates, in his *Autobiography*, that a sailor having thought proper to enclose the parish churchyard of Deskford, near Cullen, in order to keep it decent, his executor placed a tombstone over him after death, on which was the following:—

> "Hic jacet Joannes Anderson, Aberdoniensis,
> Who built this churchyard dyke at his own expenses."

That suggests another which is like unto it:—

> "Here lies the laird o' Lundie,
> *Sic transit gloria Mundi.*"

The following curious specimen of sepulchral literature is said to be copied from an old tombstone which marks the grave of a soldier in the kirkyard of Dumfries:—

> "Here lies Andrew M'Pherson,
> Who was a peculiar person;
> He stood six foot two
> Without his shoe,
> And was slew

At Waterloo."

The following is a copy of an epitaph on an old tombstone at Logiepert, in the neighbourhood of Montrose:—

"Here lies the Smith—to wit—Tam Gouk,
His Faither and his Mither,
Wi' Tam, and Jock, and Joan, and Noll,
And a' the Gouks thegither.
When on the yird Tam and his wife
Gree'd desprate ill wi' ither,
But noo, without e'en din or strife,
They tak' their Nap thegither."

In Bothwell there appears:—

"Erected by Margaret Scott in memory of her husband, Robert Stobo, late smith and farrier, Goukthrapple, who died, May 1834, in the 70th year of his age.

"My sledge and hammer lies declined
My bellows-pipe has lost its wind;
My forge's extinct; my fire's decayed;
And in the dust my vice is laid.
My coals is spent; my iron is gone;
My nails are drove; my work is done."

In Cullen churchyard, in Banffshire, there is this graphic verse:—

"Here lies interred a man o' micht,
His name was Malcolm Downie:
He lost his life ae market nicht
By fa'in aff his pownie.

Aged 37 years."

In the churchyard of Newtyle, Ruthven, Perthshire, is the following, bearing date 1771:—

"Here lies the body of Robert Small,
Who, when in life, was thick not tall;
But what's of greater consequence,
He was endowèd with good sense."

The following sublimely confused inscription will be found on the headstone, No. 41,242, of the Old Howff in Dundee:—

"1830.
In memory of James
and another son
and five other friends
Who died in infancy.
Erected by
James Stewart,
spirit merchant, Dundee,
and his spouse
and three other children."

Here is another Dundee epitaph:—

"J. P. P.,
Provost of Dundee—
Hallelujah,
Hallelujee."

Again:—

"Here lie the banes o' Tammy Messer,
Of Tarry woo' he was a dresser;
He had some fau'ts and mony merits,
And died o' drinking ardent spirits."

And again:—

> "Here lies old John Hildibrodd
> Have mercy on him, good God,
> As he would do if he was God,
> And Thou wert old John Hildibrodd."

Marion Scott died at Dunkeld, November 21, 1727, aged 100, and was buried in the Abbey. She lived in the reigns of James VI., Charles I., Oliver Cromwell (Commonwealth), Charles II., James II., William III., and Mary II., Anne, George I., and George II. Her tombstone bears this inscription:—

> "Stop, passenger, until my life you've read;
> The living may get knowledge by the dead.
> Five times five years I liv'd a virgin life;
> Five times five years I was a virtuous wife;
> Ten times five years I liv'd a widow chaste
> Now, tir'd of this mortal life, I rest.
> I, from my cradle to my grave, have seen
> Eight mighty kings of Scotland and a queen.
> Full twice five years the Commonwealth I saw;
> Ten times the subjects rose against the law.
> Twice did I see old prelacy pull'd down!
> And twice the cloak was humbled by the gown.
> An end of Stuart's race I saw: nay more!
> I saw my country sold for English ore.
> Such desolations in my time have been;
> I have an end of all perfection seen."

Thomas Tyre, pedlar, died on the 2nd day of January, 1795, and was buried in the graveyard of West Kilbride, where his monument, with the following descriptive lines, may any time be seen. He was over 72 years of age:—

> "Here lye the banes of Thomas Tyre,
> Wha lang had drudg'd through dub and mire
> In carrying bundles and sic like,

His task performing wi' small fyke.
To deal his snuff Tam aye was free,
And served his friends for little fee.
His life obscure was naething new,
Yet we must own his faults were few,
Although at Yule he sip'd a drap,
And in the kirk whiles took a nap.

True to his word in every case,
Tam scorned to cheat for lucre base.
Now he is gone to taste the fare,
Which none but honest men will share."

At Redkirk, in the parish of Gretna, Dumfriesshire, there was formerly a churchyard, which the sea has completely swept away. The only vestige of it is a monumental stone, lying about 150 feet within high water mark, and which will no doubt be soon sanded up. The inscription upon it merits preservation:—

"Here lieth I—N. Bell, who died in ye yhere
MDX., and of his age cxxx. years.
Here bluidy Bell, baith skin and bane,
Lies quietly styll aneath this stane;
He was a stark mosstrooper shent
As ever drave a bow on bent.
He brynt ye Lockwood tower and hall,
An' flang ye lady o'er ye wall;
For whilk ye Johnstone, stout and wyte,
Set Blacketh a' in low by nyght,
Whyle cryed a voice, as if frae hell,
'Haste, open ye gates for *bluidy* Bell.'"

An eccentric character named John So, a native of Inverkip, bequeathed his property to a friend, on the condition that he would get engraved on his tombstone the following epitaph written by himself:—

"Here lies John So,
So so did he so,
So did he live,
So did he die,
So so did he so,
So let him lie."

This, to be seen on the south wall of Elgin Cathedral, is repeated in various churchyards throughout the country:—

"The world is a city full of streets,
And death the mercat that all men meets,
If lyfe were a thing that monie could buy,
The poor could not live, and the rich would not die."

The next is found near Rob Roy's grave, in Balquhidder:—

"Beneath this stane lies Shanet Roy,
Shon Roy's reputed mother;
In all her life save this Shon Roy
She never had another.

'Tis here or hereabout, they say,
The place no one can tell;
But when she'll rise at the last day,
She'll ken the stane hersel'."

Andrew Sharpe, who practised the arts of the drawing-master and poet, and enjoyed some reputation as a flute-player, is thus celebrated in the churchyard of Kinnoul, Perth:—

"Halt, for a moment,
Passenger, and read—
Here Andrew dozes
In his daisied bed.
Silent his flute,
Torn off its key,
His genius scattered
And the Muse set free."

This curious example is found in Arbroath:—

"Here lyes Alexander Peter, present treasurer of Arbroath, who died 12th January, 1630.

Such a Treasurer was not since, nor yet before,
For common work, calsais,[4] brigs,[5] and schoir;[6]
Of all others he did excel;
He devised our school and he hung our bell."

---

[4] Causeway.

[5] Bridges.

[6] Sewers.

---

The following lines are said to be in the churchyards of Stirling, Ordiquhill, Dundee (Old Howff), Fort Augustus, and Hamilton:—

"Our life is but a winter day
Some only breakfast and away,
Others to dinner stay and are full fed,
The oldest man but sups and goes to bed,
Large is his debt that lingers out the day,
He that goes soonest has the least to pay."

Close by St. Regulus Tower, St. Andrews, the ashes of a sea captain and his spouse have anchored safely in their last haven, which is marked by a simple tombstone with these words:—

"Here we lie

In horizontal position,

Like a ship laid up

Stript of her mast and riggin'."

Captain Hill, who rests in the kirkyard of Cleish, has his virtues thus pithily extolled on the stone which marks the spot:—

"At anchor now in Death's dark road,

Rides honest Captain Hill,

Who served his king and feared his God,

With upright heart and will.

In social life sincere and just,

To vice of no kind given;

So that his better part, we trust,

Hath made the Port of Heaven."


The following quaint inscription, copied from the Abbey of Melrose, consecrated in 1146, is of much historical value. From it, it would appear that one John Murdo superintended most of the ancient ecclesiastical edifices in Scotland:—

"John Murdo some tym callit was I,

And born in Parysse certainly,

And had in kepying all mason werk

Of Sanctandroys, the hye kyrk

Of Glasgu, Melros, and Paslay,

Of Nyddysdale, and of Galway,

Pray to God, and Mari baith,

And sweet St. John, keep this holy kyrk fra skaith."

In Forfar cemetery we find:—

> "'Tis here that Tibby Allan lies,
> 'Tis here, or here about,
> But no one till the Resurrection day,
> Shall the very spot dispute."

Loch Ranza has this:—

> "Here lies Donald and his wife,
> Janet M'Fee;
> Aged 40 hee,
> Aged 30 shee."

In the Necropolis of Glasgow, which is separated from the Cathedral and its olden cemetery by the Molendinar Burn, stands a plain stone with the grave warning:—

> "Stranger, as you pass o'er the grass,
> Think seriously, with no humdrumming,
> Prepare for death, for judgment's coming."

In the same place may be seen:—

> "Here lies Mess Andrew Gray,
> Of whom ne muckle good can i say
> He was ne Quaker, for he had ne spirit;
> He was ne Papist, for he had ne merit;
> He was ne Turk, for he drank muckle wine;
> He was ne Jew, for he eat muckle swine;
> Full forty years he preached and leed,
> For which God doomed him when he deed."

The subject of the next epitaph, owing to her bravery at the battle of Ancrum Moor, is celebrated in heroic verse still to be seen in a country churchyard in Roxburghshire:—

> "Fair Maiden Lilliard lies under this stane,
>
> Little was her stature, but great was her fame;
>
> Upon the English louns she laid many thumps,
>
> And when her legs were cutted off she fought upon her stumps."

In the churchyard of Hoddam is found:—

> "Here lyes a man, who all his mortal life
>
> Past mending clocks, but could not mend his wyfe,
>
> The 'larum of his bell was ne'er sae shrill
>
> As was her tongue—aye clacking like a mill.
>
> But now he's gane—oh! whither nane can tell—
>
> I hope beyond the sound o' Mally's bell."

Over the last lair of a Glasgow magistrate there is written:—

> "Here lyes—read it with your hats on—
>
> The bones of Bailie William Watson,
>
> Who was famous for his thinking,
>
> And moderation in his drinking."

The following has been deciphered from an inscription on a tombstone in Skye:—

> "Here lie the bones
>
> O' Tonald Jones,
>
> The wale o' men
>
> For eating scones.
>
> Eating scones
>
> And drinking yill,

> Till his last moans
> He took his fill."

In the kirkyard of Horncliffe, on the Tweed, may be seen:—

> "Here lies the Horner of Horncliffe,
> Puir Tam Gordon, cauld and stiff,
> Wha in this narrow hole was puttin
> For his lawless love of wedder mutton."

There is a neatly expressed compliment to the memory of a dead wife in these lines, said to be copied from a gravestone in Meigle:—

> "She was—but words are wanting,
> To say what.
> Think what a wife should be—
> She was that."

The writer of William Mathieson's epitaph, in the West Churchyard, Tranent, was not nearly so happy in his diction. It runs limpingly thus:—

> "William Matthison here lies,
> Whose age was forty-one;
> February seventeenth he dies,
> Went Is'bel Mitchell from.
> Who was his married wife,
> The fourth part of his life.
>
> The soul it cannot die,
> Tho' th' body be turn'd to clay;
> Yet meet again must they
> At the last day.
> Trumpets shall sound, archangels cry,
> Come forth Is'bel Mitchell and meet

William Matthison in the sky."

Seldom has there been a better excuse for an epitaph than appears in the following, from the burial-place of Inchchapel, near Montrose:—

"Janet Milne, spouse to James Lurie, her Monument.

> We do this for no other end
>
> But that our Burial may be ken'd."

These, though the choicest specimens of their kind, form not more than a tithe of the humorous and curious epitaphs which are readily accessible to the writer. But—though we have not laughed once irreverently—perhaps, my reader, we have laughed long enough over the "cauld clay biggin's" of gloomy Death, where rests in awful solemnity much that is sainted and sacred to us both. No more, then.

www.ingramcontent.com/pod-product-compliance
Lightning Source LLC
Chambersburg PA
CBHW032125160426
43197CB00008B/521